Corpus Linguistics with *BNCweb* –

english corpus linguistics

Thomas Kohnen · Joybrato Mukherjee (eds.)

Volume **6**

PETER LANG

Frankfurt am Main · Berlin · Bern · Bruxelles · New York · Oxford · Wien

Sebastian Hoffmann/Stefan Evert/Nicholas Smith
David Lee/Ylva Berglund Prytz

Corpus Linguistics with *BNCweb* – a Practical Guide

PETER LANG
Internationaler Verlag der Wissenschaften

Bibliographic Information published by the Deutsche Nationalbibliothek
The Deutsche Nationalbibliothek lists this publication in the Deutsche Nationalbibliografie; detailed bibliographic data is available in the internet at <http://www.d-nb.de>.

ISSN 1610-868X
ISBN 978-3-631-56315-1

© Peter Lang GmbH
Internationaler Verlag der Wissenschaften
Frankfurt am Main 2008
All rights reserved.

Printed in Germany 1 2 3 4 5   7

www.peterlang.de

At the time of going to print, preparations were being made for offering free access to the BNC and *BNCweb* via a server at Lancaster University. Please consult http://www.bncweb.info for updates on this opportunity to access the corpus.

This website also provides answers and methodological clues for selected exercises and tasks used in the book.

Table of Contents

Foreword   xiii

Acknowledgments   xvii

1   Looking at language in use—some preliminaries   1

    1.1   Introduction   1

       1.1.1   Thinking about *goalless*, *shall* and cars   1

       1.1.2   Clues from a corpus—the BNC   4

    1.2   Why read this book?   10

    1.3   Organization of the book   11

    1.4   How to use this book   12

2   Corpus linguistics: some basic principles   13

    2.1   Outline   13

    2.2   Introduction   13

    2.3   Representativeness in corpora   15

    2.4   What is corpus linguistics? Why use a corpus?   18

    2.5   A brief—and more advanced—excursion: description vs. theory   20

    2.6   Types of corpora   24

    2.7   Further reading   26

3   Introducing the British National Corpus   27

    3.1   Outline   27

    3.2   Introduction   27

    3.3   Written material   28

    3.4   Spoken material   32

    3.5   More than text   38

       3.5.1   Part-of-speech tags   38

       3.5.2   Headwords and lemmas   40

       3.5.3   Words & sentences versus w-units & s-units   41

    3.6   Format   42

    3.7   Errors   43

    3.8   More information   45

    3.9   Is it Present-day English?   45

    3.10   Exercise   46

4   First queries with *BNCweb*   47

4.1   Outline   47
4.2   Introduction   47
4.3   Getting started: your first query   48
      4.3.1   Planning your query   48
      4.3.2   Running the query   49
      4.3.3   Getting basic frequency information   50
4.4   Exploring the concordance   50
      4.4.1   Navigating through a query result   51
      4.4.2   KWIC view and Sentence view   52
      4.4.3   Random order and corpus order   53
      4.4.4   Viewing the larger context of an example   54
      4.4.5   Obtaining more information about the source of an example 57
4.5   Running a query for a word sequence   58
4.6   Restricting your query to selected portions of the BNC   59
4.7   Accessing previous queries   64
      4.7.1   Query history   64
      4.7.2   Save current set of hits   65
4.8   Browse a text   66
4.9   Exercises   68

5   Some further aspects of corpus-linguistic methodology   69

5.1   Outline   69
5.2   Introduction   69
5.3   Comparing results: normalized frequencies   69
5.4   Normalized frequencies—some further issues   73
5.5   Precision and recall   77
5.6   Statistical significance   79
      5.6.1   Confidence intervals   80
      5.6.2   Hypothesis tests for frequency comparison   83
      5.6.3   Using statistical software   86
5.7   Further reading   90
5.8   Exercises   90

6   The Simple Query Syntax   93

6.1   Outline   93
6.2   Introduction   93
6.3   Basic queries: searching words and phrases   94

	6.4	Using wildcards	97
	6.5	A short tour of the Simple Query Syntax	99
	6.6	Advanced wildcard queries	103
	6.7	Queries based on part-of-speech and headword/lemma	106
	6.8	Matching lexico-grammatical patterns	109
	6.9	Proximity queries	114
	6.10	Matching special characters	116
	6.11	Exercises	117

**7   Automated analyses of concordance lines—Part I: Distribution
and Sorting**   119

	7.1	Outline	119
	7.2	Distribution	119
	7.2.1	A *lovely* example: distributional facts about the users of *lovely*	119
	7.2.2	Frequency distribution by genre	124
	7.2.3	Dispersion & File-frequency extremes: checking the influence of idiosyncratic texts on frequencies	128
	7.3	Sort	131
	7.3.1	Sorting a query result on preceding or following context	131
	7.3.2	The Frequency breakdown function	133
	7.3.3	Sorting on the query hit	136
	7.4	Exercises	137

8   Automated analyses of concordance lines—Part II: Collocations   139

	8.1	Outline	139
	8.2	Introduction	139
	8.3	Understanding the concept of collocational strength	140
	8.4	Steps in collocation analysis	142
	8.5	Which association measure should I use?	149
	8.6	Calculating collocations in sub-sections of the BNC	158
	8.7	Further reading	159
	8.8	Exercises	159

9   "Adding value" to a concordance using customized annotations   161

	9.1	Outline	161
	9.2	Introduction: why annotate your concordance data?	161
	9.3	Annotation within *BNCweb*: using the "Categorize hits" function	162
	9.3.1	Setting up a category for analysis	163

9.3.2   Categorizing concordance hits   165
9.3.3   Analyzing data categorized in *BNCweb*   167
9.3.4   Re-editing your annotations   169
9.3.5   Advantages and disadvantages of categorizing queries
        within *BNCweb*   169
9.4   Summarizing and presenting results of customized annotations 170
9.5   Exporting a *BNCweb* query result to an external database   174
9.5.1   Downloading from *BNCweb*   175
9.5.2   Importing into database software   177
9.5.3   Annotating the database   179
9.5.4   Analyzing the database   180
9.5.5   Advantages and disadvantages of the database approach   181
9.6   Reimporting an analyzed database into *BNCweb*   181
9.7   Further reading   183
9.8   Exercises   183

10 **Creating and using subcorpora**   185
10.1 Outline   185
10.2 Introduction: why create subcorpora?   185
10.3 Basic steps for creating and using a subcorpus   186
10.3.1 Defining a new subcorpus via Written metatextual
        categories   186
10.3.2 Running a query on your subcorpus   188
10.4 More on methods for creating subcorpora   190
10.4.1 Selecting a narrower range of texts for a subcorpus   190
10.4.2 Defining a new subcorpus via Spoken metatextual
        categories   191
10.4.3 Defining a new subcorpus via Genre labels   193
10.4.4 Defining a new subcorpus via Keyword/title scan   195
10.4.5 Defining a new subcorpus via manual entry of text IDs
        or speaker IDs   198
10.4.6 Modifying your subcorpora   200
10.5 Saving time by using subcorpora   201
10.6 Exercises   202

11 **Keywords and frequency lists**   203
11.1 Outline   203
11.2 Introduction   203

11.3   The Keywords function   203
     11.3.1 About keywords   203
     11.3.2 Producing keyword lists   204
     11.3.3 Interpreting and adjusting keyword list settings   208
     11.3.4 Finding items contained in only one frequency list   209
11.4   The Frequency lists function   210
11.5   Exercises   214

12 Advanced searches with the CQP Query Syntax   215
12.1   Outline   215
12.2   Introduction   215
12.3   From Simple queries to CQP syntax—a primer   216
12.4   Regular expressions   222
12.5   Part-of-speech and headword/lemma queries   226
12.6   Lexico-grammatical patterns and text structure   230
12.7   Advanced features of CQP queries   236
12.8   Exercises   241

**13 Understanding the internals of *BNCweb*: user types, the cache
     system and some notes about installation**   245
13.1   Outline   245
13.2   *BNCweb* users: standard users and administrators   245
13.3   Additional information available to administrator users   247
     13.3.1 Overview   247
     13.3.2 Administrator access to the Query history feature   247
     13.3.3 Administrator access to user-specific data stored by
             other features   249
13.4   Customizable settings in *BNCweb*   249
     13.4.1 Configuration settings available to standard users   249
     13.4.2 Configuration settings available to administrator
             users   251
13.5   The cache system   252
     13.5.1 General description   252
     13.5.2 Maintenance of the cache system   253
13.6   Installation of *BNCweb*   255
     13.6.1 Prerequisites   255
     13.6.2 Time and disk-space required   256
     13.6.3 Configuration of the Perl library *bncConfigXML.pm*   256

References 259

Glossary 263

Appendix 1: Genre classification scheme 275

Appendix 2: Part-of-speech tags 277

Appendix 3: Quick reference to the Simple Query Syntax 279

Appendix 4: HTML-entities for less common characters 283

Index 285

Foreword

This book is about two electronic objects: the BNC and *BNCweb*. The BNC (in full, the British National Corpus) is a vast collection of over 4,000 English texts, providing a unique record of contemporary spoken and written English. *BNCweb* is a piece of software—a search and retrieval system—to enable the student or researcher to extract or derive information from the BNC. Together the BNC (http://www.natcorp.ox.ac.uk/) and *BNCweb* (http://www.bncweb.info) form an arguably unparalleled combination of facilities for finding out about the English language of the present day (or, more exactly, of the very recent past).

To put this claim in context, let me trace the history of these two remarkable objects. First, the BNC, consisting of nearly a hundred million words in all, was created in 1991-5 by a consortium consisting of three publishers—Oxford University Press, Longman Group Ltd, and Chambers—two universities—Oxford University and Lancaster University—and one library—the British Library. It is by no means an accident that the three publishers involved were (and still are) leading dictionary makers in the UK: computerized lexicography was the foremost application that the commercial members of the consortium had in mind. On the other hand, the corpus is open to all uses and all users. Since its initial release many hundreds of copies have been licensed worldwide to universities, colleges, schools, and industrial organizations, making the corpus available to thousands of users.

Why does the BNC contain only British English material? The simple answer is that it was financed 50 per cent by British government grants, and was intended to be an investment in British industry. In fact, industrial users have been a small minority, and the corpus has proved its value as a research resource mainly for increasing numbers of universities and other educational users. (The corpus is described in detail in Chapter 3.) The fact that the texts and transcriptions included in the corpus were collected in the early 1990s and are now at least 15 years old has scarcely affected its usefulness. In fact, since that time, the increasing availability of computer power and the increasing use of corpora in linguistics have if anything increased its popularity.

Naturally an electronic corpus, however vast and varied, is virtually useless without the right software for searching it to investigate the language. One answer to this need is *Xaira* (in its former incarnation known as *Sara*), the retrieval tool issued as part of the official BNC distribution, but another is the *BNCweb* software, which is the topic of this book. In an introductory article on its most recent version—the CQP-edition—Hoffmann & Evert (2006) refer to *BNCweb* as "a user-friendly and feature-rich corpus tool". The term *tool* here might strike one as a terminological understatement, given that a Swiss Army knife would give a poor idea of the multi-functional nature of this interface. However, the terms *user-friendly* and *feature-rich* are more than justified. The important point is that this software, which was already a breakthrough in corpus retrieval technology when it was first launched (see Lehmann et al. 2000), has been developed and enhanced over a period of more than ten years during which it has been thoroughly trialed and explored by its authors drawing on the experience of users.

The uninitiated corpus-user, with very little introduction and practice, will already find *BNCweb* a revealing window onto the possibilities of corpus linguistics. As experience with the tool deepens, more and more features or functions can be added to one's repertoire with little fuss. In fact, *BNCweb* provides an enlightening educational experience as one progresses, until a whole range of things one can do with a corpus are at one's finger-tips. Working through *BNCweb* is the best guide to corpus linguistics that I can think of, extending the range of questions to which one can seek answers far beyond what most users could imagine.

The present guide to the BNC and *BNCweb* is structured to provide this kind of educational experience, and can be treated as a general textbook introducing corpus linguistics. From the introductory "taster" of Chapter 1, showing how the combination of *BNCweb* and the BNC can answer some simple English-language problems of interest, the book adds step-by-step to the breadth and depth of inquiries one can make of a richly varied corpus. Among the topics covered are:

- concordances of words and phrases
- the design and composition of the BNC
- its flexible division into subcorpora which can be studied as corpora in their own right, or used for both quantitative and qualitative comparisons
- quantitative aspects of corpus investigation: relative frequency, statistical significance, and precision and recall, together with the interpretation and evaluation of these features
- annotation: part-of-speech tags and lemmas, and ways of using them for more sophisticated searches
- the versatile search potential opened up by *BNCweb*'s Simple Query Syntax and the even more advanced CQP Syntax
- the ability to compare subcorpora in terms of keywords
- the ability to explore collocational strength
- the ability to make one's own subcorpora from the corpus data
- the ability to add one's own linguistic categorizations to the corpus data.

Although the BNC's built-in linguistic annotation (part-of-speech tagging and lemmatization) is essentially word-based, *BNCweb*'s query syntax gives you the power to search on syntactic and lexico-syntactic patterns, while the customizing of your own annotations enables you to extend your analyses beyond the tagging information provided with the corpus. The explanation and illustration of this rich array of features provide a clear and engaging up-to-date introduction to the methodology of corpus linguistics, leading the user through manageable tasks or exercises at each step.

BNCweb originated in 1996 at the University of Zurich, where Hans-Martin Lehmann collaborated with Sebastian Hoffmann and Peter Schneider. The latest CQP version of BNC*web* has been authored by Sebastian Hoffmann and Stefan Evert. Of the other members of the present authorial team, all have engaged in close work on the BNC. Ylva Berglund Prytz began research on the BNC about ten years ago, and has been more directly involved with the corpus in recent years, owing to her position at the Oxford University Computer Services, where she performs, among other functions, that of BNC Communications Officer. Nick Smith was part of a team at Lancaster University involved in the grammatical tagging of the BNC during the 1990s, and has considerable experience of teaching and tutoring in corpus linguistics using *BNCweb*. David Lee has also worked on the BNC from a different angle: he undertook his PhD research at Lancaster using the BNC, and on the basis of this experience, later compiled a genre classification scheme for the corpus, which provides a more complete and detailed classification of the texts of the corpus than was available in the original BNC release. This scheme is now officially issued with the corpus, and its text classification has been incorporated into the search parameters of *BNCweb*.

Writing this book has been a collaborative enterprise in which all authors are jointly involved. While Sebastian Hoffmann has been the lead author for the whole project, it may be of interest to know which authors bore particular responsibility for which parts of the book. The following list indicates who were the *main* authors of individual chapters (the authors are identified by initials):

Ch. 1: SH	Ch. 5: SH & SE	Ch. 9: NS	
Ch. 2: SH	Ch. 6: SE	Ch. 10: DL	
Ch. 3: YB	Ch. 7: SH	Ch. 11: DL	
Ch. 4: NS	Ch. 8: SH & SE	Ch. 12: SE	Ch. 13: SH

In addition, David Lee and Nicholas Smith contributed extensively to the revision of the manuscript after the completion of the first draft.

This book will be of benefit to a variety of users. Perhaps the group that springs to mind most immediately consists of researchers and students working on the English language, especially those focusing on lexical and grammatical usage. But people working within areas as diverse as discourse analysis, stylistics, psycholinguistics, semantics and pragmatics, for instance, are increasingly recognizing the value of the corpus as an empirical basis for answering questions within linguistics more generally.

Another prominent group of users, who likewise may benefit from this book, are those concerned with teaching and learning English, especially English as a Foreign Language (EFL) and English as a Second Language (ESL). There have already been some pioneering studies comparing native-speaker usage, as reflected in the BNC, with non-native usage, as reflected in corpora produced by non-native speakers. Teachers, textbook writers and even learners of English (especially at the more advanced levels) will find out how to retrieve authentic examples illustrating points of usage, and invaluable information on the frequency of target structures in different varieties of spoken and written British English.

In short, this book will no doubt provide an invaluable foundation for novices in the field of corpus exploration. But seasoned corpus linguists, too, are likely to benefit from its extensive discussions of methodological issues and the detailed description of the more advanced features of *BNCweb*. Whatever your interest, the practical orientation and thorough coverage of this book will equip you with the necessary skills for conducting well-informed corpus-based investigations into the workings of the English language.

Geoffrey Leech
Lancaster University
June 2008

Acknowledgments

We are greatly indebted to Claire Hardaker, who has provided extensive comments on every chapter of this book. She alerted us to several shortcomings in the draft version of the book and her insightful suggestions for changes have proved invaluable in the revision of the text. We are also very thankful for comments received from Gunnel Tottie on Chapters 1, 2 and 5.

Thanks are also due to Hans Martin Lehmann and Peter Schneider, for coming up with the original idea for *BNCweb*. Although its functionality and underlying code have in the meantime greatly evolved, the basic design principles of *BNCweb* remain essentially the same.

1   Looking at language in use—some preliminaries

1.1   Introduction

1.1.1   Thinking about *goalless*, *shall* and cars

Let's start by having a look at the following three questions:

a) What is the meaning of *goalless*?

b) How is the word *shall* used in Present-day British English? Suggest one or two typical examples to illustrate your description.

c) Who talks more about cars, British men or British women?

Question a) concerns the meaning of a single word—this type of question could, for example, be asked by a learner of English as a foreign language who has come across *goalless* without sufficient context to fully understand its meaning. In contrast, the second question goes beyond lexical meaning; *shall* is a modal verb (like *will*, *must* and *can*) and is therefore normally used together with other verb forms (like *run*, *sing* and *be*). In other words, rather than simply asking a question about the meaning of a certain word, question b) is about how this word can be combined with other elements of the English language to express a particular grammatical relationship or function. This question might for example be asked by an English teacher who is preparing a lesson on modal verbs. Question c), finally, broadly deals with the relationship between language and society. It is admittedly a bit of an odd question—calling up common clichés and stereotypes about the difference between the two sexes—and you are probably more likely to meet questions of this form during a dinner table conversation than as part of a linguistic enquiry. But there's a deeper reason for asking this question here, which will become apparent when we discuss possible answers, so let's just for the time being assume that this is a perfectly sensible thing to ask.

> **Task:**
> Spend a few moments thinking about possible answers to the questions above. Then ask some fellow students or friends the same questions and compare their answers to yours. Do you all agree on what the correct answers are? If not, think about the reasons why these differences may have occurred.

If you are a native speaker of English (or a highly proficient speaker of English as a second or foreign language), you may feel that your intuitions about the language will be fully sufficient to provide answers to all three of them. However, and this may have been confirmed if you did the above task as a group of people, even native speakers quite often disagree about certain aspects of language and its use, and these three questions may be no exception. For example, when answering question a), many people immediately think of *goalless* as meaning 'aimless, purposeless; having no destination'. Interestingly, typically only few people think of a second meaning of the word, namely that which is used in football to refer to 'a game in which no goals were scored on either side'.

Moving on to question b), your intuition may have told you that *shall* is quite old-fashioned and slowly dying out, while speakers nowadays prefer *will* and other future time expressions such as *going to* or *gonna*. You may also have worked out that the modal auxiliary *shall* is followed by the infinitive without *to*, and perhaps even that *shall* is used most frequently when the subject is a first person pronoun (that is, *I* or *we*). As a result, the typical example you gave might have looked something like this:

(1)   I *shall* ring you up as soon as I arrive.

Alternatively, you might also have thought of a use of *shall* in offers, suggestions, requests for instructions, and requests for advice. This use takes the form of a question, i.e. the subject (e.g. *I*) follows the modal *shall*. A typical sentence is shown in (2).

(2)   *Shall* I carry your bag?

When asked about the level of formality of this second type of use, people are usually quite undecided. However, the majority have the impression that this is a particularly polite—and therefore formal—usage. Furthermore, when asked about which of the two structures is more frequent, people often don't feel confident in providing a clear answer.

As for question c), most people would answer this by stating that men talk more about cars than women.

This quick summary clearly shows that the intuition-based approach can result in a considerable range of possible answers, and it is not clear how close to the "truth"—or perhaps better, how close to actual usage—they really are. In order to determine this, you may therefore want to find independent confirmation. Let us consider some ways in which this could be done. For example, dictionaries will easily help you with question a). Indeed, the *Oxford English Dictionary* (OED) lists both of the meanings of *goalless* that were mentioned above. Yet you may also want to know which of the two senses is more common in Present-day English: unfortunately, the OED does not give you any help there.[1]

For the second question, grammar books are an obvious source of additional information. However, in this context it is important to ask what authority the author of a particular grammar book has for writing up his or her description. If its contents are heavily based on the author's intuitions about the English language, they may in fact also not fully reflect actual usage, even considering that an author of a grammar book is likely to be very knowledgeable about such matters.[2]

Another way of trying to find answers to at least the first two questions is by asking a wide range of informants who are native speakers of English. This is best done by giving them apparently unrelated questions whose context will trigger the use of the feature in question (e.g. *shall* vs. *will*). This method of "informant testing" is often more accurate than a direct appeal to native speaker intuitions, as the information provided is less likely to be influenced by factors such as self-censorship or accommodation. For example, when asked directly, an informant may opt to use *I will* or *I'll*—instead of *I shall*—because he or she does not want to give the impression of being old-fashioned. However, the same informant may not have any problems with using *I shall* in situations where they are not aware of the fact that the questions or tasks are designed to extract information about their use of *will* vs. *shall*. Although this informant-based method is clearly more informative than relying purely on the intuitions of a single speaker, it is obviously also much more difficult and time-consuming to carry out.

Finally, you could simply decide to observe what's happening around you and draw your conclusions on the basis of the data you collect. Every time someone talks about a car, you take note of the speaker's sex. Every time someone uses *shall*, you look at the type of construction in which it is used. And every time you read or hear *goalless*, you use the context to find out more about the meaning of this word. Once you have noted down a sufficient number of instances, you will have a reliable basis for a description of what is really going on with *goalless*, *shall* and talk about cars in today's English. However, there are two major problems with this method. First, with fairly infrequent words and expressions (e.g. *goalless*), you will have to wait a very long time before you have enough data to make any general claims. Secondly, and more importantly, your language experience may differ dramatically from that of other people who also use English. If, for example, you are a student at a British university, a large

---

1   However, some learner dictionaries (e.g. the *Collins COBUILD Advanced Learner's English Dictionary* 2006) do indicate whether certain senses are particularly common or rare.

2   It has to be pointed out, however, that many modern descriptions of English are no longer purely intuition-based. Instead, grammar books nowadays are often based on exactly the kind of data and methodology that we will describe in this book.

part of your language use will take place in interactions with other students and a considerable part of what you read will be academic texts (like the one you are reading right now). This is very different from the language experience of an average coal miner, lawyer, or jazz musician. And maybe the experience of these other types of language users will be particularly different from yours just in the context of the three questions you are trying to answer.

This book is about a method—and a tool—that will allow you to eliminate these two major problems to a very large extent. Suppose you had access to a huge collection of texts and conversations produced by a cross-section of today's population in Britain—i.e. by students, lawyers, jazz musicians, coal miners and a whole range of other types of language users. Further suppose that you would have access in such a way that it is possible to easily search the complete collection in a matter of seconds, and that you would also be able to get further information about the search results that are retrieved (e.g. about the type of speaker or writer, the kind of context in which it was produced, etc.). This is exactly what the British National Corpus (BNC) and *BNCweb* will give you.

1.1.2   Clues from a corpus—the BNC

The BNC is a 100 million word collection of samples of written and spoken language from a wide range of sources. It was put together to represent a wide cross-section of current British English, and contains a large number of language samples from different kinds of texts, produced by different kinds of language users and made available in different ways. A more detailed description of the corpus—including an account of how it was compiled, what type of texts it contains and what additional information is available about these texts—will be given in Chapter 3. *BNCweb* is a user-friendly web-based interface that was created to search (or as we say, to query) the data contained in the BNC. It gives you easy access to a wide range of functions that allow you to linguistically analyze the results of your queries. Originally developed at the University of Zurich by Hans Martin Lehmann, Sebastian Hoffmann and Peter Schneider (see Lehmann et al. 2000), *BNCweb* is nowadays maintained and further extended by Sebastian Hoffmann and Stefan Evert. The functionality of *BNCweb* is described in detail in the remaining chapters of the book.

To whet your appetite, let us quickly return to our three questions and see what clues we can find with the help of the BNC and *BNCweb*. A quick search for *goalless* shows that there are only 86 instances in the whole corpus. So on average, the word occurs less than once in every million words. Figure 1.1 displays how *BNCweb* will present the results of the search—or query—to you. This kind of output is generally referred to as a concordance.

Your query "goalless" returned 86 hits in 39 different texts (98,313,429 words [4,048 texts]; frequency: 0.87 instances per million words)

| I< | << | >> | >I | (Show Page: | 1 |) | (Show Sentence View) | (Show in random order) | New Query | | (Go!) |

No	Filename			Hits 1 to 20 Page 1 / 5
1	A1N 339	and drew a large attendance. The only redeeming feature of a	goalless	, worthless event at Stamford B
2	A1N 409	were created by Gillian Coultard in midfield, and the game finished	goalless	Photograph: Peter Jay Football
3	A22 50	clear mild night, emerged as worthy winners on aggregate after a	goalless	draw. Rangers, precariously ah
4	A2E 548	had managed just two goals in their first nine games. A	goalless	first leg at Hillsborough had lef
5	A2E 568	Sansom, their former England left-back, was left behind after the	goalless	draw against Stockport County
6	A3L 237	but less interesting and inventive. As one observer put it after	goalless	draws with Castellon and Mall
7	A40 589	's final game in the Lada Classic at Luton yesterday - a	goalless	draw with the world champion
8	A4B 401	has said he noted faults in Terry Butcher's game during the	goalless	draw in Sweden last month. Bu
9	A52 40	BARCLAY in Chorzow Poland. .0 England. .0 A SECOND successive	goalless	draw saw England through to t
10	A5C 5	team made sure of a place in Italy next summer with a	goalless	draw, their third in six qualifyir
11	A5U 147	leaders, Ealing, visit Leicester. Leicester could only manage a	goalless	draw midweek with Sutton Co
12	A80 377	different locations. The rush for tickets was sparked by Sunday's	goalless	draw between the US and El S
13	A8C 364	win at Hillsborough was important for morale, but last week's	goalless	draw with QPR at Plough Lan
14	A99 281	at least with the Swedes you can be reasonably sure of a	goalless	draw. All the top seeds will wa
15	A9H 175	quantity now, their most crucial result in the qualifiers was the	goalless	draw with the Soviet Union in

Figure 1.1:   The first 15 hits of a search for *goalless* in the BNC (cropped view)

Looking at this concordance, it is immediately obvious that football appears to be the predominant context in which British English speakers make use of the word *goalless*. In fact, if you were to look at all 86 instances in more detail, you would find that every single one is from the field of sports. Now, this does not of course mean that the other meaning of *goalless*—i.e. 'aimless'—does not exist at all in Present-Day English. After all, although the BNC contains nearly 100 million words, it is actually quite tiny in comparison with the totality of language use in Britain, and it is entirely possible that some very infrequent features are not represented at all in the corpus. However, you can now safely say that the 'aimless' meaning of *goalless* is very marginal indeed. The other obvious point to note from this list of results is that *goalless* often co-occurs with *draw*, referring to a game during which no goals are scored.[3] Of the total of 86 instances, 51 (59 per cent) co-occur with *draw*. If you are a learner of English as a foreign language, this is useful information because it will not only allow you to understand the most common meaning of the word but it will also give you the opportunity to notice how it is used idiomatically by native speakers.

What can the BNC tell us about the second question, i.e. how *shall* is used in Present-day English? A simple lexical search of *shall* gives you many more hits than you will want to look at: there are 19,505 instances of *shall* in the whole

---

3   At least this is the case in British English. Speakers of other varieties of English may prefer the expression *goalless tie* instead.

BNC. However, we could restrict our investigation by looking at the spoken part of the corpus only. A good reason for doing this is that we suspect that *shall* is becoming less common nowadays: it is widely assumed in linguistics that when something changes in a language, that change generally starts in the spoken rather than the written variety.

With *BNCweb*, it is easy to restrict searches to sub-parts of the corpus, e.g. spoken texts only. This part of the BNC contains about 10 million words, but *shall* still occurs 2,735 times. This suggests that *shall* is still in common use in Present-day English—compare this to the 86 instances of *goalless* in the whole corpus—and that it is still a long way from vanishing from the language altogether. Figure 1.2 shows a screenshot of the first five hits that are returned by *BNCweb*.

As you can see, both types of uses mentioned above are found in these first few sentences, e.g. ***shall** we listen to you* (no. 1, where the personal pronoun follows *shall*) and *I **shall** be contacting him* (no. 4, where the personal pronoun is placed first). But which of the two patterns is more frequent, and can we find out more about preferences among particular (types of) speakers?

Your query "shall" in spoken texts returned 2735 hits in 482 different texts (10,409,858 words [908 texts]; frequency: 262.73 instances per million words)

|< << >> >| Show Page: 1   Show KWIC View   Show in random order   New Query   Go!

No	Filename	Hits 1 to 50 Page 1 / 55
1	D91 721	or shall we listen to you?
2	D95 182	Or shall, what do you think of haven't it petitioned?
3	D95 226	Well, what I think I shall do now is I think I should take this a little further about this union business, I think I should get in touch with Dave [gap:name] , the Editor of the T U C to find out what the exact position of these, this so called union is because it doesn't sound like a union to me, it sounds, it sounds like an .
4	D95 278	I did do that along with Ron [gap:name] and er they were speaking in terms of er a conjurer at under a pound a time and thing of that nature which should then come to a the pensioner's category at Poole, so I took it back to Stuart [gap:name] and he said oh see what I can do Norman, and at the present moment it rests there because I haven't been able to contact Stuart at the moment owed to the holiday, but I shall be contacting him and hopefully we will also be doing two days, which is the Tuesday and the Thursday, also what they, er, he's, he's promised to do is to come half way with the cost of the jazz band, which is a great help.
5	D95 279	Er, so you can say that er Mr [gap:name] is a friend of pensioner's, he said, he said he would be prepared to, what I, I, I approached him and said er, what about Harlow Caring Council, are they prepared to assist the pensioners in any way or do they wish to join in on this, oh yes he said, of course Norman he said, how much are you paying er Ron [gap:name] I said well his asking forty pound for the, for the morning, oh he said I'll go half way with that, then he came out and said to me, pull me up afterwards and ask me to go to leisure services about the Tuesday, and so I'm still following that up and hopefully we will have two days on pensioner's week, because you want to have as much impact as possible and in a few moments, when I nearly finished here, I shall be reading you something where you'll see that it is important that we make an impact on the people of Harlow.

Figure 1.2:   Result of a search for *shall* in the spoken component of the BNC

One way of proceeding from here would now be to look at every single one of the 2,735 instances of *shall* returned by the search, always noting down information about the speaker (if available) and the grammatical pattern in which it is used. However, this would be very tedious and time-consuming. Fortunately there are quicker and more convenient ways of seeing patterns in the way *shall* is used. Let's for example consider the age of speakers who use *shall*. Our intuition might tell us that older speakers are typically more conservative and might therefore more likely use an old-fashioned form. If this were true we might then expect the use of *shall* to be more frequent among older speakers than among younger ones. *BNCweb* allows you to test this hypothesis in just a few simple clicks (using the so-called DISTRIBUTION feature).

Age:

Category	No. of words	No. of hits	Dispersion (over speakers)	Frequency per million words
0-14	385,234	189	66/258	490.61
25-34	1,120,516	368	90/351	328.42
15-24	594,400	185	81/302	311.24
60+	1,137,433	311	89/318	273.42
35-44	1,075,749	287	81/335	266.79
45-59	1,638,364	400	133/436	244.15
total	5,951,696	1,740	540/2,000	292.35

Figure 1.3: Distribution of *shall* over the category "Age of speaker" in the spoken component of the BNC

As you can see in Figure 1.3, the data is not conclusive: older speakers do not use *shall* more frequently than younger ones; in fact, it is the youngest group that can be seen to use this modal most often, while the oldest age group is found somewhere in the middle of the table. Clearly, this finding does not support the view that *shall* is archaic and in the process of dying out.

But let's dig a little deeper. Another thing you can do with *BNCweb* is to find out which words occur particularly often before or after *shall*. In this way, you could confirm your hunch—if this is what you came up with in response to question b)—that the first person pronoun subjects *I* and *we* are very frequent both before and immediately after *shall*. It turns out that nine out of every ten instances of *shall* occur together with *I* or *we*. The interesting question now is whether there are any differences among the various age groups with respect to the two possible sentence types, i.e. *I/we shall* vs. *shall I/we*. Again, *BNCweb* gives you this type of information very quickly—the results are shown in Figures 1.4a and 1.4b.

Age:				
Category	**No. of words**	**No. of hits**	**Dispersion (over speakers)**	**Frequency per million words**
60+	1,137,433	183	60/318	160.89
45-59	1,638,364	192	72/436	117.19
35-44	1,075,749	118	48/335	109.69
25-34	1,120,516	106	49/351	94.6
15-24	594,400	52	30/302	87.48
0-14	385,234	11	9/258	28.55
total	5,951,696	662	268/2,000	111.23

Figure 1.4a: Distribution of *I/we shall* in the spoken component of the BNC

Age:				
Category	**No. of words**	**No. of hits**	**Dispersion (over speakers)**	**Frequency per million words**
0-14	385,234	175	62/258	454.27
25-34	1,120,516	244	69/351	217.76
15-24	594,400	126	63/302	211.98
35-44	1,075,749	149	55/335	138.51
45-59	1,638,364	197	92/436	120.24
60+	1,137,433	103	51/318	90.55
total	5,951,696	994	392/2,000	167.01

Figure 1.4b: Distribution of *shall I/we* in the spoken component of the BNC

As you can see, the two patterns show an opposite trend: *I/we shall* is most often used by older speakers (182 instances, on average 160 times per million words), but the same group of speakers use *shall I/we* the least (103 instances—about 91 instances per million words). The reverse is true for the youngest speakers, who use *shall I/we* most often (175 instances, 454 instances per million words) but hardly use *I/we shall* at all (only 11 instances).

Now that you have obtained these findings—or **DESCRIPTIVE STATISTICS**— you have quite a good foundation for answering the second of the three questions at the start of this chapter. First of all, you can say that *shall* is still quite frequent in Present-day English—although of course you haven't yet checked how much more frequent *will* is. Secondly, you can say that one of the two uses, i.e. *I shall* or *we shall* is predominantly used by older speakers, suggesting that the declarative form may indeed be old-fashioned. Furthermore, you can say that the other type of use, which includes offers, suggestions and requests for instructions expressed by *shall I?* or *shall we?*, is mainly used by younger speakers. Finally—and most crucially—you could look at this age distribution as a snapshot of a change in the English language that is still ongoing, and from this predict what the future of this use might be. Think about it: what will happen when the young speakers represented in the BNC will be sixty or older? Will they have started using *I/we shall* more frequently by then because that's simply what older speakers do? Probably not. A much more likely interpretation of the data is that the declarative use is slightly dated and indeed slowly leaving the language—it is dying out. The use of *shall* for offers and suggestions, on the other hand, is probably going to increase even further. If this is true, perhaps it would make sense for teachers of English as a second or foreign language to introduce this type of use first, and only later go on to present the more marginal and archaic uses.

Even though we have extracted all sorts of information from the corpus, we have of course not yet answered the question whether the use of *shall* in offers and suggestions is particularly polite or not. Unfortunately, the tables we have compiled so effortlessly do not help us find this answer. Instead, we will have to look more closely at a sufficient number of instances of this particular use of *shall* in context. Descriptive statistics are almost always only one side of the coin, and a comprehensive description of a linguistic phenomenon will often require both a quantitative and a qualitative analysis of the data.

Finally, let's have a quick look at the third question—but how do we do this? How can we really answer the question whether men or women talk more about cars? A very basic approach would be simply to look for the word *car* and to have *BNCweb* calculate the same kind of distributional statistics as for *shall* above, just this time for the sex of speakers rather than age. Figure 1.5 displays the result of this calculation. Interestingly, women seem to use the word *car* more often than men. Notice, by the way, that the number of actual hits is higher for men (1,789 male vs. 1,597 female uses), but we need to take into account that there are more words in this corpus uttered by men than by women. This is why measuring the frequency across the same amount of text—as occurrences per million words, for example—is important: 485 instances per million words (pmw) for women vs. 361 pmw for men. We will—or we shall?—return to this issue again in later chapters.

Sex:				
Category	No. of words	No. of hits	Dispersion (over speakers)	Frequency per million words
Female	3,290,569	1,597	333/1,360	485.33
Male	4,949,938	1,789	438/2,448	361.42
total	8,240,507	3,386	771/3,808	410.9

Figure 1.5: Distribution of the word *car* over male and female speakers in the spoken component of the BNC

But what have we actually answered by looking at Figure 1.5? If you think about it, not all that much. First of all, we have forgotten an important part of the use of the word *car*: the plural form *cars*. Secondly, and much more importantly, what does it actually mean to "talk about cars"? Do you always need the lexical item *car* to do so? If someone says *I bought a Merc yesterday*, clearly this is also talking about a car. Conversely, what about mentioning a *car boot sale*? The word *car* is used here, too, but is the speaker really talking about cars? You can probably see that finding a reliable answer to the third question involves much more than a simple search and a few clicks in *BNCweb*—and this is a valuable insight. Some research questions are much easier to answer with the help of corpora than others, and it is important to know both the opportunities and the limitations that the use of corpora involves.

1.2   Why read this book?

This book is mainly about the practical steps involved in answering relevant linguistic research questions with the help of the BNC and *BNCweb*. As you will quickly realize, *BNCweb* is a very user-friendly tool: it is easy to perform a simple search of the corpus, and a few mouse-clicks are usually sufficient to give you lots of further information about your query. You might therefore wonder: is it really necessary to read a detailed manual? Our answer to this is: first, this book is not just a software manual—it was written by linguists interested in language study, and goes beyond a description of what the software can do. It is focused on what linguistic questions you can answer using the software and how you can go about interpreting the data generated by it in a meaningful way. The ease of use of *BNCweb* makes corpus-based language study appear simpler and more straightforward than it really is, and masks some considerations that should be part of every enquiry.

First and foremost, it is necessary to know more about the corpus: What is actually in the BNC? How did the compilers of the BNC choose the texts? How much do we know about the speakers and writers of the texts and the conditions of their production?

Second, it is necessary to learn the theoretical bases and methodological steps in corpus-based research: *How do I interpret the results presented by* BNCweb? *What do they tell me about British English as a whole or the text varieties that I chose to examine? What do they **not** tell me? How do I compare results from different searches? How can I be sure the results are reliable? How do I know that my searches really are relevant to answering my research questions?* This book will help you answer these important questions, and you will learn about theory and methods as you work your way through the chapters. It will help you avoid the potential problems and pitfalls that could turn the first steps of a novice corpus user into a potentially frustrating or misguided experience.

In this book, methodological points are addressed and illustrated in the context of actual investigations of language use. It is this combination of theory with extensive hands-on practice that makes the book different from others in the field of corpus linguistics. The functionality of the various features of *BNCweb* are explained through "real-life" examples of linguistic issues, combining "how-to" with a discussion of theoretical and methodological considerations.

1.3   Organization of the book

The organization of the chapters is as follows: Chapter 2 introduces some of the fundamental concepts of corpus-linguistic methodology. This is followed by a detailed description of the British National Corpus in Chapter 3. In Chapter 4, we then illustrate the basic search functionality of *BNCweb* and show how a query result—in the form of concordance lines—can be investigated to gain insights into the use of a particular word or phrase. This is followed by a second methodology chapter—Chapter 5—which covers a number of important issues relating to the comparability and reliability of findings made through *BNCweb*. We focus on why normalized frequencies are important (and how they are calculated), introduce the concepts of "precision" and "recall", and testing for statistical significance. In Chapter 6, we offer a detailed description of *BNCweb*'s "Simple Query Syntax" and show how it can be used to perform highly sophisticated searches of the corpus.

The next three chapters are then devoted to various ways of further manipulating and analyzing your query result. Chapters 7 (DISTRIBUTION and SORT) and 8 (COLLOCATIONS) cover ways of exploring your query results automatically, i.e. without the need to look at concordance lines individually (or, as it is often called, manually). In Chapter 9, we then turn to the manual annotation of concordance lines and guide you through the process of adding your own classifications to a query result (either within *BNCweb* itself or with the help of third-party programs such as Microsoft *Excel*).

For many research questions, it will be necessary to restrict searches to a subsection of the whole BNC—a so-called "subcorpus". Chapter 10 illustrates the various ways in which subcorpora can be defined. Furthermore, we will show how user-defined subcorpora can be employed to make repeated searches of (sub-parts of) the BNC more efficient. *BNCweb* also offers two additional functions—the FREQUENCY LIST and KEYWORD features—that can be used to explore the corpus data from a more "whole-text" or macro perspective (i.e. without starting from a concordance); these will be covered in Chapter 11.

In addition to the Simple Query Syntax introduced in Chapter 6, *BNCweb* also accepts queries in something called "CQP Query Syntax", whose advanced features allow users to perform even more powerful and flexible searches of the corpus. Given the much less intuitive nature of this query syntax, however, the description offered in Chapter 12 is likely to appeal predominantly to more advanced users. Chapter 13, finally, concerns practical issues in the running of *BNCweb*. It covers such aspects as the difference between standard users and users with administrator rights, and it also describes some internal aspects of the workings of the software that have been designed to optimize access by whole groups of users. The chapter concludes by outlining some issues relating to the installation and maintenance of *BNCweb*.

1.4   How to use this book

This book is probably best read while sitting in front of a computer with access to *BNCweb*. This will make it possible for readers to gain hands-on experience in using the tool by following the step-by-step descriptions of the many sample analyses. Each chapter also contains a number of tasks and exercises that will offer further opportunities for enhancing and broadening the practical skills of readers. However, the book has been written in such a way as to make independent reading of its contents a worthwhile experience.

Several of the chapters contain a considerable amount of information—in fact, it may be too much to fully "digest" everything in one sitting. This especially applies to the two chapters which introduce the Simple Query Syntax and the CQP Query Syntax (Chapters 6 and 12), as their descriptions are designed to be useful as a comprehensive reference to the query language. Although it may be informative to read these chapters in one go, you will probably find yourself returning to their contents at some stage in the future, as your need to make more complex searches arises.

A similar comment applies to the chapter describing the BNC (Chapter 3) and to the methodologically oriented Chapters 2 and 5. While we recommend that you consult these chapters thoroughly before you conduct any serious studies on the BNC, we would like to encourage you to explore the different features and options of *BNCweb* at your own pace, so don't worry if you don't fully understand everything the first time around. As you become more experienced and more familiar with the output provided by *BNCweb*, you will likely get a better grasp of the more theoretical aspects of corpus linguistic methods that we discuss in these chapters. They are therefore well worth revisiting. In sum, we are confident that this book will give you a thorough grounding in corpus linguistic theory and methods, as you learn by doing—as we guide you through this powerful yet user-friendly program.

2   Corpus linguistics: some basic principles

2.1   Outline

This chapter introduces readers to the basic principles of corpus linguistics. It covers points such as:

- What is a corpus?
- What is representativeness in corpora?
- What is corpus linguistics and what are the advantages of using corpus data?
- What different types of corpora are there?

In addition, this chapter includes a more advanced section on the relationship between corpus data and the formation of theoretical models of language.

2.2   Introduction

The word *corpus* (plural: *corpora*) comes from Latin, and means 'body' (cf. the related English word *corpse*)—this was also its original meaning in Late Middle English (15th century). By metaphorical extension, the word over time came to refer to a more abstract type of body, such as a collection of writings, e.g. the corpus of Shakespeare's works. In the second half of the 20th century, linguists began to refer to more general collections of language data as corpora. However, not just any compilation of texts is a corpus. Here is a concise definition of this most recent meaning of the word:

> A corpus is a collection of pieces of language that are selected and or-
> dered according to explicit linguistic criteria in order to be used as a
> sample of the language.   (Sinclair, 1996)

Some aspects of this definition are particularly important and require a bit more attention. Sinclair points out that the pieces of language need to be *selected*. This suggests that a linguistic corpus is much more than, for example, a fairly random compilation of a large number of texts. Instead, the individual pieces of language need to be selected in such a way that they fulfil a particular function, namely that they can be regarded as representative of the whole (where this "whole" can be an entire language or a specific variety or subset of it, such as "academic journal articles"). In other words, although a corpus is only a (potentially quite small) subset of what it is supposed to represent, its function is to mirror the whole in such a way that linguists can use it to say something about the language variety that was sampled: observations on the basis of corpus data are generalized back to the whole from which the corpus was initially selected.

This general principle of corpus linguistics is presented graphically in Figure 2.1. The large area on the left represents the totality of the language which is used and experienced—i.e. read or heard—by speakers of British English today. Since it is impossible in practice to investigate this totality, a representative sample of it needs to be compiled. Observations of linguistic behavior in this representative corpus then make up the linguistic findings, which in turn allow the linguist to draw conclusions about what typically happens in British English overall. Note that the size of the corpus shown in Figure 2.1 is of course not to scale: in reality, even a large corpus such as the BNC can represent only a tiny fraction of the totality of language in use.

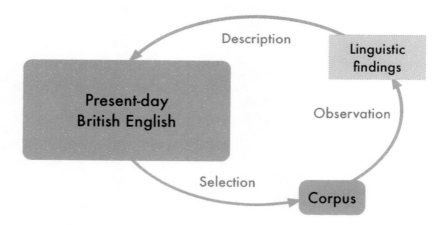

Figure 2.1:   The general procedure of corpus linguistics, illustrated with reference to the British National Corpus

Of course, corpora can also be compiled as samples of more specialized types of language use. For example, if you are interested in newspaper language or legal language, a suitable corpus will consist of a set of texts that mirrors this particular type of language use closely enough to allow you to draw generalizations about that type of language. It is important to keep in mind that not every corpus that you may have access to is suitable for all types of linguistic analysis.

It is obvious, for instance, that a corpus of British English does not form a good basis for investigating distinctive features of American English, and that a corpus of student essays will not be very informative if you are interested in spoken interaction. Sometimes, however, it may not be so obvious that a particular corpus is not truly suitable for a particular project. It is therefore very important to know the characteristics of a corpus before you start using it. Or to put it more bluntly: if you don't really know what your corpus contains and is supposed to represent, the interpretation and application of your results can be seriously compromised.

Finally, it is worth pointing out that in principle, a corpus does not need to be an electronic collection of language. In fact, some studies published in the early to mid-20th century (e.g. Jespersen 1909-49, Ellegård 1953) used the same general procedure of analysis without access to computers at all. However, when a corpus is available in electronic format, many types of analysis can of course be carried out much faster and much more efficiently and reliably. In fact, results that *BNCweb* can generate for you in seconds could take months or even years to produce if you were to attempt this by hand!

Task:
Imagine that you were given the task of compiling a representative corpus of Present-day English. What texts/pieces of language would you include in your corpus? How much of each do you think would be a "fair" representation of this type of text? Are there any kinds of language use that you would explicitly exclude from such a corpus? Try to make your selection criteria explicit—why this type of text but not that one? Why more of one than another? If you are working in a group, check whether your choices are the same as those of other group members. If not, can you agree on a "best method of selection"?

2.3   Representativeness in corpora

Compiling a truly representative corpus is not an easy task. And when it is a group effort, it is likely that different people will have different ideas about how to go about the task. Let us look at some possible replies to the questions posed above.

First of all, what types of language use should be included in a representative corpus of British English? Newspapers? Both fiction and non-fiction books? Spoken and written language? These are probably fairly uncontroversial proposals. What is far more of an issue is the question how much of each of these text types should be included. More broadsheet or more tabloid newspapers? More best-selling novels or more specialist books dealing with scientific topics? On the one hand, you could argue that tabloids have a higher circulation and that they should therefore form the bulk of the newspaper language to be included. On the other hand, you could say that there are many more different types of broadsheet newspapers than tabloids and that this variety should therefore make up a larger section of the newspaper texts in the corpus. In fact, each argument in its own way makes perfect sense. Taking the point of view of "influence", you could also argue, on the one hand, that the broadsheets are perceived as better-quality newspapers, and "represent" British English better than "low-brow" tabloids. However, the opposite may also be argued: that the tabloids better represent the "language of the common people" rather than the language of an elite group of highly proficient writers.

Let us take this one step further. What is the most common type of language produced by most speakers of a language? Clearly, the answer must be spontaneous conversation with friends, classmates, colleagues, members of the family, etc. In fact, relatively few people produce language output (spoken or written) that is intended for large audiences. If language production is the decisive factor in the choice of texts to be included, a representative corpus would consist mostly of spontaneous spoken interaction. However, if language exposure or reception were considered to be the more important factor, spoken text types such as TV and radio programmes would also make up a large percentage, and written text types such as newspapers and books would constitute a large chunk of the written part of the corpus. In both approaches, however, highly specialized texts, e.g. academic journal articles from the fields of biochemistry or linguistics, would receive marginal coverage, if any at all. To keep a balance and to ensure a wide coverage of types, therefore, a corpus compiler of a "general language" corpus may therefore also choose to include a wide variety of texts, even though no direct link to actual usage or exposure can be established.

Returning to our list of possible text types to be included: what about scripts of TV soap operas? Poetry? Shopping lists? E-mail messages and/or letters? The language used by teenagers in SMS text messages or in online chats? For all of these categories, you could argue for or against inclusion—and once you have decided in favor of inclusion, you are again faced with the question of how much you will want to add. For example, scripts of soap operas are problematic because they contain "naturalistic" dialogue rather than actual, authentic language use. Yet, if you consider that soap operas are very popular and that therefore many people will be exposed to these constructed dialogues, perhaps you might want to include more of them. Finally, you may be doubtful about including text messages because this type of language use might be considered far too non-standard and informal (consider e.g. *i got 1 u will h8* for *I got one you will hate*) to be included in a representative corpus of British English. However, you could argue that text messages are such a common aspect of our daily lives that it is important for this type of language to be included. As we will point out again below, corpus linguists tend to be interested in (impartial) language description rather than in telling people how to use language correctly. If this is the case, there is really no reason why SMS messages should be excluded purely on the grounds of being non-standard.

We could use up much more space to discuss what types of language use should or should not be included in a representative corpus. But as you might already have guessed, there really is no correct answer: corpus representativeness is something that corpus compilers can (and certainly should) strive for— but there are simply no absolute or objective criteria that can be used to gauge representativeness. However, this fact should not deter you from doing corpus linguistic research. Rather, we have discussed this issue in some detail in order to draw your attention to one important fact: that you as a corpus user need to know what is in the corpus before you can begin to interpret your linguistic findings in a meaningful way. It is essential that you find out as much as possible about the corpus which you want to use.

Let us look at an extreme example that nicely demonstrates the importance of knowing your corpus. In today's world, e-mail is an essential mode of communication for a great number of people. As a result, it would probably be a good idea to include e-mail messages in any corpus that is intended to represent Present-day British English. At the time when the British National Corpus was compiled, however, the picture was quite different: at the beginning of the 1990s, e-mail use was still very marginal and largely restricted to academic and governmental contexts. Even so, the BNC does in fact contain examples of e-mail communication—7 files with a total of 214,018 words (or slightly more than 0.2 per cent of the whole corpus). The first point you would need to consider when you want to look at e-mail language in the BNC is that it may not have had the same functions back then as it does today. For example, many e-mail messages today are written in a very informal style, but perhaps this was not the case in the early 1990s. As a result, conclusions drawn from some of the patterns that can be observed in the seven e-mail texts in the BNC may tell us little about the use of e-mail language today. However, the point we would like to highlight here has much more serious implications.

Interestingly, the word *scum* occurs very often in the e-mail texts included in the BNC—there are 342 instances in total. This is a very odd finding indeed, considering that *scum* only occurs a total of 540 times in the whole 100-million word corpus—and this figure includes the 342 instances in e-mail texts! If you only look at those numbers, you may think that, for whatever reason, *scum* is particularly frequent in e-mails. However, the fact that a corpus is reasonably representative of overall language use does not necessarily mean that all of its sub-components are equally representative. As it turns out, what is classified as e-mails in the BNC are not messages that were sent from one person to another single recipient; instead all of the messages were posted to a single electronic mailing list. And the subscribers of this mailing list were fans of the football club Leeds United. The frequent use of the noun *scum* can be explained by numerous references to the rival team Manchester United as "(the) scum"—and it therefore has nothing to do with the nature of e-mail communication as such.

Obviously, this is an extreme example of how a particular choice that was made by the compiler(s) of a corpus can lead to very wrong interpretations on the part of the uncritical corpus user. However, the same principle is relevant to all linguistic findings obtained by a corpus search: the strategies and selection methods of the corpus compiler(s) will invariably—even if only subtly—influence your results. The only way to counter this is by knowing enough about the corpus that you use to allow you to account for these potentially distorting influences in the analysis of your data.

2.4   What is corpus linguistics? Why use a corpus?

Corpus linguistics is the systematic study of linguistic phenomena using (machine-readable) collections of authentic language use, i.e. corpora. It is an essentially quantitative method, meaning that corpus linguists tend to count features of language (or have the computer count them) as part of their analysis of linguistic features. Furthermore, corpus linguists are typically interested in discovering general patterns—or norms—of language use rather than in establishing a "butterfly collection" of idiosyncrasies or peculiar features of language that speakers produce. The emphasis is on description rather than prescription, i.e. corpus linguists aim to describe rather than to establish (or uphold) rules about how language should or should not be used.

However, corpus linguistics isn't only about counting. Instead, corpus linguists typically rely on both quantitative and qualitative analytical techniques. For example, returning to our discussion about the two constructions *shall I/we* vs. *I/we shall* in Chapter 1, once you have compiled the descriptive statistics about the distribution of these constructions over different age groups, it pays to look at a subset of the instances more closely—qualitative work. For instance, if you look at the larger context of individual instances, you might discover subtle differences in the functions that these items perform in the discourse (e.g. suggestions vs. offers, different degrees of politeness, etc.) and you might therefore notice important distinctions between age groups that would have remained hidden behind the distributional figures. For most linguistic research questions, quantitative descriptive statistics are really only one side of the coin, and are usually just the starting point or launch pad for further analytical work.

Although there is some disagreement among corpus linguists themselves, it is probably fair to say that corpus linguistics is mainly a particular way of investigating language—a systematic approach rather than a proper field or branch of linguistics as such (unlike, for example, phonology, semantics or syntax). The reason for saying this is that as long as you have a suitable corpus at your disposal, you can use corpus-linguistic methods in almost any field of linguistics, to describe the sound system of a language or language variety, its morphology, lexico-grammatical characteristics, pragmatics, discourse phenomena, etc.

Linguistics is the scientific study of language. But how do you study in a scientific way something that is so pervasive yet also so varied? There are two broad approaches that are both "scientific" in their own ways, yet have very different starting points, methods, and goals. Many so-called "theoretical linguists" or "generative linguists" are mainly interested in studying what may be called the "language potential"—what the language system is like in the brain, in the abstract, in terms of various universal and local rules and principles. Other linguists are more interested in describing and accounting for how language really works in real life, as evidenced by actual linguistic output, both spoken and written. This second approach to language is the one that most corpus-based linguists adopt. Some common questions they might ask about language would be: What do speakers/writers tend to say or write in this particular genre/situation? What linguistic forms do they use to accomplish certain goals or communicate particular meanings? How do particular forms match up with particular meanings or functions? What changes can be observed in language use across regions, social classes, genders, and across time? In seeking the answers to such questions, linguists will have to look at "language in use"—actual samples of language as used by speakers and writers of the language, in order to find evidence for or against a certain hypothesis. We know that language varies from group to group, and even from person to person, so any one linguist's knowledge of language use will necessarily be limited. Many facts about language that may be pedagogically useful are also practically impossible to obtain simply by relying on introspection alone (e.g. What are the most frequent verbs in a particular variety of a language? Which social or age groups use *shall* the most, and in what type of sentence pattern?).

Reliable, empirically based statements about actual linguistic behavior are frequently only possible with corpus data. As a representative sample of the output of a particular language community, a large general language corpus (such as the BNC) gives you access to a cross-section of speakers and writers. The patterns that emerge from such data allow a much more complete description of language use than introspection, as the data is not derived from the fallible intuitions of just one or a small handful of people.

However, this is not the only advantage of using a corpus. If linguistics is to be truly the *science* of language, it should satisfy the fundamental scientific requirement of replicability. For a linguist who entirely relies on introspection, this requirement is hard to fulfill entirely. For the corpus linguist, however, this is no problem at all: anyone who has access to the same corpus—and the BNC is widely used by linguists all over the world—can replicate and objectively verify your linguistic results.

Finally, we would briefly like to mention that corpora may be particularly attractive to people who are not native speakers of the language which they are investigating. Although you will of course need sufficient knowledge about a language to interpret your linguistic findings in a meaningful way, native and non-native speakers are basically on an equal footing when it comes to discovering patterns in a corpus.

2.5   A brief—and more advanced—excursion: description vs. theory

In the previous section, we briefly mentioned a number of fields of investigation where corpora can provide important insights that would not be available via introspection alone. However, there are many other areas of linguistics— particularly in the more theoretically oriented branches of the discipline—where the role of corpora is much less prominent. In fact, until relatively recently (about the 1980s in Britain, and even later in the United States), corpus linguistics was a rather marginal way of investigating language. This was the case because for several decades, mainstream linguistics was very critical of the value of corpora, particularly as a basis for forming theories of language. For much of the second half of the 20th century, linguists such as Chomsky were working on improving their theoretical models of language, and they did not believe that a description of authentic language use could make a significant contribution to such a model. For example, Chomsky famously states that

> [a]ny natural corpus will be skewed. Some sentences won't occur because they are obvious, others because they are false, still others because they are impolite. The corpus, if natural, will be so wildly skewed that the description would be no more than a mere list.
>
> (Chomsky 1962: 159)

It is furthermore argued that other influences on speakers (e.g. whether they are tired or angry or have a cold, whether they are speaking under time pressure or in front of an audience, etc.) will result in additional disfluencies or one-off utterances that will distort the picture for those who are interested in finding out about the internal workings of language. In order to capture this distinction between a theoretical/idealized model and actual use, the two terms "competence" and "performance" are frequently used. Competence is the tacit, internalized knowledge of a (native) language while performance is what is produced on the basis of this knowledge. Chomsky and his many followers are interested in explaining competence. What is in a corpus, however, is performance data. The important question now is whether corpora can also tell us something about competence. We strongly believe that they can, and we will now use the corpus-based study of complex prepositions as an example to support this claim.

Complex prepositions are multi-word prepositions such as *in terms of*, *in front of* or *in response to* which in many ways function like single-word prepositions (consider e.g. *I like to sit in front of the fire* vs. *I like to sit before the fire*). However, are they really like single words? If so, this would mean that they should have no internal (syntactic) structure, i.e. that they are indivisible units. Also, they would presumably be retrieved from memory as a single chunk and not put together on the basis of (syntactic) rules of the language. The two options are illustrated in Figure 2.2.

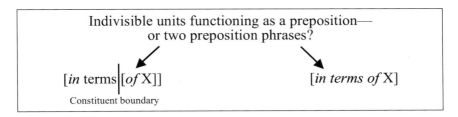

Figure 2.2:   Two possible syntactic interpretations of complex prepositions

If the version on the left is indeed correct, and we have a preposition phrase contained within another preposition phrase, complex prepositions cannot be indivisible units. Rather, this interpretation in fact suggests that there is a syntactic boundary after the nominal element *terms*. Such a view is supported by the fact that it is indeed possible to add lexical items to the inside of the complex preposition. As a case in point, consider example (1):

(1)   This service was introduced *in **direct** response* to the needs of our customer. (G29: 851)

If we pursue this type of argumentation, we are using an introspection-based approach: "I can think of a sentence where this is possible, and this is therefore proof against the claim that this construction is indivisible". However, let us for the moment propose that the version on the right side of Figure 2.2. is the norm. Complex prepositions like *in terms of* would then be stored and retrieved from the speaker's memory as single, indivisible items. Phrases like *in immediate front of* would in turn only be constructed on the basis of our knowledge of the rules of grammar when it is absolutely necessary, and no constituent boundary would have to be postulated after *terms* (or any other nominal element in a complex preposition).

Which of the two views is the correct one? It is important to note that this question is not a question about language use—instead, it is a question about how elements of language are stored and retrieved. In other words, it is a question about competence. Nevertheless, it is possible to use performance data—i.e. as reflected in a corpus—to find an answer to this question.

For this purpose, we can again make use of the spoken conversations contained in the BNC. In particular, we can look at a very frequent feature of spoken language: filled pauses such as *er* and *erm*. Think about it: why do they occur so frequently in conversations? Linguists have suggested a number of reasons. One very important one is hesitation: we use a filled pause when we are not (yet) quite sure about what exactly we would like to say next. Instead of being silent while we do the planning—which could invite interruption from our conversational partner(s)—we bridge the gap with *er* or *erm*. In other words, filled pauses can be seen as a reflection of the cognitive processes underlying the production of language.

Interestingly, these filled pauses don't seem to occur randomly. Rather, there appears to be a connection between their placement and syntactic structure. Consider the following statements about the connection between syntactic boundaries and filled pauses:

> Within sentences these boundaries are the appropriate place to stop to plan details of the next major constituent. [...] This stopping place is typically marked by a filled pause.   (Clark & Clark 1977: 267-8)

> Filled pauses occur at lesser or medial syntactic boundaries (in addition to major boundaries)[...]   (Biber et al. 1999: 1054)

Now, if people tend to say *er/erm* at syntactic boundaries, and if we wish to test the claim that there is a syntactic boundary within complex prepositions, corpus data should be able to give us some important evidence. There are four possible positions where a filled pause could occur in the context of complex prepositions: immediately before and after, and internally either before or after the nominal element, e.g. *erm...in...erm...front...erm...of...erm*. These four positions are exemplified in sentences (2) to (4), with sentence (3) containing filled pauses in two different positions:

(2) The county council thinks that ... it's a balanced approach *in line **erm** with* Secretary of State's previously stated wishes. (BNC:HVK: 140)

(3) ***Erm*** *in terms of* ***er*** forcing people to have it, well you can't <pause> er somebody has to want to, to look at the possibility ... (BNC:F86: 439)

(4) Yes, I readily accept that, er my general proposition is *in* ***er*** *connection with* the settlement pattern of York, and... (BNC:HVK: 145)

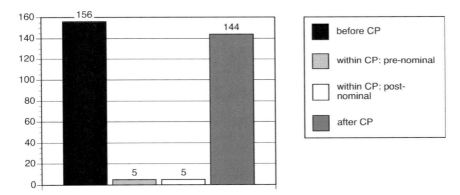

Figure 2.3:   Complex prepositions: distribution of filled pauses in the spoken component of the BNC (Hoffmann 2005: 45)

If we count all filled pauses in all these four positions in all the instances of complex prepositions in the spoken part of the BNC (a total of 310), we see an interesting picture—this is shown in Figure 2.3.

As you can see, filled pauses occur very frequently both immediately before and after complex prepositions. In contrast, few of them are found in the positions surrounding the noun. In fact, both internal positions are equally rare, with five instances of filled pauses each. This is surprising, considering that the second of the internal positions has been claimed to be a syntactic boundary. The corpus data presented in Figure 2.3 therefore strongly suggests that this boundary does not truly exist. Instead, complex prepositions are stored as single units in our lexicon. When necessary (e.g. if they want to add a pre-modifying adjective to the internal nominal element, such as in example (1) above), speakers of the language can also assemble the same sequence of orthographic words from smaller building-blocks of language. However, this is not the default option.

What we have just done is to make an informed claim about competence using performance data. In corpus linguistics, the patterns we observe can be interpreted as a window on our competence and the structures and rules which underlie the production of speech. There is thus no reason at all why corpora should be disqualified from contributing to theoretical models of language. On the contrary, corpus linguistic methodology has an important role to play in the building of such models, yielding insights that would not otherwise be available to the researcher.

2.6   Types of corpora

Earlier in this chapter, we stressed the fact that some corpora will be more suitable for the investigation of particular linguistic questions than others. We made this point with respect to content, i.e. what particular variety (e.g. American English vs. British English), mode (e.g. spoken vs. written) or specific type of text (e.g. newspapers vs. novels) the corpus was intended to represent. However, corpora can also differ on various other levels, and here again, a thorough knowledge of what kind of corpus you are using can be crucial for the success of your linguistic study. This section will mention a number of possible types, although it cannot cover all types of corpora that exist. For a more comprehensive overview of the full range of corpora, please consult David Lee's web site on corpus-based linguistics at http://devoted.to/corpora.

- Corpora can be **synchronic** or **diachronic**. The first of these terms refers to a corpus that contains texts which were all produced at about the same time (e.g. the 1990s or the first half of the 16th century). Conversely, a diachronic corpus is designed to cover a whole period of time, e.g. from Old English to Early Modern English, or from the year 1650 to the end of the twentieth century. Obviously, diachronic corpora are well-suited to the study of language change. However, because they have to cover an extended period of time, they will typically contain much less information about the whole range of language use at a particular point in time than a synchronic corpus. In turn, synchronic corpora are not well-suited for the investigation of change over time, although they can yield important clues when there is variation among forms or structures (as we saw with *shall* in Chapter 1).

- Corpora can consist of **complete texts** or **samples** (i.e. only parts of full texts); the majority of corpora are of the latter type. When complete texts are used to create a corpus, the size of the corpus will of course increase more quickly. However, there is a danger in this case that the styles and idiosyncrasies of certain authors will be overrepresented in the corpus simply because some works are considerably longer than others. On the other hand, a small sample size will mean that items that only rarely occur in a particular text type may not actually be adequately represented in the corpus. (For further information about the influence of sample size, see the discussion in Biber 1993.)

- Corpora can be **static** or **dynamic**. The contents of a static corpus are fixed once it has been compiled. In contrast, a dynamic corpus (also: monitor corpus) is one that is constantly updated and added to—and in some cases, older texts are also deleted. Such a dynamic corpus will of course be more up-to-date than a static corpus. However, since the actual content of the corpus continually changes, linguistic findings based on searches performed at different points in time may differ to some extent.

- Corpora can be **plain** or **marked-up**. A plain text corpus only contains the actual words of the included texts. Most published corpora, however, contain some types of MARK-UP that are nowadays commonly enclosed within angled brackets ("<" and ">"). Without going into too much detail, we can note that mark-up can be used to give various kinds of information about: (i) the origins/producers of a text (METATEXTUAL MARK-UP); (ii) the various sections (structural mark-up) or typographical representations (typographical mark-up) of a text; or (iii) linguistic characteristics of the text (linguistic ANNOTATION).

  Metatextual mark-up gives information about speakers/authors (e.g. male vs. female) or about the time when the texts were produced (e.g. a certain year or period in the history of the language). Structural mark-up gives us such text-level information as paragraph boundaries and sub-headings (in written texts), or speaker changes, overlaps and interruptions (in spoken texts). Finally, the term "annotation" is usually used to refer to "value-added", i.e. linguistically interpreted, TAGS which give extra information that is not part of the text, but is the result of some kind of linguistic analysis (usually by a computer program, but annotations can be added manually as well—see Chapter 9). For example, each word can be given a part-of-speech tag (e.g. distinguishing between nouns, verbs and adjectives; see 3.5.1), or information can be added about the functions of words and phrases in the sentence (e.g. subject, object, adverbial).[1] Many research questions can benefit from linguistic mark-up and annotations in the corpus. For example, the findings about the two different uses of *shall* which we presented in Chapter 1 would not have been possible without access to further information (mark-up) about the age of the speakers who used *shall*. However, mark-up and annotations (e.g. part-of-speech tags) can make it much more difficult to read the corpus texts in their raw format. Specialized corpus tools, such as *BNCweb*, are therefore usually used to display heavily annotated corpora in a human-readable format while still allowing linguists to make full use of the various kinds of mark-up.

---

1   "Tags" is a general/umbrella term that is sometimes used interchangeably with "mark-up", but many corpus linguists use "tags" mainly to refer to "linguistic tags"—i.e. annotations, particularly part-of-speech annotations.

As Chapter 3 will show in more detail, the BNC is a synchronic and static corpus which consists of a large number of text samples that are heavily marked-up with information about the texts, speakers and writers, and annotated with linguistic information (e.g. parts of speech).

2.7   Further reading

In this chapter, we have introduced you to some of the basic concepts of corpus linguistics. In doing so, we have highlighted issues that will be particularly relevant in your work with the BNC. If you wish to find out more about this methodology and its varied applications, we recommend that you consult one of the introductory textbooks available, e.g. McEnery & Wilson (2001 [1st ed. 1996]), Biber et al. (1998), Kennedy (1998), Stubbs (1996), Hunston (2002), Meyer (2002) or McEnery et al. (2006).

The topic of representativeness in corpora is covered in detail in Biber (1993).

3 Introducing the British National Corpus

3.1 Outline

This chapter presents a detailed description of the data source that *BNCweb* works with. Individual points covered are:

- The major parts of the BNC and the selection criteria applied in compiling the corpus
- Additional descriptive information about texts and speakers in the corpus
- Grammatical annotation: part-of-speech tags and headwords/lemmas
- The (internal) format of the BNC texts
- Errors in the corpus

In addition, we briefly discuss the question whether the BNC can be considered to be a representative corpus of Present-day English.

3.2 Introduction

In Chapters 1 and 2 you learned about what a corpus is and why you might want to use one. You also saw references to one particular corpus: the British National Corpus (BNC). Chapter 2 repeatedly underlined the importance of knowing your corpus, including factors relating to its compilation. The BNC is carefully documented, and comes with a reference guide, where you can find detailed information about how the corpus was compiled, what it contains, and how information about the texts and the words in the texts have been coded (or marked up) in the corpus. The *Reference Guide for the British National Corpus (XML Edition)* (Burnard 2007) is available at http://www.natcorp.ox.ac.uk/XMLedition/URG/, and at some stage you may want to explore it to gain further understanding of features of specific relevance to your particular study.[1] In this chapter, we will introduce the corpus paying particular attention to some of the characteristics that you should be familiar with when you set out to use the BNC.

The British National Corpus was created to be a balanced reference corpus of late 20th century British English. It was compiled by a team of people representing a number of research institutions, publishers and libraries. The aim was

---

1   Throughout the book, we will refer to Burnard (2007) as *BNC User Reference Guide*.

to create a very large, carefully planned corpus of contemporary British English (with the end date set in the early 1990s). The project team put considerable effort into drawing up plans for what the corpus should contain, in order to mirror the language of the time. The material to be included in the corpus was then selected according to specified SELECTION CRITERIA. Once the material was selected, it was included in the corpus together with whatever supplementary information about it that was available. That means that in addition to information about the criteria on which each text was chosen, further information about the material in the corpus may be available. As further explained below, it is important to be aware of the difference between the selection criteria, for which specific proportions were established, and the DESCRIPTIVE FEATURES, which were added where available in order to characterize the texts which had already been selected on other grounds.

All in all, the BNC consists of over 4,000 "texts"—more accurately, "files".[2] Each file is a sample of written or spoken language. The size of the samples varies, from a few hundred words up to several tens of thousands. Some of the files contain an extract of a longer text (e.g. part of a book), while others consist of several shorter texts (e.g. an issue of a newspaper, which is made up of a large number of different articles). A list of all the files included in the corpus can be found in the *BNC Reference Guide*. You can also find information about the material through *BNCweb* itself, as will be illustrated later, for example in Chapter 4 (Section 4.4.5).

3.3   Written material

The BNC contains both written and spoken material. The written component of the corpus comprises about 90 million words in all. The written texts that were included in the corpus were selected on the basis of three independent criteria (see Table 3.1):

- *domain*—subject field or broad topic area
- *time*—when they were produced
- *medium*—the type of publication in which they appeared

The corpus contains both published and unpublished material: texts from books, newspapers, and magazines; fiction and non-fiction texts; some handwritten notes; school essays, etc. The material is from the latter part of the 20th century

---

2   Each file has a unique identifier (e.g. CAE or G42), which we will refer to as "text ID" or "filename". Note that unlike some corpora, in the BNC there is no connection between the text ID and the content of the file.

and the bulk of the texts are from 1974-1993, with a small number of samples of fiction going back as far as 1960. These early texts are included to mirror their longer shelf-life and continuing influence on the language.

Table 3.1   Proportion of the corpus (number of words) sampled according to domain, time, and medium.

Written Component (~90%)		
Sampling criteria (proportion of words in the written component)		
Text domain	Time period (publication date)	Medium
• Imaginative (19%) • Natural & pure science (4%) • Applied science (8%) • Social science (16%) • World affairs (20%) • Commerce and finance (8%) • Arts (7%) • Belief and thought (3%) • Leisure (14%)	• 1960-74 (2%) • 1975-1984 (5%) • 1985-1993 (91%) • unknown (2%)	• Book (57%) • Periodical (32%) • Misc. published (4%) • Misc. unpublished (5%) • To-be-spoken (1%)
87,903,571 words		

In choosing texts for inclusion in the corpus, the compilers aimed to meet the pre-defined proportions for texts from the different domains, time periods, and types of media. Where possible, they also tried to get a wide and inclusive range of material so that there were, for example, texts written by both men and women, material aimed at children, teenagers and adults, texts covering different topics and so on. There were, however, no predefined proportions set for these descriptive features. This means that although it is possible to find, for example, unpublished material written by women, this material was not sampled to mirror the amount of such writing in the language as a whole and therefore cannot automatically be assumed to be a good, representative sample of unpublished writing by women in Britain. Likewise, although there is material written for children in the corpus, no predefined proportions were set with regard to the exact representation of such texts according to domain, time period and medium (such as books versus periodicals). This is important to keep in mind when you want to study a particular kind of text. Although the corpus may well contain a substantial amount of that kind of material, this is not necessarily a good and representative sample. We can take the newspaper material in the BNC as a case in point.

The corpus comprises a large number of newspaper extracts. They were selected so that the corpus contains examples of both national and regional papers, broadsheets and tabloids, Sunday papers and papers published on weekdays. There is material from domestic news sections, from sports pages, letters to the editor, international news and so on. That means that the BNC as a whole contains different kinds of newspaper material which contributes to the overall picture of the British English language that we can study using the corpus. However, if we wanted to study British English newspaper language in particular, we would not want our corpus to contain material that had been selected only as examples of that kind of language. Instead we would want to make sure we based our study on a corpus that adequately represents the kind of text we were examining, for example a corpus with equal proportions from all main broadsheet papers, or amounts of material from regional papers reflecting the size of the papers' readership, balanced across the days of the week or from different' times of the year, and so on. As the BNC cannot provide that kind of balance and comprehensive cover for all possible types of text, we have to be cautious in the kind of conclusions we draw from studies of a subset of the corpus. This applies not only to genre-based subsets, of course, but is equally true for other samples such as ones based on time of publication, target audience, sex of author and so on.

As you will see in later chapters, *BNCweb* makes it easy to restrict your searches to a particular part of the corpus, or a subset of corpus files that you choose. This places a particular burden of responsibility on the researcher, who should ensure they know what they are searching and what limitations, if any, their selection bring about.

Table 3.2 below lists the descriptive features (information added after texts had been selected), with an indication of the amount of written material for which this information is available. This information is also available in *BNCweb*. By using the DISTRIBUTION function, for example, (described in Chapter 7) you can easily find the number of words with a particular feature or combination of features that you have searched.

The texts for the BNC were thus selected according to certain pre-defined criteria, with further information about the material being added where available. Once the corpus was released, independent work was carried out by David Lee to categorize the material further according to GENRE (e.g. personal letters, popular magazines and job interviews; see Lee 2001). This information was included in subsequent releases of the corpus, and is also available to users of *BNCweb* in two forms: as detailed genre categories and as **DERIVED TEXT TYPES**. The latter is made up by combining the genres identified by Lee into larger units. The "Derived text types" and the proportion of text in each category are listed in Table 3.3. A list of all the genres identified by Lee is available in Appendix 1.

Table 3.2   Descriptive features and proportion of material in the written component for which the information is known and searchable via
BNCweb (% of words in the written part of the corpus).

Feature	Description	Proportion known
Age of author	Six groups with slightly different spans (10, 15 or undefined number of years)	22%
Sex of author	Male, female, mixed (where there is more than one author)	53%
Domicile of author	Where author is resident (usually UK when known)	27%
Type of author	Sole, multiple (several authors), corporate (organization or similar)	96%
Age of audience	Child, teenager, adult, any (92% adult)	89%
Target audience sex	Male, female, mixed	77%
Text sample	Sample taken from beginning, middle, end of source text; whole text; composite	60%
Perceived level of difficulty	A subjective assessment of the text's technicality or difficulty (high, medium, low)	89%

Table 3.3   Derived text types: word counts and proportions in written texts[3]

Derived Text Type	Words	Proportion
Non-academic prose and biography	24,178,674	28%
Other published written material	17,924,109	20%
Fiction and verse	16,143,913	18%
Academic prose	15,778,028	18%
Newspapers	9,412,174	11%
Unpublished written material	4,466,673	5%

---

3   Note that the category "Derived Text Type also includes two values for spoken data:
"Spoken conversation" and "Other spoken material". These values correspond exactly to
the two major components of the spoken part of the BNC (see Section 3.4).

The genre classification is an important feature, since it allows users to identify material that belongs to a more fine-grained category of text than the original sampling criteria. It also offers an alternative division of the material. It is, for example, easy to find texts that come from newspapers, irrespective of their domain, and academic writing from different disciplines can be easily retrieved whether published in books or periodicals. The use of the genre classification for research purposes is illustrated in Chapter 7.

3.4   Spoken material

As discussed in Chapter 2, spoken language makes up by far the majority of the language we encounter and produce every day. We talk to family members, friends, colleagues, shop assistants, teachers, bus drivers, and so on. It would thus be natural to expect a representative corpus to contain a large proportion of spontaneous conversations. Capturing such everyday spoken exchanges is not easy, however. You can hardly put two people in a studio and ask them to converse naturally, expecting that to be a good sample of the language we produce and encounter when we are out and about doing our normal activities. The way this problem was solved for the BNC was to select a number of speakers who would carry a portable tape-recorder and record their conversations over a certain period of time. To ensure that a wide variety of speakers were included, the speakers were recruited according to the same principles used by market research companies: in proportions that mirror the distribution of people in the country as a whole. That means that the group of recruited speakers (called **RE-SPONDENTS**) included both men and women, people of different age groups, from different social classes, and who lived in different parts of the country. The aim was not to have equal numbers of each category of speaker, but to have a mix that reflected the distribution in the country as a whole.

The recruited respondents were asked to carry a microphone and a portable tape-recorder and to capture their conversations for a specified period of time. These texts then form what is known as the **DEMOGRAPHICALLY SAMPLED COMPONENT (DS)** of the corpus, made up of conversations between the recruited respondents and a number of different people with whom they talked. The recruited respondents were not allowed to make the recordings surreptitiously but were instructed to make it known to the people they talked to that they were being recorded. Material was only collected from those who consented to be recorded. Naturally, there are many kinds of language that are not included in the corpus, such as very personal or intimate conversations, family arguments and discussions of company secrets.

The recruited respondents were asked to keep a record of the people they talked to, and to note down their sex, age and other information about them, where this was known. Needless to say, the information that is available about the people in the recordings varies greatly. We may know a lot about some people, such as the recruited respondents themselves and their closest family, while we know little or nothing about some of the other speakers. All in all, about 4.2 million words of spontaneous conversation were captured for the demographically sampled component of the BNC.

All the material gathered by a single respondent was combined as one "text" or file. That means that a demographically sampled "text" will actually include several conversations and the language of a range of speakers. Some of these speakers will be similar to the respondent, for example friends or colleagues of the same age and sex as the volunteer. Others will have different characteristics, so that as a whole, a spoken text mirrors the language environment of that respondent. It is important to be aware of the difference between a respondent and a speaker. When you search the corpus using *BNCweb*, you can restrict your search to certain parts of the corpus. If, for example, you restrict your search to a "female respondent", you will be searching the conversations recorded by a female. These may include speech produced by both men and women. If you search material by a "female speaker", however, that search runs on material spoken by women, irrespective of the sex of the person who recorded it. In nearly all instances, the speaker-based classification is to be preferred.

Spontaneous conversation is not the only form of spoken language that we encounter or produce frequently. The spoken part of the BNC also contains material that was collected in particular settings or contexts, and accordingly this is known as the **CONTEXT-GOVERNED COMPONENT (CG)**. Such texts include, for example, meetings, radio broadcasts, lectures and tutorials. As shown in Table 3.4, the texts for the context-governed component were sampled from four broad domains, based on the context in which they were produced.

Table 3.4   Composition of the context-governed component of the BNC

Domain	Description	Word count
Business	company talks and interviews; trade union talks; sales demonstrations; business meetings; consultation	1,282,416
Educational and informative	lectures, talks, educational demonstrations; news commentaries; classroom interaction	1,646,380
Leisure	speeches; sports commentaries; talks to clubs; broadcast chat shows and phone-ins; club meetings	1,574,442
Public or institutional	political speeches; sermons; public/government talks; council meetings; religious meetings; parliamentary proceedings; legal proceeding	1,672,658

In general, texts in the context-governed component tend to contain more formal language use:

- public or institutional contexts of language use, for example political speeches and sermons
- educational and informative contexts such as educational demonstrations and news commentaries
- leisure contexts such as sports commentaries, club meetings and chat shows that have been broadcast on television or radio
- business contexts, for example company talks and interviews and sales demonstrations

Some types of texts—such as meetings of different kinds—are found in all domains, while other types were sampled for only a single domain. Sales demonstrations, for example, only pertain to the domain of business.

All in all, the spoken component contains about 10 million words, or slightly over 10% of the corpus—see the overview of its composition in Table 3.5. This does not mean that spoken language is less important than written, but is a reflection of the fact that spoken material is significantly more difficult to acquire, and much more expensive to collect and convert into a suitable corpus format.

Table 3.5   Composition of the spoken part of the BNC.

Spoken Component: ~10%	
Context-governed component (CG)	**Demographically Sampled component (DS)**
Categorized by domain:	Sampled according to:
• Educational and informative	• Respondent age
• Business	• Respondent sex
• Institutional	• Respondent social class
• Leisure	• Geographical region
6,175,896 words	4,233,962 words
10,409,858 words	

The spoken material was, thus, collected in two ways: spontaneous conversations recorded by a set of demographically sampled respondents (the DS component) and material selected on the basis of the DOMAIN in which it was used (the CG component). Where possible, the material was collected in three regions: North (27%), South (45%), and Midlands (24%)[4]. The type of interaction in which the text was produced has been documented. About 15% of the spoken part of the corpus consists of monologues while the remaining 85% is classified as dialogue. Monologue material is only found in the context-governed component. Dialogues are found in both DS and CG.

Where available, information about the speakers was added to the file.[5] It is worth keeping in mind that speaker information was sometimes obtained directly from the speakers themselves and in other cases was inferred by the respondents. This means that the quality and quantity of such data contained in the corpus may vary. The respondent may, for example, not have been qualified to classify someone's accent or dialect, and they may not always have had sufficient information about someone's age, level of education, or socio-economic status. Table 3.6 lists the kind of information that you can look for when using *BNCweb* and illustrates how much of the spoken data has this kind of speaker-related information.

Table 3.6   Speaker-related information available in the BNC.

Feature (proportion where known)	Description/note	Values
Age group (57%)	Age of speaker when recording was made, defined as one of six age groups.	• 0-14 • 15-24 • 25-34 • 35-44 • 45-59 • 60+
Social Class (27 %)	Primarily available for the recruited respondents.	• AB (Higher management: administrative or professional) • C1 (Lower management: supervisory or clerical) • C2 (Skilled manual) • DE (Semi-skilled or unskilled)

---

4   About 4% of the spoken material lacks information about where it was captured.

5   Each speaker in the corpus is given a unique identifier—a so-called "speaker ID". There are a total of 5,394 such speaker IDs in the spoken part of the corpus. As with text IDs, the speaker ID gives no clues about the characteristics of the speaker (e.g. "Speaker sex" or "Speaker age").

Table 3.6 (cont.)   Speaker-related information available in the BNC.

Feature (proportion where known)	Notes	Values
Sex (79%)	The proportion of male and female speakers varies between the two spoken components.	• male • female
Education (1%)	Age at which the participant ceased full-time education.	• Still in education • Left school aged 14 or under • Education continued until age 19 or over
Dialect (49%)	Dialect or accent of speaker, as identified by the respondent. There is no definition or description of the different values that have been used. Some values appear to partially overlap.	Refers to geographical region but varies in specificity.
First Language (29%)	Relates to the country of origin of the speaker, as identified by the respondent. When known, 99% is British English.	• German • French • British English • North American English

In the section about the written part of the corpus above, we saw that it is possible to find considerable amounts of data of a particular type of text or from a certain genre in the BNC. It was stressed that although we can find, for example, a large amount of newspaper text, this is not necessarily a good and representative sample of British English newspaper language as a whole. The same applies to the spoken material. Table 3.6 gives the overall proportions of the material for which a particular feature is recorded. Often this varies considerably between the two spoken components. Social class of the speaker, for example, is recorded for about 27% of the spoken material. However, those 27% are almost exclusively material in the demographically sampled component. That means that any search based on social class of the speaker will effectively be restricted to spontaneous conversation (the kind of language recorded in that component). A similar—although less pronounced—case of imbalance is the predominance of male speech in the context-governed component, while the larger part of women's speech (69%) is of the demographically sampled kind—see Figure 3.1. Of the nearly five million words in the corpus produced by male speakers, 71% is found in the context-governed component (CG). The proportion of CG language produced by female speakers is only 31%. That means that the language you see if you look only for "female speaker" is primarily conversational (from the demographically sampled component), while a search for "male speaker" will retrieve mainly context-governed material.

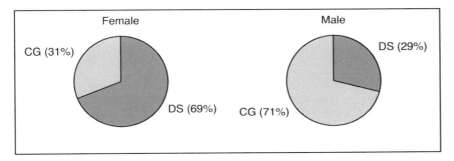

Figure 3.1   Male and female speech. Proportions of demographically sampled (DS) and context-governed (CG) material in the subsets of male and female speech in the BNC.

This can have considerable consequences for a study comparing male and female language. Assume, for example, that both sexes use a certain word in conversational language but not in more formal contexts. If you look at women's use of the word, you will find many instances (since the female language in the corpus is largely conversational). You will not find as many instances produced by men though (since there is not as much conversation by men in the corpus). Based on this difference, it might be tempting to draw the conclusion that women use the word more than men, and miss exploring the possible explanation that the use of the word varies with type of language, not with gender. By being aware of the nature of the corpus, and by exploring the data in different ways, you can avoid making such mistakes.

The BNC in its published form does not include any sound files.[6] The spoken material has been transcribed and is included as orthographic text only. That means that it is not possible to distinguish different pronunciations, accents, stress patterns, intonation contours and so on. Some typical features of spoken

6   Some of the original recordings have been deposited with the British Sound Archive at the British Library, and can be consulted there.

language have, however, been captured. These include information about pauses, overlapping speech, and non-verbal events, such as noises in the background. Punctuation was added to the transcriptions as and when the transcribers felt it was natural to do so, for example marking utterances that had a questioning intonation with a question mark, and marking whatever sounded like the end of a sentence with a full stop.

There is also information about changes in voice quality and features of the speech found noteworthy by the person transcribing the material, for example if someone is mimicking a particular accent, singing the words or laughing while speaking. Unfortunately, it is not possible to know how consistently these features were marked by the transcribers or to what degree all transcribers chose the same words to code the same kind of event. A similar source of occasional inconsistency can be found in the treatment of pronunciation variants such as *can't* vs. *cannot*, *going to* vs. *gonna* and *I am* vs. *I'm*. Here, too, we cannot always assume that the choices were consistent across all instances and that we have an accurate representation of how something was actually said. In the case of filled pauses, a fairly high level of consistency was achieved because transcribers were explicitly instructed to use *er* or *erm* to capture the wide range of potential variants (e.g. including *uh, uhm, em, errrrm, etc.*).

3.5   More than text

3.5.1   Part-of-speech tags

An important feature of the BNC which makes it more valuable is the grammatical annotation. Each word has been automatically assigned a part-of-speech tag—a code giving information about the word-class of that particular word. The tool used to tag the BNC is CLAWS, a program developed at Lancaster University, and the texts were further processed to improve the accuracy rate of the tagging to around 98-99%. With these tags, it is possible to distinguish instances of *round* used as a noun from *round* used as a verb, adverb or adjective. Table 3.7 shows a selection of the part-of-speech (POS) tags used in the corpus. The full list of tags is found in Appendix 2. As you can see, the tags not only give information about the main parts of speech, but offer more detailed information: for example, distinguishing between singular and plural uses of nouns, between positive, comparative and superlative adjectives, and between various forms of verbs. You will find some examples of how you can benefit from using this information in later chapters.

Where the automatic process was unable to definitively decide which tag to assign to a word, an **AMBIGUITY TAG** was used. An ambiguity tag consists of a hyphenated pair of tags: for example "AJ0-AV0", where the choice between adjective ("AJ0") and adverb ("AV0") is left open. The first element of an ambiguity tag may, however, be taken to be slightly more likely. There are 30 different ambiguity tags used in the BNC.

Table 3.7   Selected part-of-speech (POS) tags with descriptions

Tag	Description
AJ0	Adjective (general or positive) (e.g. *good, old, beautiful*)
AT0	Article (e.g. *the, a, an, no*)
AV0	General adverb: an adverb not subclassified as AVP or AVQ (e.g. *often, well, longer* (adv.), *furthest*)
CJC	Coordinating conjunction (e.g. *and, or, but*)
ITJ	Interjection or other isolate (e.g. *oh, yes, mhm, wow*)
NN1	Singular common noun (e.g. *pencil, goose, time, revelation*)
PNP	Personal pronoun (e.g. *I, you, them, ours*)
PRP	Preposition (except *of*) (e.g. *about, at, in, on, with*)
PUN	Punctuation: general separating mark (. , ! , : ; - and ?)
VVB	Lexical verb in the finite base form, comprising the indicative, imperative and present subjunctive (e.g. *forget, send, live, return*)

You can find more information about the part-of-speech tagging, including a description of the different tags, the basis upon which they were assigned, and a discussion of how ambiguous and problematic cases were solved by referring to Garside (1996), Garside & Smith (1997), and Leech & Smith (2000). (The last of these articles has been incorporated into the *BNC Reference Guide*).

Although this type of detailed part-of-speech information is valuable, there are instances where a less fine-grained distinction is useful. For example, if you are looking for "any verb", it is awkward to have to list all tags that are used for verbs. Conveniently, the words in the BNC have also been annotated with a less detailed tagset. This simplified tagset only contains 11 high-level tags, which were assigned on the basis of the more detailed tagging, by combining the detailed tags into larger categories, as illustrated in Table 3.8.

It is worth noting that the SIMPLIFIED TAG "ADJ" includes not only canonical adjectives but also the part-of-speech tag "DT0", i.e. "General determiner pronoun". As a result, demonstrative pronouns such as *this* and *that* will be included in any search using the tag "ADJ". Also, the infinitive marker *to* (POS-tag: "TO0") is subsumed under the simplified tag "PREP".

Table 3.8   The simplified tagset

Simplified tag	Description	Original tag(s)—see Appendix 2
ADJ	adjectives, numerals, general determiner pronouns	AJ0, AJC, AJS, CRD, DT0, ORD
ADV	adverbs, negative particles	AV0, AVP, AVQ, XX0
ART	articles	AT0
CONJ	conjunctions	CJC, CJS, CJT
INTERJ	interjections	ITJ
PREP	prepositions and infinitival marker *to*	PRF, PRP, TO0
PRON	personal, wh-, and possessive pronouns; existential there	DPS, DTQ, EX0, PNI, PNP, PNQ, PNX
STOP	punctuation	PUL, PUN, PUQ, PUR
SUBST	substantive/noun; alphabetical symbols	NN0, NN1, NN2, NP0, ZZ0, NN1-NP0, NP0-NN1
UNC	unclassified, uncertain, or non-lexical words	UNC, POS, AJ0-AV0, AV0-AJ0, AJ0-NN1, NN1-AJ0, AJ0-VVD, VVD-AJ0, AJ0-VVG, VVG-AJ0, AJ0-VVN, VVN-AJ0, AVP-PRP, PRP-AVP, AVQ-CJS, CJS-AVQ, CJS-PRP, PRP-CJS, CJT-DT0, DT0-CJT, CRD-PNI, PNI-CRD, NN1-VVB, VVB-NN1, NN1-VVG, VVG-NN1, NN2-VVZ, VVZ-NN2
VERB	verbs	VBB, VBD, VBG, VBI, VBN, VBZ, VDB, VDD, VDG, VDI, VDN, VDZ, VHB, VHD, VHG, VHI, VHN, VHZ, VM0, VVB, VVD, VVG, VVI, VVN, VVZ, VVD-VVN, VVN-VVD

3.5.2   Headwords and lemmas

The words in the BNC have been annotated not only with POS-tags, but also with information about their **HEADWORDS**. A headword is a set of wordforms consisting of a basic uninflected form and its inflectional variants. The headword FORGET, for example, represents the wordforms *forget, forgets, for-*

got, forgetting and *forgotten* while the headword BE comprises the wordforms *am, is, are, was, were, being, been, 's, 're* and *'m*. Notice that these forms share the same grammatical wordclass (in these cases, verb). However, headwords can also span across two or several wordclasses. For example, LOOK can be a noun (e.g. *the look of love*) or a verb (e.g. *you look nice*). In such cases, it is usually preferable to focus on the individual wordclasses separately. This can be achieved by combining the simplified tags introduced in the previous section with the headword annotation; in the context of the BNC, such a combination is referred to as a LEMMA.[7] Searching for lemmas is straightforward in *BNCweb*—see Chapter 6.

3.5.3   Words & sentences versus w-units & s-units

So far, we have been referring to words (and word counts in different parts of the corpus) without specifying what we mean by "word". You may think that the concept of a word is simple and straightforward. In many cases this is so. The phrase *The cat sat on the mat* contains six orthographically distinct units, each separated by a space, and this is what we traditionally mean by "a word". Looking closer at these units here, you notice that two of them are the same—*the* occurs twice. So if you were to say how many words this sentence contains, would that be six (the number of units) or five (the number of different units)? This problem can be solved by differentiating between tokens and types, where tokens is the number of running words (here six) and types is the number of different words (here five). Distinguishing between tokens and types can be useful, for example when you are looking at the lexical complexity of a text. Lexical richness is sometimes measured by type/token ratio (TTR), a measurement calculating the number of different of words divided by the number of running words in a text. Texts with varied vocabulary will have a higher TTR, while texts where the same words are used repeatedly have a lower TTR.[8] When we use "word" in this book and in *BNCweb*, we are counting the number of running words (tokens), not the number of different words (types).

However, differentiating between types and tokens is not enough. Look at the sentence *The cat sat on the mat.* Here the last word ends with a full stop. The full stop is not part of the word *mat*, but it is not separated by a space either. In the BNC, all punctuation marks are counted as separate tokens (called C-UNITS).

---

7   Notice that this book follows the standard convention of marking lemmas (or their corresponding headwords) in capital letters.

8   The type/token ratio is sensitive to text length, and should not be used when comparing texts of different size. There are different ways to compensate for this, such as calculating averages across smaller chunks of the text. Many readability scores and other text complexity measures include calculations of type/token ratio in some form.

The sentence can thus be said to contain seven tokens, six of them words, and one a punctuation mark. What, then, do we do with an item such as *I'm*—the contracted form of *I am?* Is that one token (no spaces), two tokens (*I* + *'m*), or even three (*I* + *'* + *m*)? The BNC, and *BNCweb*, uses something called **w-units**. A w-unit is the smallest linguistic unit recognized by the automatic word-class annotation program CLAWS. In the case of *I'm*, CLAWS identifies that as consisting of two w-units: the personal pronoun *I* (tagged PNP) and a present-tense form of the verb BE: *'m* (tagged VBB). One benefit of this is that a search for all instances of the first person singular pronoun will retrieve also those found in such constructions (e.g. *I'm, I'll*). You can find a list of all the con-tracted forms recognized by CLAWS in the *BNC Reference Guide,* Section 9.7. These include not only enclitic verb contractions but also negative contractions, such as *can't, isn't, won't* and other combinations. The orthographic unit *gonna*, for example, is analyzed as two w-units: *gon na,* and *Sara's* consists of the w-units *Sara* and *'s* (where *'s* is either a form of BE or marks the possessive). It is particularly important to remember how orthographic units are divided into w-units when searching for such items using *BNCweb*. If you enter *gonna* as your search (or "query") term, you will not find a single example in the corpus, while a search for *gon na* retrieves over 12,000. Chapter 6 describes in more detail how to search for contracted forms and punctuation marks using *BNCweb*.

The smallest units of a BNC text are thus the w-unit (used for word-like elements) and the c-unit (used for punctuation marks). The w-units and c-units are combined into larger, sentence-like units, called **s-units**. The s-units are numbered sequentially, and these are the numbers you will see next to the con-cordance lines when you retrieve examples from the corpus using *BNCweb* (see Chapter 4 for more details).[9] The spoken texts have also been divided into s-units, even though it can at times be difficult to decide what should constitute a sentence-like unit, for example when people interrupt each other or for other reasons do not finish their turn.

3.6   Format

The underlying source files of the BNC are in a format called XML. This type of encoding is ideally suited to represent the metatextual categories used in the

---

9   The XML-edition of the BNC is the third version of the corpus since its original release in the 1990s. Some of the changes made between versions meant that a small number of s-units were deleted from the corpus (e.g. because duplicate stretches of text were re-moved—see Section 3.7). However, the numbering of the remaining s-units in the corpus texts was not changed as a result of this. Some s-units may therefore appear to be "miss-ing". The benefit of keeping the original numbering is that it is possible to compare ex-amples and references between different versions of the corpus.

corpus (e.g. text domains, categories of speaker, textual features, etc.). However, the text format of the corpus is generally of little consequence to users of *BNCweb*. The information contained in the XML codes is captured and then made available in different ways through the *BNCweb* interface. The example from a BNC XML text shown in Figure 3.2 illustrates the benefit of using *BNCweb*: the raw XML file is practically unreadable, and difficult to process without special software. Those wishing to learn more about the BNC XML format can find detailed information in the *BNC Reference Guide*.

```
<u hns:added="start"><s n="5136"><w c5="CJS" hw="if" pos="CONJ">If </w>
<w c5="PNP" hw="you" pos="PRON">you </w><w c5="VVB" hw="like"
pos="VERB">like</w><c c5="PUN">!</c></s></u><u who="PS06H"><s
n="5137"><align with="KBLLC173"/><shift new="laughing" /><w c5="ITJ"
hw="yeah" pos="INTERJ">Yeah </w> <shift/><c c5="PUN">!</c></s></u><u
who="PS06A"><s n="5138"> <align with="KBLLC173"/><vocal
desc="laugh"/><align with="KBLLC174"/> <pause/><w c5="DTQ" hw="what"
pos="PRON"> What </w><w c5="PNP" hw="i" pos="PRON">I </w><w c5="VVB"
hw="want" pos="VERB">want </w><w c5="VBZ" hw="be" pos="VERB"> is </w><w
c5="PNI" hw="something" pos="PRON">something </w><w c5="TO0" hw="to"
pos="PREP">to </w><w c5="VVI" hw="eat" pos="VERB">eat</w><c c5="PUN">,
</c> <w c5="AV0" hw="now" pos="ADV">now</w><c c5="PUN">!</c> </s></u><u
who="PS06H"><s n="5139"><align with="KBLLC175"/><w c5="VDB" hw="do"
pos="VERB">Do </w><align with="KBLLC176"/><w c5="PNP" hw="you"
pos="PRON">you</w><c c5="PUN">?</c> </s></u><u who="PS06A"> <s n="5140">
<w c5="ITJ" hw="mm" pos="INTERJ">Mm</w><c c5="PUN">.</c></s></u>
```

Figure 3.2   Extract of a BNC XML text.

3.7   Errors

Compiling a corpus like the BNC is a complex process. For the process to be possible at all, a large degree of automation is needed. In other words, large corpora, by their very nature, consist of so much data that humans must rely on software (that is, automated processes) to carry out certain tasks for them, such as annotating words for POS and headwords. Although the output of automated processes can be checked and manually corrected, time constraints and limited funding make it impossible to do that thoroughly for the whole corpus. That means that errors in the corpus are inevitable. We summarize here some of the main known types of error so that you will be able to apply caution when necessary.

The corpus contains many aspects of what could be called an error from a prescriptive point of view. These include false starts in speech, odd choices of words and non-standard grammatical uses (e.g. *He done it*). From the descriptive linguist's perspective, these features should not be called errors since they are the kind of irregularities we encounter in natural language—of which the BNC is intended to be an accurate representation. As a consequence, such perceived "errors" and irregularities have not been corrected or changed, but are left in the corpus as illustrations of the variation in the language as it is actually used.

Other errors are those introduced in the production of the corpus. At the time when the corpus was compiled, the amount of readily available text in electronic format was limited. That meant that the texts that were selected for the corpus had to be converted into computer-readable format, either by scanning the text or by somebody keying it in by hand. Although both processes were monitored carefully, it was unavoidable that some errors crept in, such as typos and misspelled words, or passages where one or several words were accidentally left out or repeated.

Very occasionally, you may come across duplicate passages in the corpus. In some cases, these were introduced as a result of the sampling procedure. For example, a text about sporting injuries may have been identified as belonging to both the domain "Science (medicine)" and "Leisure". This is a natural feature of the language—some texts do belong in more than one category, and it is only natural that such instances are found in the corpus. Another natural repetition is in newspaper articles and news stories, which may be repeated in more than one paper or broadcast more than once on a news programme. In some cases, however, the duplicated material was included in the corpus by accident. Someone typing in a text from the paper version may accidentally have typed in the same paragraph twice or transcribed the same stretch of speech twice. Likewise, material may be missing, for example due to the typist or transcriber accidentally skipping a paragraph when converting the text to computer-readable format.

As mentioned above, the part-of-speech annotation has been done automatically. The process is generally very accurate, but errors do occur. The type of errors and their frequency has been described in detail by Leech and Smith (2000), which is available on the BNC website. As the detailed part-of-speech tags were used as the basis for assigning the simplified wordclass tags, any errors in the original tagging will be carried over to the simplified tags. The headword information was also generated automatically, and similarly resulted in occasional errors, not least where unusual or foreign words are concerned.

As described above, information about non-verbal events is indicated in the spoken part of the corpus. Features such as changes in voice quality and overlapping speech have also been recorded for many conversations. One problem with the overlapping speech, further described in Chapter 4, is that the annotation is incomplete, sometimes making it impossible to say where an overlap starts or ends, even when an overlap is marked.

3.8 More information

The British National Corpus is a large and diverse resource. It cannot be emphasized enough how important it is that you know your corpus if you want to use it for language study or research. You will soon find that in order to use *BNCweb* to the full, you will need to become familiar with the BNC. At the same time, as you use *BNCweb*, you will certainly come to understand more about the composition, strengths and limitations of the corpus itself. As you will see when you start using *BNCweb*, you can, very easily, get information about the amount of text that belongs to a text category, and see how large a proportion of the corpus you search when you restrict your query according to one or more criteria. Information about individual texts, such as title, author, text category and so on, is available at a click of the mouse. The following chapters will demonstrate how you find and can use the information that is available. As you become more familiar with *BNCweb* and the kind of questions you can answer using it, you may also want to learn even more about the corpus or check a particular detail of relevance to your work. You can find more information about the corpus and details about how it was compiled and annotated in the online *BNC Reference Guide*.

3.9 Is it Present-day English?

In this book, we will occasionally refer to the BNC as a corpus that represents "present-day", "contemporary" or "modern" English. Given that all of its texts are at the time of writing this at least 15—and a few of them almost 50—years old, you may feel that this is not an accurate description. However, we believe that these labels are nevertheless generally valid. It is of course true that the BNC cannot be used to investigate some of the most recent lexical developments of the language. For example, the vocabulary of English has certainly been enriched as a result of the dramatic rise of Internet usage—and a search in the corpus for the nouns *blog* or *webpage* (or the verbs *to google* or *to facebook*) will not return any results. However, many other aspects of language are fairly stable over long periods of time. The history of English spans a period of more than 1,500 years, and changes in areas such as grammar or morphology are typically much slower than the type of lexical developments we have just mentioned. When looked at from this perspective, the BNC can certainly be described as containing "Present-day English". As we have repeatedly stressed, a good understanding of the composition of the corpus is essential if you want to make use of it in a meaningful way. The BNC clearly has its limitations. However, in view of its size, vastly varied contents and its wide range of annotation levels, it is still an excellent source of data for investigations into how British English is used today.

3.10   Exercise

Re-evaluating representativeness. In Chapter 2, you were asked to think about the kinds of text—and their proportions—you would include in a representative corpus of British English. Return to your notes and compare your list to the contents of the BNC (given in Tables 3.1 and 3.3). Where do your suggestions match the decisions made by the BNC compilers? Where do they differ? Can you explain any of these differences with reference to the limitations under which the BNC compilers worked (time restraints and financial limitations)? Do you think any of the decisions they made would match yours, had the BNC been commissioned today?

4 First queries with *BNCweb*

4.1 Outline

In this chapter we cover the following topics:

- searching for a single word
- restricting a query to specific written or spoken parts of the BNC
- interpreting frequency information from a query result
- exploring the concordance part of a query result
- accessing previous query results

4.2 Introduction

The main purpose of this chapter is to introduce and discuss the first practical steps in analysis using *BNCweb*. *BNCweb* queries can vary considerably in their complexity. This chapter deals with the simplest types of query, i.e. those that search for a word (e.g. *goalless*, *data*, *she*) or a sequence of words (e.g. *part and parcel*). We will also show how you can explore *BNCweb* concordances and how to save your query for future reuse. In addition, you will learn how to restrict the scope of queries to selected written or spoken portions of the corpus, using metatextual categories. In Chapters 6 and 12, we will look at more complex types of query and explore how to search for, for example, contracted forms and special characters (as in *won't* and *café*); grammatical categories (POS-tags, see 3.5.1); headwords and lemmas (e.g. the lemma WASH, which covers all forms of the verb—*wash*, *washes*, *washed*, *washing*—see 3.5.2); and non-adjacent combinations of words and/or POS-tags.

We will introduce the functionality of basic *BNCweb* searches with the help of the following research question:

What evidence does the BNC hold of a new sense of wicked?

Let's assume you've recently heard or somehow become aware that this word has acquired a new sense or meaning: in addition to its traditional sense of 'evil', 'morally wrong', 'malicious', etc., *wicked* is nowadays also found in a radically different, very approving sense, roughly equivalent to 'excellent' or 'wonderful'. You are now curious to know if this sense is indeed evidenced in the BNC. As well as finding examples, perhaps you'd also like to find out what proportion of the time (approximately) *wicked* is used in the 'excellent' sense; and whether the word *wicked* (in any of its senses) is more a feature of spoken or written language. Given the recency of the new sense of *wicked*, you might further want to see which age groups of speaker have already started adopting it.

BNCweb offers three different query options for searching the corpus. The default search mode is referred to as STANDARD QUERY—it can be used to search for words or word sequences across three predefined sections of the BNC: the whole BNC, the whole "Spoken" component and the whole "Written" component. However, there will be times when you will want to limit your search to smaller sub-sections of the corpus, e.g. to specific text types or classifications of speaker, such as newspaper texts or language produced by speakers between 0 and 24 years old. This is where the search modes WRITTEN RESTRICTIONS and SPOKEN RESTRICTIONS come in.

When you make a corpus query, most corpus analysis programs present the results as a CONCORDANCE listing and provide basic frequency information. That is, they display a list of all the instances in the corpus matching the expression you searched for, each surrounded by a few words or a sentence of context from the source texts; and they tell you how often the item occurs in the corpus, or in any selected parts of it. In *BNCweb*, these two outputs, the concordance and frequency information, appear together in a single window, the QUERY RESULT page.

4.3   Getting started: your first query

4.3.1   Planning your query

Let's return to the research question introduced above—*What evidence does the BNC hold of a new sense of* wicked*?* Before making a corpus search, you may wish to consult one or two dictionaries to see what senses are listed. The information you get will naturally depend on the date of the publication, and the "culture" of the dictionary regarding splitting or lumping closely related senses. All dictionaries, however, should list one or more senses that for present purposes can, without too much distortion, be collapsed and labeled the "Evil" sense. Newer dictionaries may list the further sense that we are interested in, describing it variously as 'excellent', 'remarkable', 'wonderful', 'very good'. Let us call this the "Excellent" sense. Our query in *BNCweb* will allow us to determine, very approximately, how prevalent the "Excellent" sense is in 1990s British English. (Recall that for our purposes we treat the English of the 1990s as more or less contemporary—see 3.9.) Where dictionaries comment on usage, they generally state that the "Excellent" sense is colloquial in style, or that it is "used mainly by young people". We will therefore also explore how the frequency of *wicked* varies across different genres, and across different age groups of speakers.

4.3.2 Running the query

The first page you will see when you first log in to *BNCweb* is called the "Standard query" page. To start your query for *wicked*:

1. Enter `wicked` in the box below the heading "Standard query".
2. For this query, do not make any changes to the other available options.
3. Click on [Start query].

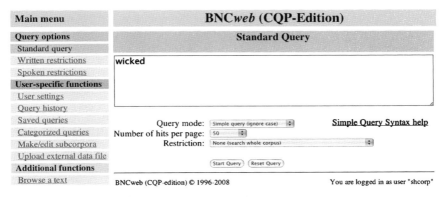

Figure 4.1:   Entering a Standard query for *wicked*

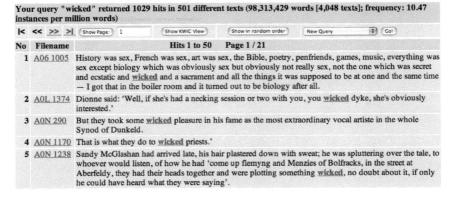

Figure 4.2:   Query result of a search for `wicked` in the whole BNC

Figure 4.2 shows the Query result page, which shows the concordance lines of a search for the word *wicked* together with frequency information at the top. Also available are various options for changing how the concordance is displayed, and for proceeding to further stages of analysis. We'll begin by reviewing the frequency information.

4.3.3   Getting basic frequency information

From the top line of the *BNCweb* Query result page—referred to as the "title bar"—we can see that *wicked* has 1,029 "hits" or occurrences. We also find that these 1,029 occurrences are spread across 501 different texts. These numbers together give an idea of the DISPERSION of the query term—i.e. how well spread the occurrences are across the available data. At this stage, it may not seem very helpful to you to know that *wicked* occurs in 501 texts (or even that this averages at nearly 1 hit for every 2 texts in which it occurs). But suppose all the hits were found in just 20 texts: that would be a sign that usage of *wicked* is highly constrained, being limited to a handful of writers/speakers or to a very small number of text types or usage contexts. As your experience with using *BNCweb* increases, you will have a better basis for comparing dispersion values for different queries and you will be able to use them to discover restrictions on usage that could otherwise have remained hidden. (See also Chapter 7 for further discussion.)

Following the information about the frequency and dispersion, we have, in parentheses, a word count—the number of words in the corpus that your query was run over. In this case, because you have just searched the whole BNC, the number is just under 100 million words—98,313,429, to be precise.

Based on the word count, *BNCweb* tells you how many instances were found *per million words*. For *wicked*, this works out to be 10.47 instances per million words. (For convenience, we often abbreviate "per million words" to "pmw"). This NORMALIZED FREQUENCY is particularly relevant when you want to compare the frequencies of query items (such as *wicked*) across different parts of the BNC. We will return to a detailed discussion of the calculation and importance of normalized frequencies in Chapter 5.

4.4   Exploring the concordance

Having obtained an initial overview of the frequency of *wicked*, let's start exploring the concordance part of the query result. Our aim here is twofold: to get a general idea about the range of different uses of our query item, and in doing so, to become acquainted with the various viewing options afforded by *BNCweb*.

Task:
Browse through the first page of the concordance, briefly reading through the examples of *wicked* as you go down. Try to get a general idea about the range of different uses of the word. Can you find any examples where *wicked* matches the "Excellent" sense described above? You might like to jot down the hit numbers of any relevant examples. You may also like to revisit the "Evil" sense category proposed above. On looking at the data, you may decide that it is not sufficiently refined for your purposes.

Looking at the first 50 hits of the query result, you will probably have arrived at the conclusion that most of the concordance lines contain clear examples of the "Evil" sense of *wicked*—a possible exception is line 13 ("*Wicked* French dressing"). This would therefore seem to suggest that the "Excellent" sense is very rare in Present-day English. But how reliable is this finding? For example, how sure can you be that the first 50 hits displayed are actually representative of the full set of 1,029 hits? Furthermore, in some cases it will have been necessary for you to guess since you wouldn't have been able to see enough of the surrounding text, and might therefore have struggled to work out the meaning of *wicked* that was intended. The following sections give some guidance on how to navigate through the concordances, manipulate the way concordance lines are displayed and ordered, get more linguistic context and obtain more information about the source texts.

4.4.1 Navigating through a query result

If you want to make sure that the "Excellent" sense is indeed very rare, one obvious solution is to read through all 1,029 concordance lines. This is, of course, not really practical in the present case, but we will use the example to show how **|< << >> >|** you can navigate through a concordance in *BNCweb*. Use the arrow links pictured left to advance or backtrack through the pages of your concordance. As you might expect, the last of these links takes you straight to the last page of the concordance, and the first one takes you back to the beginning. Clicking the second or third link takes you one page back or forward, respectively.

(Show Page:) 7   Use the [Show page] button to navigate directly to a specific page of the concordance results. For instance, you may remember seeing a particularly juicy example of *wicked* on page 7. To save yourself navigating a page at a time back to the example, just enter '7' and press [Show page].

4.4.2   KWIC view and Sentence view

By default, your concordance will be displayed with each example within a whole sentence (as in Figure 4.2 above). You may find it more convenient to view the concordance with the query item aligned in a fixed, central position, within a single line of context. This position is usually referred to as the **NODE**

> (Show KWIC View)

position. In this format it is often easier to detect recurrent language patterns. To switch to this view, simply click on the [Show KWIC View] button (KWIC means "Key Word in Context"). The result of this is shown in Figure 4.3:

No	Filename		wicked	
		Your query "wicked" returned 1029 hits in 501 different texts (98,313,429 words [4,048 texts]; frequency: 10.47 instances per million words)		
		I< << >> >I (Show Page:) 1 (Show Sentence View) (Show in random order) New Query ▾ (Go!)		
		Hits 1 to 15 Page 1 / 69		
1	A06 1005	really sex, not the one which was secret and ecstatic and	wicked	and a sacrament an
2	A0L 1374	she's had a necking session or two with you, you	wicked	dyke, she's obviou:
3	A0N 290	laird, not elected by the people. But they took some	wicked	pleasure in his fam
4	A0N 1170	'Take off his frock. That is what they do to	wicked	priests.' 'Is that so.
5	A0N 1238	at Aberfeldy, they had their heads together and were plotting something	wicked	, no doubt about it,
6	A0U 2352	beds were horrid filthy and full of vermin. There was very	wicked	carryings on. I can
7	A12 464	contrast to another leitmotif that marks the entrances of Carabosse, the	wicked	fairy. The two tune
8	A12 1055	to marry and save Odette after she has told him how the	wicked	Von Rothbart turn
9	A14 1044	Rowland in the guide of Fairy Godmother — or is it the	Wicked	Witch? — offering
10	A1L 8	The Baby's Catalogue win children over with ripping yarns and a	wicked	sense of humour. T
11	A1Y 240	security. 'They are suicidal and nuclear threats by anybody are	wicked	.' But he maintainec
12	A2C 91	do it again anyway for the effect. These children are not	wicked	or evil — but the l
13	A2U 87	, as a script-writer for 'Allo 'Allo. ROCK /	Wicked	French dressing: A
14	A36 16	head in a restaurant? BOOK REVIEW /A buried treasury of	wicked	wits: Claire Tomali
15	A36 27	brother Samuel, who admonished her thus: Repent, renounce all	wicked	wit: ... So may the

Figure 4.3:   A concordance for the query `wicked` in KWIC view (cropped view)

The button you just pressed is a toggle button. Having pressed it once to activate the KWIC view, the button now displays the words "Show Sentence View"; if you click this, the display will revert to Sentence View and the button will read "Show KWIC View" once more. Which view to apply is merely a matter of personal preference.

4.4.3   Random order and corpus order

By default, the concordance hits in the Query result page are displayed in the order in which they appear in the texts of the BNC, ordered alphabetically by filenames. This order is called "corpus order" in *BNCweb*.

Corpus order is not in itself a bad way to look at your data. However, it may prove problematic if you are not careful and make linguistic generalizations based on only the first page, or even first several pages, of your concordance results. This is because texts in the BNC are not randomly ordered; instead, similar types of texts tend to be grouped together. For example, the text IDs of 102 texts with content taken from *The Guardian* begin with A7-, A8-, A9-, or AA-. As a consequence of this, many of the hits displayed on the first couple of concordance pages will tend to come from newspaper data—and they may therefore represent a usage of your query term that is specific to this particular text type.

Looking at a concordance in corpus order may therefore give you a skewed impression of actual usage—unless of course you look at all the concordance lines in the query result. Exhaustive manual checking of concordance results is often not a practicable solution. In the case of our example query term, *wicked*, it could take you several hours to read and analyze all the instances (more than 1,000 of them), and many queries performed with *BNCweb* will return far more hits than that.

This problem can be solved by putting the data into random order. In order to do this, simply click the [Show in random order] button at the top of the concordance. As a result, the title bar will have the words "(displayed in random order)" appended. The button is a toggle button, so it will now say "Show in corpus order", giving you the option to restore the original corpus order view. Note that if you click [Show in random order] again, you will obtain the same randomized order of examples as the previous time you selected this option.

> **Task:**
> Switch the display of the query result for *wicked* to random order and have a look at the first 50 or 100 concordance lines. Do you notice any difference? Are there more instances of the "Excellent" sense of the query term?

Since your query result is now in random order, the chances of seeing the full variety of uses of *wicked*—and gauging how frequent they are—even in the first 50 or 100 instances is greatly increased. In fact, you are likely to have found quite a few instances of the "Excellent" sense of *wicked*.

You may now ask yourself whether it is not still necessary to look at the complete set of 1,029 concordance lines to arrive at a reliable description of the use of *wicked* in the BNC. If you want to know the exact number of uses of the "Excellent" sense of *wicked*, this is indeed correct. However, let's say that you found 10 instances of this use in the first 100 randomly ordered hits. From this count, you can estimate—or extrapolate—the relative frequency, or percentage share, of this meaning in the complete query result: if 10 per cent of the first 100 instances of *wicked* are examples of the "Excellent" sense, it is likely that a similar proportion of this sense would be found in the full set. In other words, you could estimate that approximately 103 of the 1,029 instances (i.e. again 10 per cent) of *wicked* are used in this sense. Obviously, the larger the number of (random) instances you look at, the more reliable your estimate will be—see 5.6.

Tip:
You can change the default settings for KWIC vs. Sentence view and Corpus order vs. Random order with the USER SETTINGS command— see 13.4.1. This command is accessible from the MAIN NAVIGATION PANEL of *BNCweb*.—i.e. the list of links on the left hand side of the "Standard query" page.

Another option for changing the order of the concordance lines is SORTING. This function is described in Chapter 7 (Section 7.3).

4.4.4   Viewing the larger context of an example

One of the problems you may have faced when determining the sense of *wicked* was that the sentence in which it occurred did not provide enough information to come to a reliable decision. To see more context for any example, simply click on the query item in the relevant line of the concordance. (It will be displayed as hyperlinked text, e.g. *The naval officer is as <u>wicked</u> as the boys...*) This takes you to a new page, as shown in Figure 4.4—this is an extract from a written text. The title bar of the page lists the filename (here, it is text 'A0U'), and the sentence, or s-unit, numbers of the text that is displayed. The query item *wicked* is highlighted in red. (*BNCweb* will also attempt to find other matches of the query term on the same page and color them blue.) The grayed out words within square brackets (e.g. *[orig: incomphrehensible]*) indicate original misspellings of words that were corrected in the BNC. You can move backwards and forwards through the text surrounding the example by clicking on the arrow links ("<<" and ">>" respectively).

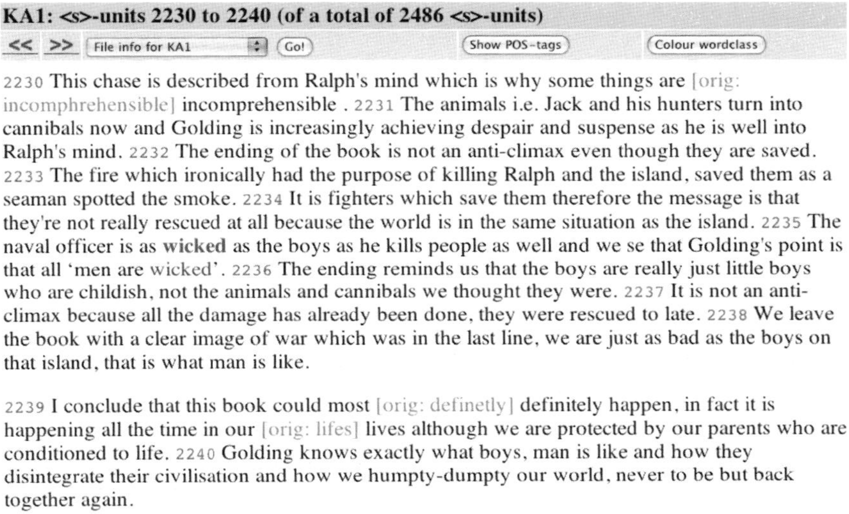

KA1: \<s\>-units 2230 to 2240 (of a total of 2486 \<s\>-units)

`<<` `>>` `File info for KA1` `⬍` `Go!`   `Show POS-tags`   `Colour wordclass`

2230 This chase is described from Ralph's mind which is why some things are [orig: incomphrehensible] incomprehensible . 2231 The animals i.e. Jack and his hunters turn into cannibals now and Golding is increasingly achieving despair and suspense as he is well into Ralph's mind. 2232 The ending of the book is not an anti-climax even though they are saved. 2233 The fire which ironically had the purpose of killing Ralph and the island, saved them as a seaman spotted the smoke. 2234 It is fighters which save them therefore the message is that they're not really rescued at all because the world is in the same situation as the island. 2235 The naval officer is as **wicked** as the boys as he kills people as well and we se that Golding's point is that all 'men are wicked'. 2236 The ending reminds us that the boys are really just little boys who are childish, not the animals and cannibals we thought they were. 2237 It is not an anti-climax because all the damage has already been done, they were rescued to late. 2238 We leave the book with a clear image of war which was in the last line, we are just as bad as the boys on that island, that is what man is like.

2239 I conclude that this book could most [orig: definetly] definitely happen, in fact it is happening all the time in our [orig: lifes] lives although we are protected by our parents who are conditioned to life. 2240 Golding knows exactly what boys, man is like and how they disintegrate their civilisation and how we humpty-dumpty our world, never to be but back together again.

Figure 4.4:   Larger context display of a concordance line for the query `wicked` in a written text of the BNC[1]

Other options available on this page allow you to do the following:

- see information about the file (text) from which the example is drawn (see Section 4.4.5 below)
- see a larger/smaller window of context for the example. The smallest possible window is 10 s-units and the largest window is 50 s-units
- return to the concordance (*BNCweb* Query result)
- start a new query

If the instance of *wicked* that you are interested in comes from a spoken text, *BNCweb* will group the s-units into speaker turns and also display the names of the speakers (if known). The text may also contain some additional information such as changes in voice quality (e.g. "laughing", "singing"), pauses and indications of non-linguistic events that may have an impact on the conversation (e.g. "baby gurgling"). A sample context view of a spoken text is shown in Figure 4.5.

---

1   You can browse the same extract as shown in Figure 4.4 without running a query first: simply use the BROWSE A TEXT function on the main navigation panel—see Section 4.8.

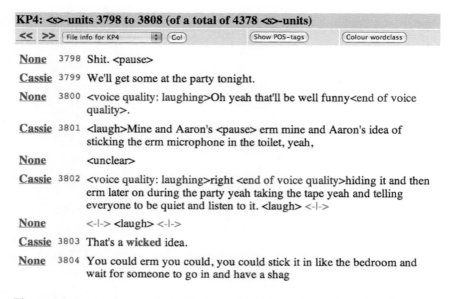

None   3798   Shit. <pause>

Cassie 3799   We'll get some at the party tonight.

None   3800   <voice quality: laughing>Oh yeah that'll be well funny<end of voice
                   quality>.

Cassie 3801   <laugh>Mine and Aaron's <pause> erm mine and Aaron's idea of
                   sticking the erm microphone in the toilet, yeah,

None   <unclear>

Cassie 3802   <voice quality: laughing>right <end of voice quality>hiding it and then
                   erm later on during the party yeah taking the tape yeah and telling
                   everyone to be quiet and listen to it. <laugh> <-|->

None   <-|-> <laugh> <-|->

Cassie 3803   That's a wicked idea.

None   3804   You could erm you could, you could stick it in like the bedroom and
                   wait for someone to go in and have a shag

Figure 4.5:   Larger context display of a concordance line for the query
               wicked in a spoken text of the BNC (first 7 s-units only)

Two additional features of spoken texts in the BNC are worth noting: firstly,
when the conversations recorded for the BNC were transcribed, it was occasionally not possible to decipher everything that was being said. In these cases, the
transcribers inserted a tag "unclear" into the text (cf. Figure 4.5, immediately
preceding s-unit 3802). This tag may stand for a single indecipherable word—or
for a whole stretch of words. Secondly, many conversations involving two or
several participants will contain some overlap of speaker turns. These are indi-
cated by red "<-|->"-symbols in *BNCweb*. Unfortunately, no distinction is made
between starting and end points of such stretches of overlap.

> **Note:**
> If you look carefully at the text displayed in Figure 4.5, you will no-
> tice that the indications of overlap are not complete: the end of Cas-
> sie's utterance in s-unit 3802 appears to overlap with laughter by an
> unknown participant. However, the beginning of this overlap in Cas-
> sie's utterance is not shown.

This is the result of an error that was introduced in the automatic conversion of the corpus from its earlier SGML-format to XML, which resulted in approximately a quarter of all indications of overlap being lost. Other elements that were affected (to a lesser degree) by this type of error are pauses, unclear passages and indications of non-linguistic events. For further information, see the detailed description available at http://www.bncweb.info.

4.4.5   Obtaining more information about the source of an example

Each text in the BNC has associated with it a rich set of information about the source from which it comes, for example:

- for written texts: the name and sex of the author(s), full title of the source, its date of publication, etc.

- for spoken texts: the speakers' names (pseudonyms), and, if known, their birthplace, sex and age as well as the situational context of the recording.

BNCweb offers three ways to obtain this information:

1. Click on the entry in the "Filename" column in the query result, i.e. the filename and the s-unit number (e.g. "A0U 2352"). This will take you to a page entitled "BNC header information for file XYZ", displaying the complete set of metatextual information that is available for the text in which the hit is found. (When you have finished reading this information, click the [Back] button of your browser to return to the concordance.)

2. Hover your mouse pointer over (but without clicking) the link in the filename column. The metatextual information pops up as a so-called "tool-tip" box, which disappears when you move your mouse away.

3. The same information is also available from the larger context display page (cf. Figure 4.5).

Task:
Returning to your randomly ordered query result for *wicked*, check whether any of the instances representing the "Excellent" sense come from the spoken part of the corpus.

4.5   Running a query for a word sequence

Once you have finished looking at a concordance for a query term, you can think about searching the corpus for further items. Sooner or later you will want to search for a sequence of consecutive words (or "tokens" as we often say in *BNCweb*). The sequence could be, for example, part or all of:

- an idiomatic expression (e.g. *beat about the bush, kettle of fish*)
- a grammatical construction (*supposed to, in terms of*)
- a foreign expression naturalized into English (*en route, persona non grata*)
- a place or company name (*New York, World Health Organization*)
- any other item, whether or not it is normally recognized as a structural unit (*women tend to, nothing to be*)

To run a new query you need to be on the *BNCweb* STANDARD QUERY page. If you are already on this page, simply follow the procedure described in Section 4.3.2 above. If you are not on the STANDARD QUERY page, it is usually possible to start a new Standard query by selecting "New query" from one of the drop-down menus. For example, in the *BNCweb* Query result page, in the top-right there is a drop-down menu. Make sure that "New query" is selected and click [Go!].

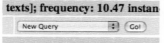

When you reach the STANDARD QUERY page, enter into the box a word sequence of your own choosing (or one of those listed above if you cannot think of one), putting a space between each token, e.g.

    beat about the bush

and click [Go!]. Note that in contrast to many Web search engines (e.g. *Google*), it is not part of the *BNCweb* search syntax to put quotation marks around a sequence of words that you wish to match exactly; in fact, doing this would result in no hits being found at all.

> **Note: the post-query options menu**
> The drop-down menu shown above accesses the other major functions of *BNCweb* which we will explore in later chapters. For the rest of the book, it will be referred to as the POST-QUERY OPTIONS MENU.

Briefly explore the resulting concordance as outlined in Section 4.4. As you read through, you could ask yourself, for example: *Is the word sequence always used in ways that I would have expected? Is more than one meaning involved? In what kinds of text do the examples seem to occur most often?* etc.

Later, in Chapters 6 and 12, we will show you how to introduce increasing degrees of optionality into the above kinds of query, enabling you to find patterns such as:

- *supposed to* preceded, but not necessarily immediately, by a form of BE
- GET *on* + possessive pronoun or genitive + *wick*

4.6   Restricting your query to selected portions of the BNC

Sometimes it is preferable to search only a portion, or selected portions, of a corpus. Taking *wicked* as a worked example again, you could study its frequency and use in the BNC fiction texts, for instance. You may wish to know: What is the most typical sense of *wicked* in fiction? Does that sense appear to be related to the stereotype of the villainous character in fiction? What is the frequency of *wicked* in fiction compared to other genres of writing, such as academic writing or newspaper reportage?

If you are looking at the "Excellent" sense of *wicked*, you may want to check whether it is indeed slang and a feature of youth language, as some dictionaries state. For this purpose, you would want to check the frequency of *wicked* in spoken conversation texts, and across different social classifications of speaker. (As explained in Chapter 3, the conversational part of the BNC distinguishes speakers according to demographic criteria such as their age, sex and class.) *BNCweb* can help you answer questions such as the above by allowing you to conveniently search in selected portions of the corpus.

Let's begin with the most basic type of text restriction: searching for *wicked* in the spoken part of the BNC only. There are two simple ways to do this is. Either:

1. Enter a Standard query as normally, typing `wicked` into the search box.

2. Select "Spoken Texts" in the drop-down menu next to the "Restriction" box and click [Start query].

Alternatively:

1. In the main navigation panel of *BNCweb*, under the heading "Query options" click on SPOKEN RESTRICTIONS. The page will refresh, showing a

new panel in the center of the screen, entitled "Restricted Range of Spoken Texts".

2. Type in `wicked` in the "Query term" box, then click [Start query] (for now, ignore the other options on the page).

As in standard queries, *BNCweb* returns a query result consisting of general frequency information, a set of display options, and underneath these the concordance.

The second method above has the advantage of allowing you to restrict your query further: to one or several subsections of the spoken part of the corpus. Let's use it now to search for *wicked* in the demographically sampled spoken data.

1. Return to the SPOKEN RESTRICTIONS page (you can do this by using the [Back] button of your browser), and ensure that the query term is `wicked`.

2. Under "General Restrictions for Spoken Texts" check "Demographically sampled" (see Figure 4.6).

3. Click on [Start query].

General Restrictions for Spoken Texts:	
Overall:	**Interaction Type:**
☑ Demographically sampled ☐ Context-governed	☐ Monologue ☐ Dialogue

Figure 4.6:   Restricting a search for *wicked* to the demographically sampled part of the BNC

The result of this query is displayed in Figure 4.7 below. It is worth making a note of the frequency information here, before you move on to search other parts of the corpus. We can see that *wicked* occurs 151 times in the demographically sampled part of the corpus, across 37 different texts. Notice that the word count has changed, from 98,313,429 (the figure for the whole BNC) to 4,233,962, because of the restriction to demographically sampled texts. It is from the latter word count that the frequency per million words (35.66 for *wicked*) is calculated.

Your query "wicked" restricted to "*Text type: Demographically sampled*" returned 151 hits in 37 different texts (4,233,962 words [153 texts]; frequency: 35.66 instances per million words)		

|<	<<	>>	>|	(Show Page:) 1	(Show KWIC View)	(Show in random order)	New Query	⬩	(Go!)

No	Filename	Hits 1 to 50 Page 1 / 4
1	KBB 127	You wicked girl!
2	KBF 8303	she was saying that you know mother is [unclear] very evil and wicked.
3	KBF 12659	It's wicked!
4	KBG 195	What a wicked dog!
5	KBH 6	Of, one of the words that she was talking about, people have started using wicked for [unclear] a normal phrase.

Figure 4.7:   Query result for the search for *wicked* in the demographically sampled part of the BNC

Now go back to the STANDARD QUERY page. Do a search for *wicked* in the written part of the BNC by selecting the appropriate option in the drop-down menu called "Restriction". The results will show that the word occurs only 9.64 times per million word. Remember that when we searched the whole BNC, the frequency was 10.47 pmw. Comparing the three normalized frequencies, we can now safely suggest that *wicked* is indeed predominantly used in spontaneous spoken conversations.

Before leaving the concordance you might like to study the examples to see what meanings are evidenced, and ones occur most often. Again, it may help to use the different display formats of *BNCweb* to obtain this picture: e.g. random order, KWIC view, increasing the context size of short examples, and obtaining information about a text from the filename column. Notice, by the way, that the participants in the conversation in text KBH—see for example hit (5) in Figure 4.7—actually talk about just the phenomenon we are investigating here: they point out that *wicked* can also be used in the "Excellent" sense.

Let's now refine our query a little, to see how age groups differ in their use of *wicked*. First we'll look at the two youngest age groups, 0-14 and 15-24.

1. In the main navigation panel of *BNCweb*, again select SPOKEN RESTRICTIONS and enter wicked as the query term.

2. Under "General Restrictions for Spoken Texts" again check "Demographically sampled".

3. Scroll down the page to "Speaker restrictions", and in the "Age" section check "0-14" and "15-24".

4. Scroll back to the top and click on [Start query].

Make a note of the frequency per million words, and read the examples to see which sense predominates.

5. Use your browser's [Back] button to return to the SPOKEN RESTRICTIONS query page, and this time uncheck the age groups "0-14" and "15-24".

6. Now check the higher age groups "45-59" and "60+".

7. Click on [Start query].

How do the younger and older speakers compare in their usage of *wicked*? (Use frequency pmw for the comparison.) In terms of senses, do the younger and older groups of speaker generally use *wicked* in the same way or differently?

Using restricted queries of this type, you can confirm that *wicked* is predominantly used by younger speakers—in fact, its frequency is considerably higher for speakers in the age band 0-14 (177.13 pmw) than for any other age group. In addition, it will have become apparent that many of these uses by younger speakers are indeed examples of the "Excellent" sense of *wicked*.

Your query *"wicked"* restricted to *"Text type: Demographically sampled* and *Age: 0-14"* returned 63 hits by 20 different speakers (355,673 words [201 speakers]; frequency: 177.13 instances per million words)

Figure 4.8:   Title bar for a query with metatextual restrictions

Notice that for this type of query the dispersion information (cf. Section 4.3.3) has changed from indicating number of texts to number of speakers—see Figure 4.8. This is because the restrictions we have introduced here apply to speakers rather than whole texts.

> **Tip:**
> Later we will explore an alternative—and more convenient—method for searching first for one age group and then another: using the post-query DISTRIBUTION function. See further, Chapter 7.

There are many alternative restrictions you can apply to standard queries. You could change the restriction from "Demographically sampled" to the more formal "Context-governed" category (see Chapter 3). However, to finish this worked example, we'll take a brief look at *wicked* in fiction—i.e. in the written part of the BNC.

1. Click on WRITTEN RESTRICTIONS on the main navigation panel. The page will refresh, showing a new section in the center of the screen, entitled "Restricted Range of Written Texts".

2. Type `wicked` into the "Query term" box.

3. Under "Domain", select "Imaginative prose" (the term used in the BNC for fiction).

4. Click on [Start query].

Can you see any general patterns in the way *wicked* is used in fiction? (Unless you have time to read all 445 hits, we recommend again that you apply [Random order] before you start analyzing them: see 4.4.3). As suggested earlier, you could jot down a short description of each sense that you feel it is important to distinguish, and keep a running tally of cases that match each sense, for one or two pages of concordance results (or as many as you have time for).

There are many additional types of restrictions you may choose in order to investigate the use of *wicked* in more detail. You could, for instance, look for *wicked* in texts written by female authors and published between 1960-74, in the domain of imaginative prose (i.e. prose fiction). It is also possible to select several check boxes in the same category. In such cases, *BNCweb* will interpret your input as alternative options and return hits that match any of the selected criteria. For example, you can search for *wicked* in the text domains "Imaginative prose" OR "Informative: Arts" OR "Informative: Leisure".

It is worth remembering that when you restrict your search, you will be investigating a smaller part of the corpus. The more restrictions you choose, the smaller the number of texts or speakers will be. Although *BNCweb* always calculates frequencies per million words that can be used to directly compare search results from subsections of different sizes, the reliability of your findings will be reduced along with any reduction in the size of your data base. As a case in point, consider the title bar displayed in Figure 4.9.

Your query "wicked" restricted to "*Text Domain: Imaginative prose* and *Age of Author: 35-44* and *Sex of Author: Female* and *Type of Author: Sole* and *Age of Audience: Adult*" returned 10 hits in 5 different texts (550,114 words [16 texts]; frequency: 18.18 instances per million words)

Figure 4.9:   Title bar of a query result with several metatextual restrictions

Here, the restrictions that were chosen meant that only about 550,000 words from five texts of the corpus were searched. Although *BNCweb* indicates that the frequency per million words is 18.18, this frequency is calculated on the basis of only 10 hits. Even a small difference in the absolute numbers of hits—let's say a single text that adds another 10 hits—can have a dramatic effect on the frequency pmw. In cases such as this, your interpretation of the data therefore needs to be very tentative. We will return to this issue again in Chapter 5 when we introduce the concept of statistical significance.

> **Note:**
> The text restriction choices do not cover all possible features of texts,
> or all possible combinations. For example, they do not allow you to
> combine demographic conversation texts with academic written texts.
> If you want to search a combination of texts that you cannot easily de-
> fine using SPOKEN RESTRICTIONS or WRITTEN RESTRICTIONS, you can
> choose to build your own specialized subset of the corpus (a "subcor-
> pus"): e.g. a corpus of medical texts, or one of spoken and written
> law-related texts. This can also be a useful time saver as you wouldn't
> then have to tick many text restriction boxes each time you want to
> make a search on a predetermined set of texts. Read more about this in
> the chapter about subcorpora (Chapter 10).

4.7   Accessing previous queries

4.7.1   Query history

BNCweb automatically stores all the queries you make so that you can easily
recreate them at a later date. They are accessible via the QUERY HISTORY function, off the main navigation panel. In addition to the actual query, this function
lists the date and time of the query and the number of hits that were retrieved—
see Figure 4.10. To recreate the query result—i.e. to display the concordance
matching your query—simply click on the number in the "No. of hits" column.

BNC*web* (CQP-Edition)

Query history

No.	Date	Query (Show in CQP Syntax)	Restriction	No. of hits
1	14.06.2008, 12:15:48	beat about the	-	20
2	14.06.2008, 12:15:25	wicked	Metatextual categories: Text type: *Demographically sampled* Age: *0-14*	63
3	14.06.2008, 12:15:12	wicked	Metatextual categories: Text type: *Demographically sampled*	151
4	14.06.2008, 12:14:46	wicked	-	1029

Figure 4.10:   The QUERY HISTORY function

You may wish to have the query term from an earlier search copied into a fresh Standard query, so that you can edit it before re-running the query. For example, you may want to change the query term from `wicked` to `wickedly` or to restrict the search to spoken texts only. To make modifications of this kind, first click on the query term itself (in the column headed "Query").

The query history function also displays any metatextual restrictions you may have applied to a previous query—they are listed in the "Restriction" column. If you wish to perform a search for a different query term but with the same restrictions—or with minor changes—simply click on "Metatextual categories" in the "Restrictions" column. This will place your query term in the search box on either the "Spoken restrictions" page or the "Written restrictions" page, depending on your earlier selection. In addition, all previously chosen restrictions will be selected.

4.7.2   Save current set of hits

When you have worked with *BNCweb* for a while, it may be difficult to find a particular query in a long list of previously executed queries. Also, the Query history only stores the form of the query and a link to recreate the initial concordance. It does not allow you to retrieve a set of concordance lines that has been put into random order, or manipulated in any other way (e.g. by any of the post-query actions discussed in later chapters). The SAVE QUERY feature provides a convenient way to store individual concordances for later access.

To save your current hits exactly as they are displayed in the concordance (and also save the query):

1. In the *BNCweb* Query result page, select "Save current hits" in the post-query options menu and press [Go!].

2. Give the set of hits a meaningful name, and click [Go!] to save (see Figure 4.11).

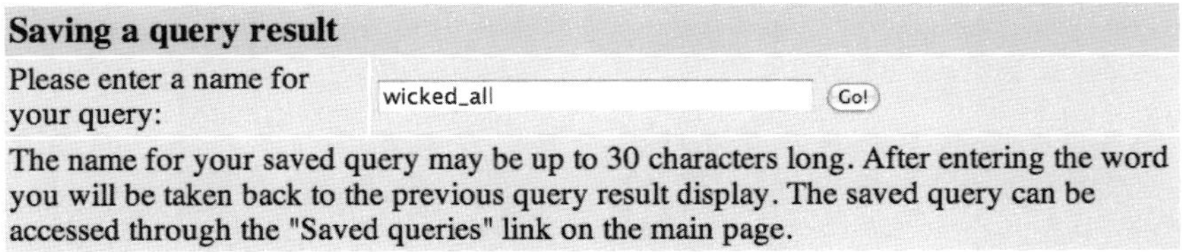

Saving a query result

Please enter a name for your query: | wicked_all | (Go!)

The name for your saved query may be up to 30 characters long. After entering the word you will be taken back to the previous query result display. The saved query can be accessed through the "Saved queries" link on the main page.

Figure 4.11:   Saving a query result

Some restrictions apply to the name of a saved query. Up to 30 characters—comprising only letters, numbers and the underscore—are permitted.

Later, you can access the same data again by the following steps:

1. Click on SAVED QUERIES on the main navigation panel.
2. Find the name of the saved query in the column "Name" and click on it to reload the results of the named query (see Figure 4.12).

You can also use this menu to rename or delete a set of results. Please note that if you delete a saved query, the action cannot be undone.

BNC*web* (CQP-Edition)

Saved queries

No.	Name	No. of hits	Date	Action
1	bottle_literal	7	14.12.2007 15:30:08	Rename Delete
2	bottle_metaphorical	5	14.12.2007 15:30:08	Rename Delete
3	bottle_other	1	14.12.2007 15:30:08	Rename Delete
4	bottle_unclear	2	14.12.2007 15:30:08	Rename Delete
5	politely	706	06.01.2008 16:15:42	Rename Delete
6	wicked_all	1029	04.05.2008 06:39:24	Rename Delete
7	you_know_discoursal	759	26.03.2008 13:50:08	Rename Delete
8	you_know_lexical	164	26.03.2008 13:50:08	Rename Delete
9	you_know_unclear	77	26.03.2008 13:50:09	Rename Delete

Figure 4.12:   List of saved queries

4.8   Browse a text

The BROWSE A TEXT facility offers a direct way to access any text in the BNC in order to browse its contents. For this, specify the three-character name of a text—or "file" (e.g. HEW)—in the first box (see Figure 4.13). Optionally set a sentence number (e.g., 20) as the point at which to start browsing. If the sentence number box is left empty, the beginning of the text will be displayed. A list of BNC filenames and their corresponding titles can be found in the *BNC Reference Guide*.

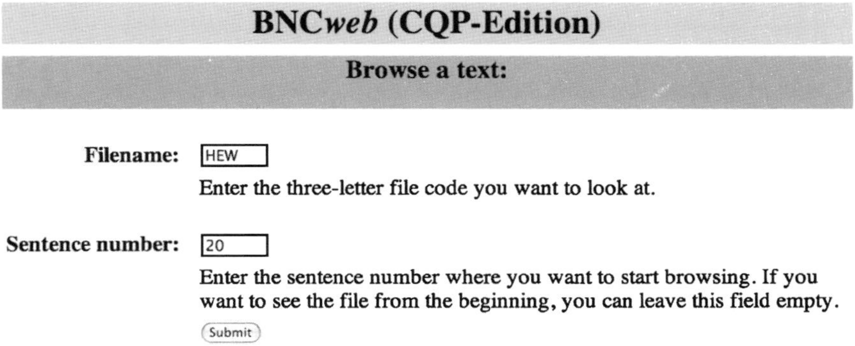

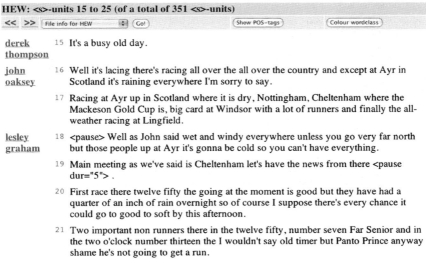

Figure 4.13: Options for the BROWSE A TEXT feature

Figure 4.14: Browsing a text—s-units 15 to 25 of file HEW (partial view)

Figure 4.14 shows the contents of file HEW, which is the transcript of a live sports commentary on horse racing broadcast on TV. The request was for sentence number 20, so *BNCweb* shows sentence numbers 15 to 25 on this page, putting sentence 20 in context. The default, as shown in Figure 4.14, is 10 s-units. This can be adjusted in the USER SETTINGS (see 13.4.1).

4.9   Exercises

1. *A closer look at* wicked. Pursue the *wicked* example further by revising the provisionally labeled "Evil" sense of the word. With the aid of a dictionary, and based on the examples you've encountered, refine the "Evil" category into more fine-grained senses and sketch brief definitions on paper. Jot down the examples, or example numbers, under each definition. Now, display the concordance of *wicked* in random order. What proportion of the first 50 random hits belongs to each of the revised senses?

2. *Which is the normal pattern of comparison of adjectives in English?* There are two main ways of turning adjective forms into comparatives and superlatives: inflectional formation (where *-er* or *-est* is added to the stem of the adjective, e.g. *small* ➔ *smaller, smallest; lively* ➔ *livelier, liveliest*) and periphrastic formation (where the word *more* or *most* is added in front of the adjective, e.g. *difficult* ➔ *more/most difficult; lively* ➔ *more/most lively*). Most textbooks state that the inflectional pattern is preferred with short, typically monosyllabic, adjectives (e.g. *tall, cold*), and that longer adjectives consisting of two or more syllables (e.g. *difficult, handsome*) tend to take periphrastic comparison. But there are some well-known qualifications to this general rule, particularly in the area of disyllabic adjectives ending in unstressed vowels such as /i/, /əl/ or /əʳ/, such as *easy, noisy, lively, gentle, noble, simple, bitter*. These adjectives allow variation in usage, but can you find whether one pattern is more common for a particular adjective?

   a) Start by comparing the frequencies of the inflectional (*easier*) and periphrastic (*more easy*) forms of *easy*. Is the pattern you observe the same in spoken and written language? Is it the same for the comparative and the superlative forms? Do any of the adjectives mentioned above pattern in a different way?

   b) Given what you currently know about the functionality of *BNCweb*, think about whether it would be possible to use the STANDARD QUERY search mode to look at adjective comparison in general. For example, does it allow you to check whether inflectional comparison or periphrastic comparison is the preferred method in British English? If not, explain why this is the case and think about the type of functionality a corpus tool needs in order to overcome these restrictions. Later chapters of this book will introduce features of *BNCweb* that make this type of task much easier (or more easy?) to carry out.

3. *How literal is* literally? Make a *BNCweb* search and examine the query result in random order. Does *literally* always mean 'in a literal sense'? In other words—do people always use it literally?

5   Some further aspects of corpus-linguistic methodology

5.1   Outline

This chapter complements Chapter 2 by dealing with the following important aspects of corpus-linguistic methodology:

- the calculation of relative frequency counts
- the interpretation of relative frequency counts
- the concepts of "precision" and "recall"
- the evaluation of statistical significance

5.2   Introduction

This chapter deals with a number of points that are intended to increase the accuracy and reliability of your corpus-based investigations. As already alluded to in previous chapters, the use of relative frequency counts—e.g. frequencies per million words—is of fundamental importance when you want to compare findings from different subsections of a corpus—or, in fact, from different corpora. In our experience, however, novices in the field often find it difficult to put this principle into practice when they conduct their first studies. We therefore feel that it is particularly important to alert readers to some possible pitfalls in using relative frequency counts. A further area of focus relates to the concepts of PRECISION and RECALL. An understanding of these terms will help you evaluate whether the data you retrieve via a particular corpus search is both accurate and sufficiently complete—and this in turn will enable you to optimize your searches. Finally, we will also offer some general guidance in evaluating how "trustworthy" your findings are. If, for example, you observe a difference in use between male and female speakers, how sure can you be that this difference is not merely a result of chance? In other words, we will be concerned with some questions of STATISTICAL SIGNIFICANCE.

5.3   Comparing results: normalized frequencies

The first important methodological issue to be discussed in this chapter is how results from different corpus searches can be compared. Let's say you would like to investigate the construction *in fact*. For example, you could be interested in finding out more about how speakers of English are using *in fact* in argumentative discourse. For this purpose, you would definitely want to look at individual instances in context—this is the qualitative part of the analysis. However, in order to select relevant occurrences for further analysis, you may want to start your investigation by finding out in what contexts this construction is particularly frequent. As shown in the previous chapter, these types of descriptive statistics can be easily obtained with *BNCweb*, making use of the metatextual information that is provided about the texts in the corpus. Here are some findings you would be able to make:

- There are 13,237 instances of *in fact* in the written part of the BNC, but only 2,994 in the spoken part
- In written texts, 2,047 instances of *in fact* are found in the text domain "World affairs" but only 662 in the domain "Belief and thought"
- In spoken texts, 518 instances of *in fact* occur in monologues, while 2,476 instances are found in conversations involving several speakers

Based on this information, you could come to the conclusion that *in fact* is more common in written language—and here particularly in texts dealing with the topic area of "World affairs". Furthermore, you could also claim that *in fact* is almost five times more frequent in dialogues than in monologues. If this sounds reasonable to you, pause for a moment to reflect whether this is really what you can claim on the basis of the information given above. You may be surprised to hear that these conclusions are in fact very wrong!

The problem is that these claims are based on absolute numbers of occurrences, i.e. **RAW FREQUENCIES**. This type of comparison is only meaningful if you are dealing with equal amounts of text. This is represented visually in Figure 5.1, where both rectangles represent parts of a corpus that are four million words in size.

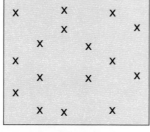
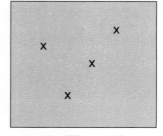

4 million words   4 million words

Figure 5.1:   Comparison between two corpus parts of equal size

In the rectangle on the left side, there are 16 instances of a particular linguistic feature (indicated by the crosses), whereas the one on the right only contains four. Since both these rectangles are of equal size, we can rightfully claim that the item is four times more frequent in the left than in the right rectangle.

However, let us now look at a situation where the corpus parts are not equal—this is shown in Figure 5.2.

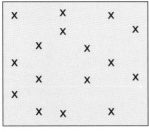

4 million words

1 million words

Figure 5.2:   Comparison between two corpus parts of different sizes

Here, the texts contained in the right rectangle only amount to one million words, while the left rectangle is still the same as in Figure 5.1 above. The rectangles contain the same number of instances of the item we are interested in as before: 16 on the left and four on the right. There are therefore still four times fewer instances overall in the right than in the left rectangle.

However, it will be obvious to you that if the comparison of frequencies is to be valid, the calculation needs to take account of the different sizes of the rectangles. This can be done by reducing the size of the left rectangle to one million words—i.e. the same size as the right rectangle—while at the same time proportionally reducing the number of instances of our linguistic feature. If there are 16 instances in four million words, how many would you expect to find—on average—if you only looked at one million words of the same texts? The answer is of course that you would expect to find only four instances (i.e. 16 divided by 4). And since we also have four instances in the right rectangle, we can now say that the linguistic feature occurs at the same frequency rate in both rectangles, even though the raw frequency figures differ considerably.

What we have done here is to calculate **RELATIVE**—or **NORMALIZED**—**FREQUENCIES**. In our example, we have decided to use frequency per million words, commonly abbreviated to "fpmw" or "pmw". This value is calculated by the following simple arithmetic:

$$\text{Frequency pmw} = \frac{\text{number of instances}}{\text{number of words}} \times 1,000,000$$

There are other ways to calculate relative frequencies than "per million words". For example, you may find corpus studies presenting frequencies per 100,000 or even 10,000 words. Using smaller numbers makes sense if you are using small corpora (or small sub-sections of a large corpus) or if you are dealing with very common features that would result in very high per-million-word frequencies. However, it is important to point out that the actual basis of comparison is in principle irrelevant. In fact, there is nothing really wrong with presenting normalized frequencies "per 246,577 words"—except that it is not very intuitive or easy to conceptualize. Nevertheless, as long as what you compare is normalized to the same number of words, you can still make valid statements.

Returning to the figures for *in fact* presented above, let us have a look at what the picture looks like when you normalize the frequencies per million words. Figure 5.3 presents the normalized frequencies of *in fact* in spoken and written data.

Category	No. of words	No. of hits	Dispersion (over files)	Frequency per million words
Spoken	10,409,858	2,994	549/908	287.61
Written	87,903,571	13,237	2,247/3,140	150.59
total	98,313,429	16,231	2,796/4,048	165.09

Figure 5.3: The frequency of *in fact* in the spoken and written components of the BNC[1]

As you can see, the big difference in size between the two components—the written part of the BNC is almost nine times the size of the spoken part—has a big impact on the number of hits. Although there are more than four times as many instances of *in fact* in the written part (13,237 vs. 2,994), the normalized frequencies are the other way round: the construction is almost twice as frequent in spoken data. It is the same case for the other two raw results mentioned earlier—and we urge you to confirm these findings for yourself using *BNCweb*: although there are 2,047 instances of *in fact* in the category "World affairs", this is the text domain with the lowest relative frequency in the corpus. In contrast, the

---

1   This is a screenshot of the output produced by the DISTRIBUTION feature—see further, Chapter 7.

662 instances found in "Belief and thought" represent almost double the relative frequency (218 pmw vs. 119 pmw), and "Belief and thought" is in fact the domain with the highest frequency. Finally, *in fact* is slightly more frequent in monologues than in dialogues (332 pmw vs. 280 pmw) even though there are almost five times as many instances in dialogues. To emphasize the point, then, relative frequencies can sometimes be the very opposite of what absolute (or raw) frequencies will tell you.

We have discussed the calculation of normalized frequencies in great detail because in our experience, this is the number one source of error for novices in corpus linguistics. Therefore, even if everything in this section has seemed commonsensical or obvious to you, we would nevertheless urge you to make a mental note of returning to this description when you conduct your first serious corpus study. As the example of *in fact* has shown, results can be drastically different when findings are not normalized, and unless you are aware of this, you may unwittingly be claiming something very different from what is actually the case.

5.4   Normalized frequencies—some further issues

In this section, we will be looking at two additional issues that may arise when working with normalized frequencies. The first of these concerns the reliability of the conclusions one can draw from the observed frequencies. The second asks whether relative frequencies of the per-million-word type are always the most meaningful measures for use in comparisons.

For the first of these issues, let us return to *in fact*. We have already looked at some categories and discovered clear differences in the frequencies of use of this construction, e.g. with respect to mode (spoken or written), domain ("World affairs" or "Belief and thought) or interactivity (monologue or dialogue). As Figure 5.4 demonstrates, there also appears to be a clear difference in use between male and female speakers: men use *in fact* about twice as often as women do (332 pmw vs. 164 pmw).

Category	No. of words	No. of hits	Dispersion (over speakers)	Frequency per million words
Male	4,949,938	1,641	591/2,448	331.52
Female	3,290,569	541	230/1,360	164.41
total	**8,240,507**	**2,182**	**821/3,808**	**264.79**

Figure 5.4:   The frequency of *in fact* by female and male speakers in the BNC

> **Note:**
> You may be wondering why the total number of words in Figure 5.4 is
> only 8.2 million words, even though the spoken part of the BNC con-
> tains over 10 million words (cf. Figure 5.3 above). This has to do with
> the fact that there are almost two million words in the corpus for
> which no information about the sex of the speaker is available. Unfor-
> tunately, this is not an uncommon situation: for the category "Age of
> speakers", for example, we only have information for less than six
> million of the total ten million words (cf. also Chapter 3).

As Figure 5.4 suggests, men use *in fact* about twice as often as women do
(332 pmw vs. 164 pmw). However, how can we be sure that this is indeed generally true? Remember that in the previous section, we said that in order to calculate normalized frequencies, we work on the assumption that the item in question occurs **on average** *n* number of times per million words. Sometimes, it is
worth checking whether that assumption can actually be confirmed. Without doing this, it is possible to miss other important influences that may be hidden behind a single frequency figure.

Category	No. of words	No. of hits	Dispersion (over speakers)	Frequency per million words
Female	2,264,094	227	98/559	100.26
Male	1,454,344	139	75/509	95.58
total	**3,718,438**	**366**	**173/1,068**	**98.43**

Figure 5.5:   The use of *in fact* by male and female speakers in the
demographically sampled part of the BNC

Category	No. of words	No. of hits	Dispersion (over speakers)	Frequency per million words
Male	3,495,594	1,502	516/1,939	429.68
Female	1,026,475	314	132/801	305.9
total	**4,522,069**	**1,816**	**648/2,740**	**401.59**

Figure 5.6:   The use of *in fact* by male and female speakers in the context-
governed part of the BNC

This is nicely demonstrated by the data presented in Figures 5.5 and 5.6, which show the use of *in fact* in the demographically sampled and the context-governed parts of the BNC. First of all, it can immediately be seen that the frequency of *in fact* differs quite a lot between the two sub-parts of the spoken component of the BNC: in spontaneous conversational English, *in fact* is about four times less frequent than in the context-governed part (98 pmw vs. 402 pmw). More importantly, in the demographically sampled part, no strong difference between male and female use of *in fact* can be observed. If anything, it is actually the women who use *in fact* slightly more frequently (100 pmw vs. 96 pmw). However, given that absolute figures are not very high (227 vs. 130), this difference should not be given too much weight. Thus, although there seems to be an overall difference between how often men and women use *in fact*—as indicated by Table 5.4 above—the picture is clearly more complex. Tables 5.5 and 5.6 suggest instead that the difference in use is the result of (at least) two factors, sex of speaker and context of use. For some reason, male speakers appear to prefer *in fact* in more formal contexts only, and it would certainly be worthwhile to look at this in more detail. When using the descriptive statistics provided by *BNCweb*, it is therefore always a good idea to check whether the results actually only give a partial picture of a more complex reality (which may involve other hidden factors).

The second issue with normalized frequencies we would briefly like to raise concerns the question whether it always makes sense to normalize "per *n* number of words". If we are using such a word-based frequency analysis to compare two sub-parts of a corpus (or, in fact, two different corpora), we are working on the assumption that equal amounts of text will give us the same number of opportunities for the feature that we are interested in to occur. But is this truly the case? Let's say we are interested in the use of relative clauses (e.g. *This is the man **who won the lottery***) and we would like to determine whether certain text domains use this type of construction more frequently than others. Let's also simply assume that we have successfully retrieved all relative clauses from our corpus. (In fact, this is anything but a trivial thing!) Our (constructed) data looks as shown in Table 5.1: we have three differently-sized parts of a corpus, containing 10, 20 and 30 million words, respectively. In the smallest part, i.e. Domain A, we retrieved 1,000 relative clauses—this therefore gives us a normalized frequency of 100 relative clauses per million words (i.e. 1,000 divided by 10 million and multiplied by 1 million). Using the same calculation, we see that Domain B has the same frequency of relative clauses: there are twice as many clauses in twice as many words, i.e. again 100 instances per million words. Domain C, finally, is the biggest in the corpus part, and it contains the highest number of relative clauses, namely 6,000. If we calculate normalized frequencies, we see that the feature is also relatively more frequent in Domain C than in the other domains: the frequency is 200 instances per million words.

Table 5.1:   Relative clauses in three different parts of a corpus

Domain	N words	N relative clauses	Frequency pmw
Domain A	10,000,000	1,000	100 pmw
Domain B	20,000,000	2,000	100 pmw
Domain C	30,000,000	6,000	200 pmw
Total	60,000,000	9,000	150 pmw

However, this calculation is potentially problematic. What we have done in Table 5.1 is to work on the assumption that relative clauses have the same opportunities of being used in all three domains. But is this necessarily so? Think for a moment about what it needs for a relative clause to occur: there has to be a noun which it can modify (e.g. *the* **man** *who won the lottery*). So, if for example Domain A has many more nouns than Domain B, there are more opportunities —or potential "slots"—for relative clauses to be used. But in our data, this higher number of possible slots did not lead to a larger number of relative clauses. So even though a word-frequency based calculation suggests that the two domains contain equal frequencies of relative clauses, one could claim that they are, in fact, less frequently used in Domain A.

Biber et al. (1999:65) show in their reference grammar that different types of language situations indeed lead to considerable differences in the overall number and distribution of word classes: nouns are much more common in newspapers and academic texts than they are in fiction and conversation. Furthermore, "nouns and verbs are about equally frequent" in conversation while "in news reportage and academic prose, there are three to four nouns per lexical verb". Unless we take this into account in our interpretation of the normalized frequencies presented in Table 5.1, our conclusions may be to some extent unreliable.

Despite these cautionary remarks, we would like to emphasize that "frequency per million words" is a widely used, trusted and very convenient yardstick for discovering many of the differences between individual parts of the corpus. It is also extremely useful if you want to compare frequencies from one corpus to another. However, we feel that it is necessary to point out even at this early stage that thinking about your data and about the accuracy and usefulness of the methods you use to draw conclusions from this data is an extremely important part of being a corpus linguist. As you become more experienced, you will become aware of potential problems in your analysis more quickly. And of course the best way to go about gaining this experience is by using corpora. There will be plenty of exercises in the remaining chapters of this book that will illustrate the methodological points we have raised here.

5.5 Precision and recall

Let us briefly go back to the first of the three questions we asked in Chapter 1, i.e. the question about the meaning of the word *goalless*. You may remember that we showed how a search with the help of *BNCweb* gave us 86 instances of this word, all of which came from the area of sports. However, did we really look at all of the relevant instances and can we therefore truly make a definite claim about how *goalless* is used in the BNC? In fact, we cannot. Although all of the retrieved instances of the word are indeed relevant, we did miss something in our search: we failed to realize that *goalless* can also be written with a hyphen! And a quick search in the BNC reveals that there are 16 instances of *goal-less* in the corpus. Furthermore, there are actually two instances where *goalless* is misspelled—in both cases, the word is spelled with only one *l*. In other words, our initial search missed 18 out of a total of 104 relevant instances. Luckily, our conclusion still remains valid: all of these 18 additional instances refer to the area of sports too. However, those instances we originally missed could very well have changed the picture.

Very often, missing something in your search is not the only problem. To illustrate this, we will return to our discussion of *shall* in Chapter 1. One of the points mentioned was that *shall* is considered to be fairly old-fashioned and that nowadays, *will* is usually used instead. But we did not check whether *will* is in fact much more frequent than *shall*. As Figure 5.7 shows, this is indeed the case: with 19,808 instances, *will* occurs over seven times more often than *shall* (only 2,735 instances).

No.	Lexical item(s)	No. of occurrences	Percent
1	will	19808	87.87%
2	shall	2735	12.13%

Figure 5.7: The modals *will* and *shall* in the spoken component of the BNC

Yet, things are unfortunately not as easy as that. There are two aspects which we have not taken care of yet. In fact, the figure of 19,808 instances of *will* is bigger than it should be: not every instance of *will* we retrieved is relevant. Can you think about why this is the case? The problem here is that *will* can be not only a modal verb but also a noun, as in *This happened against her **will*** or *We have made our **wills***. Again, the influence of this oversight is fortunately not very great: there are only 373 instances of the noun *will* in the spoken part of the BNC, so the overall difference in frequency is not greatly changed. However, the second oversight is much more dramatic: what about the contracted forms *'ll* and *won't?* As it turns out, *'ll* is even more frequent than the full form *will*, and *won't* also occurs more than 5,000 times—in contrast, only 148 instances of the contracted form *shan't* are found. The actual proportions are shown in Figure 5.8, where the numbers for *will* have been adjusted to exclude nouns: with 31,712 instances, the contracted form *'ll* is far more frequent than the full form. If the three forms of *will* are grouped together, they cover more than 95 per cent of all relevant instances, which makes *shall* look like a much more marginal variant than our initial results suggested.[2]

No.	Lexical item(s)	No. of occurrences	Percent
1	'll	31712	52.75%
2	will	19808	32.95%
3	wo n't	5714	9.5%
4	shall	2735	4.55%
5	sha n't	148	0.25%

Figure 5.8:   The modals *will/'ll, won't, shall* and *shan't* in the spoken part of the BNC

In an ideal world, a corpus tool would find all and only the relevant instances necessary to answer your research question. In reality, this is often not the case. In discussions of these two issues, corpus linguists usually use the terms **PRECISION** and **RECALL**. "Recall" measures the proportion of all relevant in-stances (i.e. what you intended to find) that are retrieved by a corpus search. It is usually given as a percentage figure. Assuming that the forms *goalless, goal-less* and *goaless* indeed cover all possible cases, the recall for our search of *goalless* in Chapter 1 was therefore 86 out of 104 items, or 82.7 per cent. "Precision" measures the proportion of all retrieved instances that are actually relevant, i.e. they match what was targeted in the search. For our *goalless* search, the preci-sion was 100 per cent, because all the retrieved instances were actually uses of the lexical item that we were interested in. In the search for the modal verb *will*, the precision was quite good too: the noun *will* only accounts for a very small proportion of all retrieved instances and the precision rate is therefore at over 98%. However, the recall was very bad indeed: because we did not initially take the contracted forms into consideration, the 19,808 instances correspond to a re-call of only about 34% (out of a total of 56,877 instances of *will, 'll* and *won't*).

As just mentioned above, a corpus linguist would ideally want to have searches with 100 per cent recall and 100 per cent precision. To get as close to

---

2   However, some people regard *'ll* as the contracted form of both *shall* and *will*. If this is the case, it is of course impossible to arrive at exact frequencies for the two modal verbs.

this as possible, it is necessary to refine the search strategy. In the cases we have discussed so far, we were able to radically improve the situation simply by making sure that we added the forms that we had previously missed. Unfortunately, such a simple remedy is not always available. Typically, improving precision reduces recall, and vice versa. The important question, then, is: which is better—to optimize recall or to optimize precision? If you are doing serious language research, then the answer is definitely "recall". The reason for this is that a high level of recall (i.e. more data, rather than less) means that you do not run the risk of making claims that are based on a minority of all relevant items. A low level of precision is much less problematic: although you will end up with a potentially large number of irrelevant instances, they can usually be discarded by manually inspecting the results (see Chapter 9). This is of course more work than having the computer do it for you—but at least you can then have greater confidence in your findings.

Unfortunately, optimizing recall is also often more difficult than optimizing precision. The problem is that you don't normally know what you have missed in your search. After all, if you had known it before, you would have looked for it in the first place. And as you may have seen with the example of contracted *'ll* and *won't*, it is in fact very easy to miss something that would represent a major part of your relevant data. It therefore pays to constantly question your search procedures, trying to guess whether there is anything you could have missed or left out.

5.6   Statistical significance

Before you can draw any firm conclusions from corpus frequency data, it is essential to establish the significance of your results with statistical tests. The necessity of a statistical analysis becomes most obvious in the fairly common situation where accurate data can only be obtained by manual counting. Let us therefore return to the example of *wicked* and its relatively new "Excellent" sense. In Chapter 4, you wanted to find out how well-established the new sense is in general English by determining its frequency in the BNC. Since it would have been tedious to go through all 1,029 instances of *wicked* and decide for each one whether it is used in the "Evil" sense or the "Excellent" sense, you only looked at a random sample of 50 instances (i.e. the first page of 50 randomly ordered hits). Recall that it was important to take a random sample because the first page of hits in corpus order would not be representative of the whole BNC.

Let us assume that you found 5 cases out of 50 in this sample where *wicked* is used in the "Excellent" sense, i.e. a proportion of 10%.[3] Then, following the

---

3   You may have arrived at a slightly different count because it is sometimes difficult to be sure precisely what the intended sense is.

reasoning of Chapter 4, you would conclude that there are approximately 103 examples of the "Excellent" sense in the entire BNC—the same proportion of 10% out of 1,029 instances of *wicked*. The crucial point, of course, is the word "approximately". Why can't you be sure that your extrapolation is correct and there are in fact 103 examples in the BNC? To answer this question, take a look at the second page of 50 hits, where you will very likely find a different proportion of the "Excellent" sense than on the first page. You might find only 3 instances, and thus extrapolate to a total of approximately 62 examples. On the third page, you might find 8 instances and extrapolate to a total of 165 examples. But which of these figures is the right one? After all, each page of 50 randomly ordered hits is an equally valid random sample.

The problem here lies in SAMPLING VARIATION. For each page, 50 hits are picked randomly from the entire result set. Therefore, the page will usually not contain exactly the same proportion of the "Excellent" sense as the full set does. This is just like tossing coins: if you toss a coin 10 times, it will also not necessarily land heads up exactly 5 times as you might have expected; any count between 2 and 8 is likely to occur. As a result, from observing 5 cases out of 50, you cannot be sure that the actual proportion in the full result set is 10%. Your extrapolation is subject to a certain degree of uncertainty.

Fortunately, statisticians have developed methods to correct for sampling variation and determine the precise amount of this uncertainty. You can find detailed information about these methods in any good statistics textbook (e.g. De-Groot & Schervish 2002) under the keywords "hypothesis test" and "confidence interval". The purpose of this section is to familiarize you with the most elementary statistical techniques required for analyzing corpus frequency data. You will also learn how to apply such techniques using on-line tools or statistical software packages.

5.6.1   Confidence intervals

In our example, you want to find out how reliable your estimate for the proportion of the "Excellent" sense of *wicked* is. This is accomplished by calculating a CONFIDENCE INTERVAL, i.e. a range of plausible values for the "true" proportion in the full result set, given the number of "positive" cases (i.e. "Excellent" readings) that you observed in your sample. The easiest way to determine confidence intervals is to use one of many online "statistics calculators" that are available on the World Wide Web. For your convenience, we provide an online *Corpus Frequency Wizard* at http://sigil.collocations.de/wizard.html which offers the most commonly needed statistical procedures in a clear and uncluttered interface. We will use this wizard for the examples discussed below. Other online tools that you might like to consult are Paul Rayson's *Log-likelihood Calculator* at http://ucrel.lancs.ac.uk/llwizard.html and the comprehensive online lab *Vas-*

sarStats at http://faculty.vassar.edu/lowry/VassarStats.html. The latter site offers a much greater range of algorithms, but it may be very confusing unless you are already familiar with statistical methods and the relevant terminology. If you want to use such advanced methods, we recommend that you obtain specialized statistical software (see Section 5.6.3). Once you have become acquainted with such programs, you will find them much easier and convenient to use than Web-based calculators.

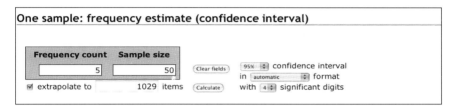

Figure 5.9   Calculating confidence intervals with the *Corpus Frequency Wizard*

In order to calculate a confidence interval for your initial observation of 5 positives out of 50 manually checked items, go to the *Corpus Frequency Wizard* and enter the information in the box on the left-hand side under the heading "One sample: frequency estimate" (see Figure 5.9). You have to enter the number of positives under "Frequency count" and the number of manually checked items under "Sample size". Since you want to estimate the number of positives in the full result set, tick the "extrapolate to" field below the box and enter the total number of results (1,029 items). Now click [Calculate]. This will display the result page shown in Figure 5.10.

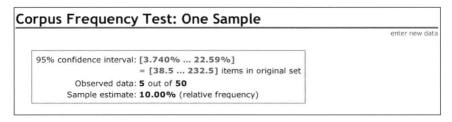

Figure 5.10   Result of calculating the confidence interval for 5 positives out of 50 manually checked items, extrapolated to 1,029 hits.

The confidence interval for the true proportion of positives ranges from 3.74% to 22.59%, and is shown in the first line. Therefore, all we can tell from manual inspection of the first page of 50 random hits is that the "Excellent" sense accounts for somewhere between 3.74% and 22.59% of all occurrences of *wicked*. This corresponds to any number between 38 and 232 instances in the full result set of 1,029 hits, as the second line in Figure 5.10 shows. It is now obvious that the extrapolation to exactly 103 instances in Chapter 4 gave a very misleading impression of high accuracy.

What we have calculated here is a so-called 95% confidence interval, indicating a certainty of 95% that the true proportion is indeed within the specified range. In other words, there is a risk of 5% that the prediction made by this confidence interval is wrong. If you have used statistical tests before, you may be more familiar with the "risk of error" view, which is often called a significance level in this context and written as $p < .05$ rather than 5%.

The 95% (or $p < .05$) level is a standard confidence level used by most statisticians and statistical software packages. If you prefer a higher degree of certainty, you can also calculate more conservative confidence intervals. In the *Corpus Frequency Wizard*, use the topmost drop-down menu on the right-hand side of Figure 5.9 to select the customary confidence levels of 99% and 99.9%. The other drop-down menus allow you to change the output format for the confidence intervals. Note that such conservative confidence intervals can become very wide; at the 99.9% level, extrapolation to the full result set predicts between 22 and 338 instances of the "Excellent" sense.

If you calculate 95% confidence intervals for all three samples (assuming 5, 2 and 8 positive cases, respectively), you will find that these intervals overlap. A true proportion of 10% would be consistent with all the samples (since it falls within each of the confidence intervals), so that the results are in fact not contradictory. We are still uncertain about the true proportion—a value of 8% is also consistent with all three samples, and so is a value of 14%—but we should be able to obtain a narrower confidence interval: we have three times as many data now (from the three pages of query hits checked by hand), and larger samples reduce the amount of uncertainty. With a total of $5 + 2 + 8 = 15$ positives out of 150 items, the 95% confidence interval for the proportion of the "Excellent" sense is 5.9%…16.2% (note that this interval includes the values 8%, 10% and 14%, which we found to be consistent with the three individual samples), corresponding to somewhere between 61 and 167 instances in the full result set. In statistics, combining samples in such a way is known as "pooling".

The reasoning that convinced us of the necessity of statistical tests for manual counts on random samples at the beginning of this section also applies to full query results obtained on the BNC, or on any subset of the BNC defined by textual or speaker restrictions. After all, a corpus like the BNC is nothing else than a sample of language (though it may not be as perfectly random as one would like it to be). In Section 5.4 above, you found that the expression *in fact* is used 541 times by female speakers in the BNC and estimated its relative frequency to be 164.41 instances per million words (541 instances among 3,290,569 words uttered by female speakers). However, if the compilers of the BNC had chosen other texts from the same years, genres, etc.—even from exactly the same speakers—you would have obtained a different result. If you enter these numbers into the *Corpus Frequency Wizard* (not ticking the "extrapolate" field this time, since you do not want to extrapolate to any finite set, but to female native speakers of English in general), the confidence interval reveals that the true relative frequency of *in fact* among female speakers may lie anywhere between 151 pmw and 179 pmw. Again, the precise estimate of 164.41 pmw above gave a very misleading impression of accuracy.

Statistical analysis is particularly important whenever you are dealing with small sets of occurrences, as was the case for the manually checked samples above. You do not need to calculate confidence intervals if you want to estimate the relative frequency of the definite article *the* in written English; they would be extremely narrow (between 6.40% and 6.41% of all words). However, if you are interested in the frequency of the word *wormhole* (which has only 3 instances in the written BNC), the confidence interval shows that it might occur as often as once per 10 million words or less than once per 100 million words on average.[4]

5.6.2   Hypothesis tests for frequency comparison

A common situation in corpus linguistics is the comparison of frequency counts between two corpora (or subsets of a corpus). For example, if you look at instances of *wicked* in the spoken and written parts of the BNC, you will quickly come up with the hypothesis that the "Excellent" sense is more frequent in spoken than in written English, in line with its colloquial nature (according to standard dictionaries). Let us assume for the sake of argument that you find 8 instances of this sense among 50 random hits from the spoken part, and only 2 among 50 random hits from the written part. If you compare the extrapolated proportions—16% vs. 4%—you might think that there is a clear difference between the two subsets; but human intuition tends to underestimate sampling variation. The large confidence intervals we have found above should have given you ample warning of this fact.

---

4   The precise range is 8.8 ... 108.8 occurrences per *billion* words (i.e. 0.0088 pmw ... 0.1088 pmw), obtained by entering the values 3 and 87,903,571 into the *Corpus Frequency Wizard* (the commas separating groups of digits are optional here, but note that many software packages will not accept such separators).

You can—and should—apply a statistical hypothesis test to establish the significance of such a frequency comparison. Statisticians have developed a number of tests that can be applied in the frequency comparison setting. You may already have read about the chi-squared test, but other procedures are more accurate especially for corpus data. Most people recommend using either the log-likelihood test[5] or Fisher's exact test (cf. Section 5.6.3). The *Corpus Frequency Wizard* offers such frequency comparison tests under the heading "Two samples: frequency comparison". In the box on the left-hand side, you need to enter the sample sizes and the number of positive cases in each sample, as shown in Figure 5.11. Then click [Calculate]. The result of the calculation is displayed in Figure 5.12.

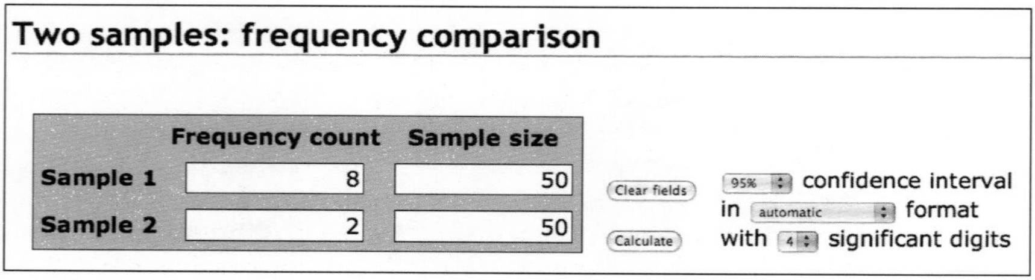

Two samples: frequency comparison

	Frequency count	Sample size	
Sample 1	8	50	Clear fields
Sample 2	2	50	Calculate

95% $\updownarrow$ confidence interval
in automatic $\updownarrow$ format
with 4 $\updownarrow$ significant digits

Figure 5.11   Frequency comparison with the *Corpus Frequency Wizard*—entering values

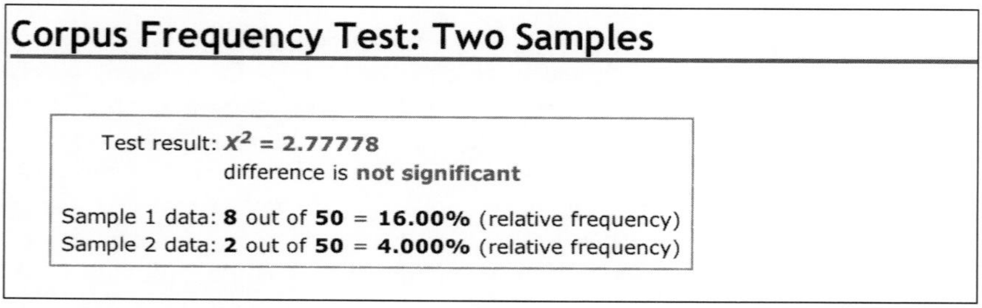

Corpus Frequency Test: Two Samples

Test result: $X^2 = 2.77778$
difference is **not significant**

Sample 1 data: **8** out of **50** = **16.00%** (relative frequency)
Sample 2 data: **2** out of **50** = **4.000%** (relative frequency)

Figure 5.12   Frequency comparison with the *Corpus Frequency Wizard* — result display

---

5   In mathematical statistics, this test is simply known as *likelihood-ratio test* or G^2. The name *log-likelihood* was coined by Dunning (1993), who popularized the procedure in the field of computational linguistics.

The wizard automatically chooses between chi-squared (X^2) and log-likelihood (G^2), depending on which test is deemed to be more accurate for your data. Here, it has selected the chi-squared test. Both chi-squared and log-likelihood scores are interpreted by comparison with the same set of standard "critical values" shown in Table 5.2, which determine how certain you can be that there is indeed a difference between spoken and written English, and that your observation is not just an accident of the random sampling procedure. In our example, the score of 2.78 is below the first critical value of 3.841, so the observed difference is not considered significant (because the risk of error is too high), and the wizard points out this fact.

If we had observed 10 positive instances in the spoken sample, the score X^2 = 4.64 would have been above the threshold. In this case, the "error rate"—the risk of a false result—would be sufficiently small for the observed difference to become significant. Statisticians call this error rate the p-value (for "probability"). The third column of Table 5.2 shows that a score above 3.841 is significant at the level $p < .05$, i.e. with an error rate below 5%. We might alternatively say that our confidence in the result is 95% (cf. the second column of the table).

Table 5.2:   Critical values for the chi-squared and log-likelihood tests

3.841	95% confidence	$p < .05$	minimum level of significance
6.635	99% confidence	$p < .01$	better confidence in result
10.827	99.9% confidence	$p < .001$	widely accepted as "almost certain"

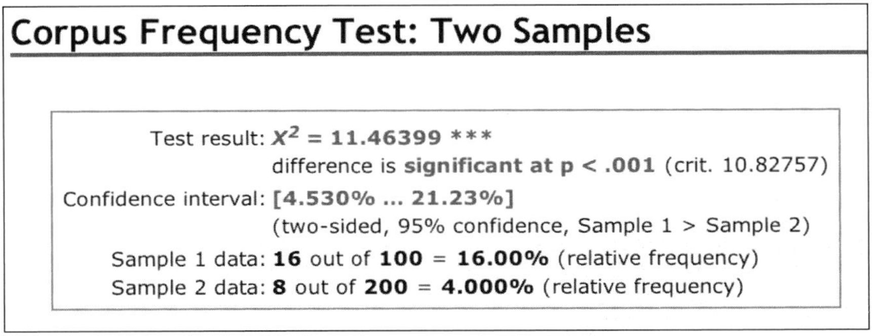

Corpus Frequency Test: Two Samples

Test result: X^2 = 11.46399 ***
difference is **significant at p < .001** (crit. 10.82757)
Confidence interval: **[4.530% ... 21.23%]**
(two-sided, 95% confidence, Sample 1 > Sample 2)
Sample 1 data: **16** out of **100** = **16.00%** (relative frequency)
Sample 2 data: **8** out of **200** = **4.000%** (relative frequency)

Figure 5.13   Significant result and confidence interval

Again, larger samples result in a lower error rate and better confidence. If you had looked at two pages of random hits for the spoken data and four pages for the written data (i.e. a total of 100 and 200 hits, respectively), and observed 16 positive cases for spoken and 8 for written texts (the same relative frequencies of 16% and 4%), you would have obtained the highest level of 99.9% confidence ($p < .001$) with a score of $X^2 = 11.46$. Note that you can use samples of different sizes: the statistical tests will adjust automatically. Figure 5.13 shows the output of the *Corpus Frequency Wizard* for a significant difference: the level of significance achieved is customarily indicated by one to three asterisks, with three asterisks denoting the highest level of significance. In addition, the critical value and corresponding error rate are displayed.

Once significance has safely been established, you may also be interested to find out how much more frequent the "Excellent" sense of *wicked* is in spoken English than in written English. Statisticians refer to this difference between true proportions as EFFECT SIZE. If you were to extrapolate directly from the observed counts (resulting in proportions of 16% and 4%, respectively), you would obtain an effect size of 12 percentage points. Because of sampling variation, however, the true effect size may be much smaller – or larger – than this value. The online wizard automatically corrects for sampling variation and computes a 95 per cent confidence interval for the effect size, which indicates in this case that the "Excellent" sense is at least 4.5 percentage points more frequent in spoken English (Sample 1) than in written English (Sample 2). The difference might in fact be as large as 21.2 percentage points, but you should always base your linguistic arguments on the lower bound of the confidence interval: only this difference has been established with sufficient confidence. As in the single sample case, you can select the confidence level and output formatting for confidence intervals with the drop-down menus seen on the right-hand side of Figure 5.11.

5.6.3   Using statistical software

While the online calculators we have used in the preceding sections are very convenient, they rely on approximations that may not be valid for low-frequency data. Specialized statistical software allows you to carry out more complex "exact" tests that avoid such approximations and give reliable answers in all situations. Various commercial software packages are available, e.g. *SPSS*, *SAS* and *S-Plus*. We recommend the *R statistical environment* (R Development Core Team 2008), which is freely available open-source software just like *BNCweb* and has a very active and friendly community of users and developers. While *R*'s text-based interface may seem unfamiliar and daunting to you at first, the enormous range of statistical techniques it offers and the enthusiasm of its user community make it well worth the effort of learning. There are numerous intro-ductory textbooks on statistical analysis with R, some of which are specifically aimed at linguists (Baayen 2008; Gries in press).

Later in this section, we will see how significance tests are carried out in R and how confidence intervals can be calculated. But first, you need to under-stand the precise logic of exact significance tests with the help of an artificially simple example.

If you have a precise quantitative hypothesis about the full set, you can fal-sify it with the help of a hypothesis test (see Baroni & Evert in press for an ex-planation of why statistical methods cannot directly confirm a hypothesis). For instance, when you looked at the first pages of hits for *wicked* in corpus order at the beginning of Chapter 4, you may have formed the impression that the new "Excellent" sense is still very rare and accounts for less than 1% of all instances (which would be in line with the claim made by various dictionaries that it is "used mainly by young people"). Does your observation of 5 cases out of 50 on the first page of randomly shuffled hits suffice to rule out this initial assumption, which is called a "null hypothesis" in statistical terminology? In order to validate the null hypothesis—that the proportion of the "Excellent" sense in the BNC is less than 1%—you can apply a so-called exact binomial test (see Baroni & Evert in press) by typing the following command into the main R window.

```
> binom.test(x = 5, n = 50, p = 1/100)
```

Here, x is the number of "positive" instances you found (5), n the size of the sample (50 random hits), and p the hypothesized proportion (1% = 1/100). Most of the command output just repeats this information:

```
    Exact binomial test

data:  5 and 50
number of successes = 5,
number of trials = 50,
p-value = 0.0001457
```

The important part is the *p*-value calculated by the test, which tells you exactly how confident you can be to rule out the initial hypothesis. The *p*-value specifies the risk of error when rejecting the null hypothesis on the basis of your observa-tion. Keep in mind that small *p*-values stand for lower error rates and hence greater confidence. There are certain commonly used levels of significance, which correspond to the critical values in Table 5.2: if the *p*-value is less than 0.05, you may reject the null hypothesis although some doubt remains; if it is less than 0.01, you can be fairly sure that your result is correct; and any value below 0.001 is accepted as virtually certain. If the *p*-value is larger than 0.05, though, you cannot draw any valid conclusions from your data. In our case, we have a *p*-value below 0.001 and can rule out the hypothesis with a high degree of certainty.

The use of such arbitrary thresholds has been extensively criticized in the statistical literature. One advantage of exact tests and statistical software packages is that they calculate a precise *p*-value, which can be interpreted directly as the risk of an incorrect rejection of the null hypothesis. Instead of using predefined thresholds, you (and your readers) can simply decide whether you are willing to take the risk indicated by the *p*-value. It is important to note that our *Corpus Frequency Wizard*—like most other online tools—does not calculate *p*-values, so you have to rely on fixed critical values when interpreting the test results.

If you do not have a hypothesis to begin with and just want to estimate the proportion of the "Excellent" sense in the entire result set, the `binom.test` command also allows you to determine a range of plausible values for the "true" proportion, i.e. a confidence interval (cf. Section 5.6.1). Simply omit your null hypothesis about the proportion when entering the command. Since the full output produced by `binom.test` can be confusing, we have highlighted the important information below.

```
> binom.test(x = 5, n = 50)

    Exact binomial test

data:  5 and 50
number of successes = 5,
number of trials = 50,
p-value = 4.21e-09
alternative hypothesis: true probability of success is not
equal to 0.5
```
```
95 percent confidence interval:
 0.03327509 0.21813537
sample estimates:
probability of success
                0.1
```

The "sample estimate" corresponds to the direct extrapolation you have performed in Chapter 4, resulting in an estimate of 10% = 0.1 (i.e. about 103 examples in total). If this estimate is corrected for sampling variation, you obtain a wide range of plausible values, the confidence interval. In our example, it ranges from a proportion of 3.3% (about 34 instances in the entire BNC) to 21.8% (about 224 instances in the entire BNC). This result is slightly different from the confidence interval calculated by the online wizard in Section 5.6.1, but indicates the same degree of uncertainty.[6]

For frequency comparisons, R offers a so-called "proportions test" (prop.test), which uses the same approximation as the online wizard, but computes precise p-values rather than relying on critical values for the test score. You can also perform Fisher's exact test (fisher.test) and avoid potentially inaccurate approximations altogether.[7] The data you need to specify for a proportions test are the numbers of "positive" instances for both samples (8 and 2) and the sample sizes (both 50 in this case, but the test can also be applied to samples of different sizes). There is no need to understand all details of the command syntax shown below: think of it simply as a template into which you can insert the relevant counts and sample sizes.

```
> prop.test(c(8,2), c(50,50))

    2-sample test for equality of proportions with
    continuity correction

data:  c(8, 2) out of c(50, 50)
X-squared = 2.7778, df = 1,
p-value = 0.09558
```

The resulting p-value of 0.09558 is considerably larger than 0.05, so there is no significant evidence at all for a difference between the proportions of the "Excellent" sense in spoken and written English.

If you are convinced that there is a real difference between spoken and written English, you will have to look at more data in order to increase the "power" of the test and achieve significance. If you find the same proportions in samples of 150 hits each (i.e. 24 positive cases for spoken and 6 positive cases for written English), the difference becomes highly significant and almost reaches the level of virtual certainty ($p < .001$). In the output from R shown below, we have again highlighted the most important information. Like the online wizard, the prop.test function also computes a confidence interval for the difference between the true proportions, which is often referred to as "effect size". In this case, the 95% confidence interval indicates that there is a difference of at least 4.68 percentage points in the frequency of the "Excellent" sense of *wicked* between spoken and written English.

---

6   You can also carry out the approximate computation of the online tool in R with the command prop.test(5, 50) to get exactly the same confidence interval.

7   We do not show Fisher's test here because the fisher.test function is more difficult to use and requires data to be provided in the form of a contingency table (see e.g. Baroni & Evert 2008). Fisher's test computes an exact p-value of 0.09165, confirming the non-significant result of the online wizard and the p-value calculated by the proportions test.

```
> prop.test(c(24,6), c(150,150))

     2-sample test for equality of proportions
     with continuity correction

data:   c(24, 6) out of c(150, 150)
X-squared = 10.7037, df = 1,
```

```
p-value = 0.001069
```

```
alternative hypothesis: two.sided
```

```
95 percent confidence interval:
 0.04680995 0.19319005
```

```
sample estimates:
prop 1 prop 2
   0.16    0.04
```

5.7   Further reading

Ball (1994) presents an excellent discussion of the issues covered in Sections 5.4 and 5.5, i.e. possible pitfalls in using normalized frequency counts and the concepts of precision and recall.

With the brief introduction to the statistical analysis of corpus frequency data presented in Section 5.6, we have barely scratched the surface. Many important details relevant to successful corpus-based analyses of language are far beyond its scope. You can find more information on hypothesis tests, p-values, significance levels and confidence intervals in Baayen (2008), Baroni & Evert (in press), Oakes (1998), and to some extent also McEnery & Wilson (2001). If you feel courageous, you may also want to consult a textbook on mathematical statistics (DeGroot & Schervish 2002 is an excellent choice) to learn about the theory behind the statistical procedures. We recommend Baroni & Evert (in press) as a starting point and the references cited therein for further reading. In particular, Evert (2006) discusses some limitations of statistical methods that make their application to corpus data problematic. You should always keep such difficulties in mind when interpreting the chi-squared and log-likelihood scores, p-values and confidence intervals that you have obtained.

5.8   Exercises

1. *Evaluating precision and recall.* Let's say that you are interested in finding all instances of present progressives that are in the passive (e.g. *The house is being built* or *The man is being interviewed*). One way of retrieving these constructions is by simply looking for the word sequence *is being.*

a) Do a BNC search for *is being* and look at the precision of the query result. In other words, what percentage of the retrieved hits are actually instances of present progressive passives? Remember to switch the display of the query result to "random order" first if you wish to look at only a subset of the query result.

b) Now think about recall. What have you missed with your simple search for *is being*? In other words, are there different ways of forming the present progressive passive that your search didn't retrieve? How good was the recall of your initial search? Hint: apart from different forms of the headword BE, you might want to think about items that could be found between BE and *being*. Just to give you one example, you could find the negative form *not* in this slot (as in *he is **not** being asked*). Note that retrieving all (or rather, most) instances of the present progressive passive requires several individual queries. In Chapter 6, we will show you how such queries can be conveniently combined into a single query.

2. *Comparing corpus frequencies.* The chi-squared and log-likelihood tests can not only be applied to small, manually inspected samples, but can also be used to compare the frequencies of a word or phrase in two subsections of a corpus. For example, idiomatic expressions are often specific to particular genres. In this exercise, your task is to make a list of at least ten common idioms (famous examples include *a bird in the hand is worth two in the bush* and *off the beaten track*), and then check for each expression whether it is more frequent in written or in spoken English.

a) Use *BNCweb* to search for the idiomatic expression in the written and spoken part of the BNC. Since you have only learned how to search for fixed phrases so far, you will have to try and identify an "invariant nucleus" for each idiom that you can use in your queries. For instance, you might simply type `bird in the hand` to find variants ranging from *a bird in the hand is still worth two in the bush* to *A bird in the hand is worth two votes for Bush* (a creative exploitation of the idiom). Some manual inspection will be necessary to make sure that such queries do not return too many false positives.

b) Write down the number of instances of each expression in the written and spoken part of the BNC, as well as the corresponding relative frequencies ("per million words") displayed by *BNCweb*. You will also need to note down the total number of words in the written and spoken BNC, which is displayed in the title bar of the Query result page.

c) Use the online *Corpus Frequency Wizard* to compare the spoken and written frequencies of each expression, entering the appropriate information in the box under the heading "Two samples: frequency comparison" (cf. Figure 5.11). Compare the results of the statistical test with the impression you got from looking at the "raw" relative frequencies. How many idioms with a significant difference between written and spoken English can you find?

d) As an instructive example, you might repeat the same frequency comparison for the frequent word *time* (which has more than 150,000 instances in the entire BNC). You will find that the difference between written and spoken English is statistically significant. Considering the confidence interval, do you think that it is also linguistically meaningful? Discuss this point, comparing the results e.g. to those obtained for the pronoun *you*.

6 The Simple Query Syntax

6.1 Outline

This chapter introduces the query language used to perform linguistic corpus searches in *BNCweb*. Readers will learn how to:

- Find all words with a particular prefix or suffix
- Use wildcards to match more complex word form patterns
- Perform part-of-speech and headword/lemma queries
- Match flexible word sequences and lexico-grammatical patterns
- Include sentence boundaries, typographic mark-up, etc. in their queries
- Search for co-occurrences of words

6.2 Introduction

You have already learned in Chapter 4 how to perform a simple lexical search for a single word or phrase. In this chapter, we describe the other features of *BNCweb*'s SIMPLE QUERY SYNTAX. Using this query language you can search for words with a specific prefix (e.g. *anti-*) or suffix (e.g. *-phobia*), words that belong to a particular part of speech (e.g. noun), and even complex lexico-grammatical patterns such as *to <verb> <noun phrase> away*. This query language has been designed specifically to be easy to learn and has a clear, uncluttered syntax for Simple queries, while being powerful enough to support the most common needs of *BNCweb* users. A concise "Quick reference sheet" can be found in Appendix 3 and also accessed on-line through the "Simple Query Syntax help" link on the STANDARD QUERY page.

The present chapter is intended both as an introduction to the Simple Query Syntax and as a comprehensive reference for users who want to explore its full potential. In Sections 6.3 through 6.5, you will find a short overview of the basic features of Simple queries. The remaining sections give detailed systematic descriptions of each aspect of the query language: wildcards for matching arbitrary characters (6.6), part-of-speech and lemma queries (6.7), flexible lexico-grammatical patterns (6.8), proximity queries for co-occurrences, i.e. words that occur within a certain distance of each other (6.9), and details on how to search for foreign letters and other special characters (6.10). Some of the later sections in this chapter (especially 6.9 and 6.10) may look daunting to first-time readers. If you are new to *BNCweb*, you might therefore prefer to focus on Sections 6.3

to 6.5—this should be sufficient to understand and adapt the query examples in the following chapters. Later on, you can return to Chapter 6 to read up on the details of the query syntax and extend your repertoire of query options.

Chapter 12 introduces the advanced CQP Query Syntax for expert users, which offers even greater flexibility, but has a less intuitive syntax. For this reason, even experienced users prefer to formulate most of their queries in Simple Query Syntax and turn to the advanced syntax only if they need to search for very complex patterns (e.g. the reduplication of nouns in expressions such as *from time to time, day by day*).

6.3   Basic queries: searching words and phrases

BNCweb's Simple Query Syntax makes it very easy to search for a particular word form or phrase in the entire BNC, in selected portions of it, or in a user-defined subcorpus (cf. Chapter 10). Just type the word you are looking for into the search box, optionally restrict the search to the written or spoken part of the BNC (in the STANDARD QUERY mode) or apply metatextual restrictions (in the WRITTEN RESTRICTIONS or SPOKEN RESTRICTIONS modes), and press the [Start Query] button. For example, to find instances of the word *loveliest*, you would enter `loveliest` (see Chapter 4). In order to find a phrase like *birds of a feather*, separate the individual words by blanks: `birds of a feather`, as shown in Figure 6.1.

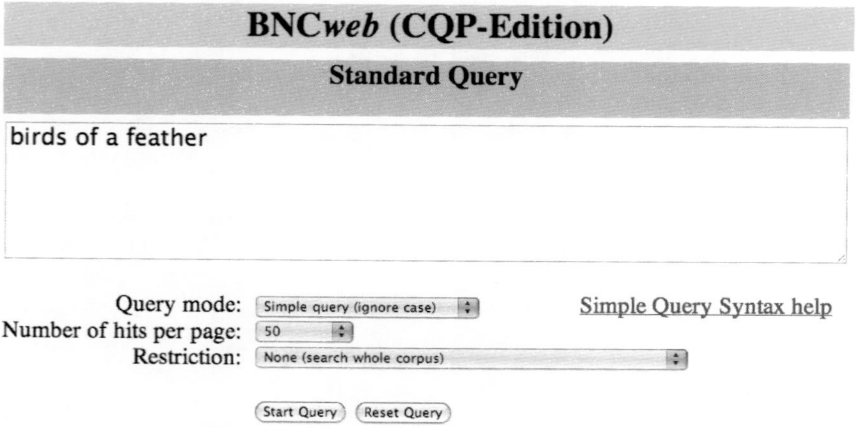

Figure 6.1:   Entering a Simple query

There are two important things you need to be aware of when writing such queries. Firstly, many punctuation characters have a special meaning in the *BNCweb* query language: they are so-called METACHARACTERS. Searching for a comma

,

or parenthesis

(

will return a syntax error, while the query ? works but does not return the expected list of question marks. In order to search for such metacharacters as literal symbols, they have to preceded by a backslash (\); programmers say that you need to "escape" the metacharacter with the backslash. For instance, type

\ ,

to find all commas and

\ ?

to find all question marks. The complete list of metacharacters is shown in the box below for reference, but when in doubt you can just add the \ before every punctuation symbol; unnecessary backslashes will be ignored. You do not have to use the backslash with alphanumeric characters, i.e. letters and digits.

> **Metacharacters in the *BNCweb* query language:**
> The following punctuation characters have a special function in the standard *BNCweb* query language and must be escaped by preceding them with a backslash (e.g. \ ?) if they are used literally.
>
> ? * + , : @ / ( ) [ ] { } _ ~ < >

Secondly, when looking for a phrase, it is not always sufficient to separate individual words by blanks. *BNCweb* queries are not based on typographic whitespace, but on the smallest linguistic units identified in the BNC annotation (i.e. the units which carry individual part-of-speech tags, cf. 3.5.1). While these TOKENS often correspond to orthographic words, punctuation symbols are treated as separate tokens even when they are attached to an adjacent word. Similarly, contracted forms like *Peter's*, *they're* and *can't* are split into two tokens that correspond as closely as possible to the original words: *Peter* + *'s, they* + *'re* and *ca* + *n't*. Thus, to find corpus examples of tag questions like *[he] will, won't he?*, you have to separate all tokens by blanks and escape the metacharacters with a backslash:

```
will \, wo n't he \?
```

Note that the results page displays the query hits as they are conventionally written, without the extra whitespace. Detailed information on the BNC tokenization conventions can be found in Chapter 3 and in the *BNC Reference Guide*. The table below gives an overview of the most common contracted forms and how to search for them with *BNCweb*.

Querying contracted forms in *BNCweb*:			
they've	they 've	*ain't*	ai n't
he'll	he 'll	*gimme*	gim me
she's	she 's	*gonna*	gon na
doesn't	does n't	*innit*	in n it
won't	wo n't	*dunno*	du n no

Keep in mind that the BNC distinguishes between straight vertical apostrophes in contractions (such as *can't* and *rock'n'roll*) and curly "typographic" quotation marks (as in *I said to him, 'What's up, Sam?'*). In Simple Query Syntax, only straight single and double quotes are used: ' for an apostrophe, and " for any quotation mark (both opening and closing). Be careful if you copy and paste queries from a text document: curly typographic quotation marks (which are often inserted automatically by word processing software) are not supported and the query will fail if you use them, displaying the error message shown on the right.

Error message

Syntax error

Sorry, your simple query "truth" contains a syntax error.

Task:
Which BNC document contains the following word sequence?

> *I said to him, 'What's up, Sam?'*

Try to write a query that matches the entire sequence.

Simple *BNCweb* queries are CASE-INSENSITIVE by default. Thus, bath will find both the common noun *bath* and the city *Bath*; Bath and BATH will return exactly the same results. If you are only interested in the capitalized form *Bath* (which could refer to the common noun at the start of a sentence, of course) or if you want to find all-uppercase spellings such as *NEW*, you have to select "Simple query (case-sensitive)" from the "Query mode" drop-down menu. Alternatively, you can append the case-sensitive modifier :C to your query: Bath:C. This modifier applies only to a single word, allowing you to match only some words in a phrase in case-sensitive mode, e.g. to ensure that *Sun* is capitalized in

    from Sun:C and

while the other words may be either in lowercase or in uppercase. If you have selected case-sensitive mode, you can use the complementary :c modifier to ignore case for individual words.

A second modifier :d tells *BNCweb* to ignore diacritics (i.e. accents on letters such as *é* or *ô*) altogether. This is often the easiest way to search for words with accented letters. Thus, the query fiancee:d finds *fiancée* and its unaccented spelling variant in the BNC.[1] Note that :d has to be written in lowercase just like the :c modifier; there is no global setting as for case-sensitivity. Case-insensitive matching also works for accented letters, so the query results for

    deja:d vu

include the all-uppercase spelling *DÉJÀ VU*. Modifiers can be combined: type Fiancee:Cd to find the capitalized form *Fiancée*. More options for matching accented and other special characters (including Greek letters) can be found in Section 6.10.

6.4   Using wildcards

So far, you have learned how to find all the instances of a specific word or word sequence in the BNC and build a traditional concordance. It is usually more interesting to search for generalizations, though. You might want to list all words beginning with *super-* or—if you are a crossword aficionado—to find the missing letters in *imp☐ss☐ble*. *BNCweb*'s Simple Query Syntax uses a number of metacharacters known as WILDCARDS for such generalizations on the level of

---

1   There is also one instance *fiancèe*, where an incorrect accent has been used. Ignoring diacritics sometimes leads to unwanted matches (so-called "noise"); in other words, this potentially reduces the precision of your queries. For instance, mere:d finds both the English word *mere* and the French word *mère*.

individual word forms. In this section, we briefly introduce some elementary and frequently needed wildcard functionality; more advanced options are described in Section 6.6.

The three basic wildcards ?, * and + may already be familiar from other software tools, e.g. Microsoft *Word*. They are used to search for a string of letters where some of these are unspecified:

> ? stands for a single, arbitrary character
>> s?ng will find *sing, sang, song, sung,* etc.
> * stands for zero or more arbitrary characters
>> sing* will find *sing, sings, singer, singingly, single* etc.
> + stands for one or more arbitrary characters
>> sing+ will find *sings, singer, singingly, single,* etc. but not *sing*

Thus, the ? wildcard can be used to write "crossword puzzle" queries like

> imp?ss?ble

(yes, there is more than one possibility!), while * and + are often used for prefix and suffix searches:

> super*

finds all words beginning with *super-*; super+ does the same, but excludes the word *super* itself (because at least one character needs to follow the prefix *super-*). Of course, prefix, suffix and so-called infix specifications can be freely combined:

> super+listic+ous

matches all words that begin with *super-*, end in *-ous*, and contain the character sequence *-listic-* in between.

A second type of wildcard expression allows you to search for precisely specified variants: separate any number of alternatives with commas (,) and enclose them in square brackets ([...]). For instance,

> neighb[our,or]

finds both the British spelling *neighbour* and the American spelling *neighbor*. Intuitively speaking, the query expression indicates that the word should begin with the letters *neighb*, and then continue either with *our* or with *or*. Of course, the variant part can be isolated in different ways, and the following query finds exactly the same hits (i.e. *neighbour* and *neighbor*):

```
neighb[ou,o]r
neighbo[u,]r
neighbo[ur,r]
```

Notice the empty alternative in the second variant, which indicates an optional element (i.e. [u,] matches either *u* or nothing at all). You must also take care not to put blanks before or after the comma, since they are used to separate tokens in the Simple Query Syntax and will confuse *BNCweb*. You can list as many alternatives between the brackets as you like. If you want to find all inflected forms of the verb *to show*, type

```
show[s,ed,n,ing,]
```

> **Task:**
> The word *artefact* can also be spelled *artifact*. Write a wildcard query that matches both spellings. Is it sufficient to use the ? wildcard? In a second step, try to find derived words such as *artefactually*, again for both spelling variants. How does the + wildcard help you to exclude the word *artefact* itself from the query hits? Can you also get rid of the plural *artefacts*, so the derivations are easier to see on the results page? Hint: make sure you understand why the query ???? matches all four-letter words (but don't try it while minors are around).

6.5   A short tour of the Simple Query Syntax

This section introduces the most important features of Simple Query Syntax—in addition to the basic wildcards—by guiding you step by step through an extended example: the inflectional and periphrastic patterns of adjective comparison, which have already been introduced in the second exercise at the end of Chapter 4. Recall that English can form comparatives and superlatives either by adding the inflectional suffixes *-er* and *-est* (e.g. *small* ➔ *smaller, smallest*) or by periphrasis with *more* and *most* (e.g. *difficult* ➔ *more difficult, most difficult*). In general, the inflectional pattern is preferred for monosyllabic and other short adjectives, while longer adjectives typically use the periphrastic pattern. There are many exceptions to this rule: for instance, both *more pleasant / most pleasant* and *pleasanter / pleasantest* are attested in the BNC. We will now look at the class of adjectives ending in *-ly*, which are said to prefer inflectional comparison even though they are not monosyllabic.

It is straightforward to search for individual examples of such adjectives, say *deadly*: the queries `deadlier, deadliest, more   deadly` and `most deadly` reveal that both patterns are possible, but periphrasis is somewhat more frequent. Suppose now that you would like to obtain the same information for *all* adjectives in *-ly*. Let's begin with the inflectional pattern. The comparative of an adjective in *-ly* ends with the letters *-lier*, the superlative with the letters *-liest*. What you want to do, then, is to find all words in the BNC that end in a certain sequence of letters, regardless of which and how many characters precede the suffix. You can use the *wildcards* introduced in the previous section to perform such searches, in particular * to match an arbitrary sequence of characters before the suffix. This leads to the following four queries for inflectional and periphrastic comparison:

```
*lier
*liest
more *ly
most *ly
```

Run these queries now, and take a look at the hits. Which pattern seems to be more frequent for adjectives in *-ly*? (Hint: after running all four queries, go to the QUERY HISTORY page to see how many hits each one returned.) Did you notice any problems when inspecting the query results?

> **Task:**
> One thing you may have noticed is that the results of the second query include the word form *[thou] liest* (because * also matches a sequence of zero characters before the suffix). The other queries return similar "accidental" hits such as *fly, ply, sly* and *flier*. A possible strategy for weeding out such "false positives" is to require that the stem of the adjective (the part before the suffix) must consist of two or three letters at least. Use the additional wildcards + (one or more characters) and ? (exactly one arbitrary character) to ensure that there are at least three characters before the suffix.

Even a superficial look at the query hits for `more  *ly` and `most  *ly` will reveal that most of them are not adjectives, but adverbs formed with the suffix *-ly* (*more recently, most importantly,* etc.). Comparing the total number of hits for the inflectional and the periphrastic pattern is entirely meaningless under these circumstances. Fortunately, you can make use of the grammatical annotation in the BNC to target adjectives specifically. First, look up the part-of-speech tag for the basic ("positive") form of an adjective in 3.5.1 or in the complete table in Appendix 2; it is "AJ0". Second, specify the desired part-of-speech tag in the query, separated from the word form pattern by an underscore (the _ character).

```
more *ly_AJ0
most *ly_AJ0
```

The part-of-speech tags have been assigned automatically by tagging software, so you may still find a few adverbs that were incorrectly tagged as adjectives.

If you do not remember the precise part-of-speech tag for adjectives, you can also use the abbreviation {A}, which stands for the general word class of adjectives (including comparative and superlative forms). A full list of word class abbreviations can be found in Section 6.7. Make sure you do not forget the curly brackets when you use such abbreviations in your queries:

```
more *ly_{A}
most *ly_{A}
```

You can apply the same strategy to avoid false positives like *flier*, *supplier* or *outlier* among the inflectional pattern:

```
*lier_{A}
*liest_{A}
```

If you run these four queries now, you will find that the frequencies have changed quite dramatically and that the inflectional pattern is indeed much more frequent. You will probably also find it rather inconvenient that you have to run two queries for each pattern, write down the numbers of hits, and add them up manually. You can save time and effort by combining the queries for comparatives and superlatives into a single query each. This is achieved in different ways for the two patterns.

For inflectional comparison, your query has to match words ending either in *-lier* or in *-liest*. Such alternatives within a single word can be expressed in wildcard notation. They are separated by commas (,) and have to be enclosed in square brackets ([...]), as has been described in Section 6.4:

```
*[lier,liest]_{A}
```

Make sure you understand why the following queries produce exactly the same results, and re-read the corresponding discussion in 6.4 if necessary.

```
*li[er,est]_{A}
*lie[r,st]_{A}
[*lier,*liest]_{A}
```

For periphrastic comparison, on the other hand, there is a choice between two different phrases. The Simple Query Syntax emphasizes this contrast by using a different notation for phrase alternatives, which are separated by vertical bars (|) instead of commas and enclosed in round parentheses ((...)) instead of square brackets:

```
(more *ly_{A} | most *ly_{A})
```

Again, there are different, but fully equivalent ways of writing this query, depending on which is considered to be the variant part:

```
(more | most) *ly_{A}
m[ore,ost] *ly_{A}
```

BNCweb also supports purely grammatical queries that are based on part-of-speech tags only: simply omit the word form pattern before the underscore character, e.g. _AJ0 instead of fast_AJ0. Such grammatical queries allow you to search inflectional and periphrastic comparatives and superlatives for *all* adjectives. The inflectional pattern is matched by the queries _AJC (comparative adjective) and _AJS (superlative adjective). Again, the two expressions can be combined into a single query using the same notation as for alternatives within word forms:

```
_[AJC,AJS]  or equivalently _AJ[C,S]
```

The analogous query for the periphrastic pattern is

```
(more | most) _AJ0
```

Section 6.8 explains how more flexible lexico-grammatical patterns can be formulated, e.g. to match noun phrases with an optional determiner and an arbitrary number of adjectives.

While working on this example, you may occasionally have wanted to look up all instances of a particular adjective, say *lovely*. In order to do so, you have so far had to spell out all three forms of the adjective, e.g.

```
love[ly,lier,liest]  or (lovely|lovelier|loveliest)
```

A much more convenient solution makes use of the headword annotation in the BNC (cf. 3.5.2). Simply enclose the base form of the adjective in curly brackets to match the entire headword:

```
{lovely}
```

Some forms, e.g. *kindly*, are ambiguous between adjective and adverb. In this case, you can specify the desired wordclass of the headword to define a lemma (cf. 3.5.2):

```
{kindly/ADJ}
```
or shorter
```
{kindly/A}
```

This matches only the adjective reading of *kindly*. For further discussion of this type of query, see Section 6.7. Of course, you could also combine the headword query with a specific part-of-speech tag (or set of tags):

```
{kindly}_[AJC,AJS]
```

This query matches only comparative and superlative adjective forms of *kindly*.

> **Task:**
> Check whether adjectives ending in *-ly* still prefer the inflectional comparison pattern if they are prefixed with *un-*. Recall that wildcard queries allow you to search for a prefix and a suffix at the same time.

We have now covered the basics of the Simple Query Syntax. The following sections explore these themes in more detail, providing a comprehensive reference guide to wildcards, part-or-speech and headword/lemma queries. We will illustrate how these features can be utilized to search for a variety of lexico-grammatical patterns. The chapter ends with a description of two further aspects of the Simple Query Language, namely proximity queries (e.g. "find all instances of *British* within ten words of *gentleman*") and searches involving special characters. Since you are now sufficiently equipped to proceed with subsequent chapters of the book, you may prefer to move on and consult Sections 6.6 to 6.10 individually when you wish to extend your repertoire of query options.

6.6   Advanced wildcard queries

In the previous section, the query `[*lier,*liest]_{A}` may have caught your attention. It shows that alternatives listed between square brackets do not have to be fixed strings, but may contain wildcards themselves (and even further nested alternatives). This flexibility allows you to express quite complex patterns even in the Simple Query Syntax. As a warm-up exercise, consider the query:

```
*[rr+rr,ss+ss,tt+tt]*y
```

Can you figure out what it does (without running it first)?

In addition to these standard wildcard metacharacters, some ordinary letters are interpreted as wildcards when they are escaped with a backslash, allowing you finer control over the characters or substrings matched. These special wildcards are sometimes referred to as ESCAPE SEQUENCES (see the table below for a complete listing). The escape sequence \a matches an arbitrary letter (*a ... z*), but no punctuation signs or other special characters. For instance, type

```
\a-grade
```

to find the words *A-grade*, *B-grade*, *C-grade*, etc. The escape sequences \l (for a lowercase letter) and \u (for an uppercase letter) only make sense if case-sensitive matching is enabled (e.g. by adding a :c modifier at the end of the word). The corresponding escapes \A, \L and \U match sequences of one or more letters, lowercase letters, and uppercase letters, respectively. For example, the query

```
\u\L:C
```

finds all capitalized words (which consist of an uppercase letter followed by one or more lowercase letters). Escape sequences do not match accented letters, and you will have to add a :d modifier to find the word *fiancée* (e.g. with fianc\a\a:D). In addition, \d matches a single digit and \D matches a sequence of one or more digits. You can find ISBN book numbers like *0-345-39180-2* with this query:

```
\d-\D-\D-\d
```

Can you guess now what the hits of the query \D\:\D look like? The following complex example finds words written in mixed case like *SoHo* and *KaDeWe*:

```
*\u\L\u\L*:C
```

This type of query is sometimes called an "infix query", in analogy to prefix and suffix queries. Because of the * at the start and end of the expression, the sequence \u\L\u\L—two single uppercase letters, each followed by one or more lowercase letters—can be matched anywhere within the word form. Without the asterisks, it would only match words that consist of exactly two capitalized components (*SoHo*, but not *KaDeWe*). For convenience, the escape sequence \w matches any character that can typically occur in a word (i.e. letters, digits, hyphen and apostrophe), and \W a sequence of such characters. If you are looking for hyphenated word forms that start with an uppercase letter, try \u\W-\W:c, which finds e.g. *French-speaking*, *King-to-be* and *Do-It-All*. On the other hand, the query \u\A-\A:c matches *French-speaking* but not the other two examples. If you had simply used the + wildcard (i.e. \u+-+:c), the query hits would have included abbreviations such as *Lt.-Col.* and *V.-C.*

Overview of Simple query wildcards:		
?	single character	
	s?ng ➔ *sing, sang, sung, song, ...*	
*	zero or more characters	
	sing* ➔ *sing, sings, singer, ...*	
+	one or more characters	
	sing+ ➔ *sings, singer, ...*	
[x,y]	alternatives	
	hum[our,or] ➔ *humour, humor*	
\a	single letter	
	\a-team ➔ *A-Team, b-team, ...*	
\A	one or more letters	
	anti\A ➔ *antibody,...* [not *anti-war*]	
\l, \L	lowercase letter(s)*	
	\u\L \u\L ➔ *New York, ...*	
\u, \U	uppercase letter(s)*	
	\U-\U ➔ *CD-ROM, WARM-UP, ...*	
\d, \D	digit(s)	
	\D-fold ➔ *1-fold, 2-fold, 3-fold, ...*	
\w, \W	"word" character(s)	
	anti\W ➔ *antibody, anti-war, ...*	
(* = case-sensitive mode only)		

Wildcards can be used freely among the items of a phrase query, but they only apply to single word tokens and do not match across multiple tokens. Hence, black*white matches *black-and-white*, but not *black and white* (the following section explains how to search for the latter).

> **Task:**
> Use wildcard queries with suitable escape sequences to look for place
> names like *Stratford-upon-Avon* and *Stoke-on-Trent*. Don't forget to
> activate case-sensitive mode or add the `:c` modifier.

6.7   Queries based on part-of-speech and headword/lemma

Many English word forms are ambiguous between different grammatical categories. For instance, *light* can be an adjective ('not heavy'), a noun ('illumination')
or a verb ('ignite, illuminate'). While you might sort a concordance for `light`
by hand into adjectives, nouns and verbs, sometimes one of the readings is so
predominant that it would be tedious to filter out manually. A rather extreme
case is the noun *can*: more than 99% of the occurrences of the word form *can*
are instances of the modal verb. It is virtually impossible to single out the noun
occurrences (slightly over 800 of them) from a simple concordance. Fortunately,
the information about parts of speech incorporated in the BNC (POS-tags, cf.
3.5.1) can help us here. For instance, singular (common) nouns are identified by
the POS-tag NN1. The complete tagset is listed in Appendix 2. Further information and a detailed explanation of the tags can be found in the *BNC Reference
Guide*.

The *BNCweb* Simple Query Syntax allows you to add a POS-tag to any token in a query, separated from the word form specification by an underscore
character (_). In order to find the singular noun *can*, you would therefore type

```
can_NN1
```

Keep in mind that the POS-tags have been annotated by a tagging program, so
they are not always correct (for an amusing example, try the query `beer
can_NN1`). You can use wildcards both in the word form part and the POS part
of a query item. This feature becomes particularly useful in combination with
the systematic naming scheme of the BNC tagset. If you take a closer look at the
listing of POS-tags in Appendix 2, you will notice that all tags starting with the
letter *N* refer to (common or proper) nouns, those starting with *V* refer to verbs,
etc. In order to find common nouns ending in the letters *-ice* (including plurals
like *mice* and invariant forms like *dice*) you might thus execute the query

```
+ice_NN*
```

The wildcard `*` is also convenient for matching ambiguity tags that have been
included in the BNC wherever the tagger was less certain of a tagging decision.

Compared to the first example above, can_NN1* finds 39 additional matches
that are considered ambiguous between noun and (lexical) verb reading. POS-
tags also allow you to distinguish between the different readings of contractions
like *she's*:

> she 's_VB* → *she is*
>
> she 's_VH* → *she has*

You can match tokens purely by part-of-speech category if you omit the word
form pattern to the left of the underscore. For example, _NN* matches any common noun, and _V?Z the third person singular present of any verb (or type
_V?Z* to include ambiguity tags).[2] The query

> _VH* _V?N

matches simple examples of perfect tense.

While POS queries like _N* and _V* are very intuitive, the full details of
the BNC tagset can be difficult to memorize especially for casual users. For this
reason, *BNCweb* offers abbreviations for the most frequently needed POS categories on a more coarse-grained level. These abbreviations are enclosed in curly
brackets ({ ... }).[3] To search for *can* as a noun, you could therefore type
can_{N}. Simple prepositional phrases of the form *for a long time* are identified by the query

> _{PREP} _{ART} _{A} _{N}

More complex examples of searches based on grammatical patterns can be
found in Section 6.8. Note that some of these general categories fail to pick up
ambiguity tags. A complete listing of simplified tags (including their shorthand
alternatives) and an equivalent wildcard expression for the matching POS tags is
shown in the box below. The full set of tags matching the third column of this
box is listed in Table 3.8.

It was already pointed out in 3.5.1 that the definitions of some categories are
not entirely intuitive (e.g. demonstrative pronouns such as *this* and *that* with tag
"DT0" are treated as adjectives). They are also fairly restrictive and will usually
not include ambiguity tags, which are assigned to the simplified tag category

---

2   If you find leading underscores visually confusing, you can also type these purely gram-
    matical patterns as *_NN* and *_V?Z (since * matches any word form, it has no effect
    in this case).
3   Wildcards are not allowed in such abbreviations, but they would also make little sense:
    queries like _{A*} do not encode any meaningful generalizations.

"UNC".[4] Moreover, the actual BNC tagging does not always agree with the specification of the simplified tagset in the official documentation. For these reasons, you may prefer to work with the full tagset in order to have complete control over the parts of speech included in the search. The rightmost column in the box below specifies wildcard expressions for POS tags that are equivalent to the general categories and that can be used as a convenient starting point.

Simplified tags	Description	Matching POS patterns
`{A}` or `{ADJ}`	adjective	`[AJ?,CRD,DT0,ORD]`
`{ADV}`	adverb	`[AV?,XX0]`
`{ART}`	article	`AT0`
`{CONJ}`	conjunction	`CJ?`
`{INT}` or `{INTERJ}`	interjection	`ITJ`
`{N}` or `{SUBST}`	noun	`[N??,N*-N*,ZZ0]`
`{PREP}`	preposition	`[PR?,TO0]`
`{PRON}`	pronoun	`[DPS,DTQ,EX0,PN?]`
`{V}` or `{VERB}`	verb	`[V??,V*-V*]`
`{$}` or `{STOP}`	punctuation	`PU?`
`{UNC}`	unclassified or uncertain	

Lemmatization addresses a problem that is in a sense the opposite of part-of-speech ambiguities: what we intuitively (and linguistically) perceive to be the same word can appear in entirely different forms in the corpus (e.g. *show*, *shows*, *showed*, *shown* and *showing*, but also less obviously related forms like *goose* and *geese*). It is straightforward but tedious to write a wildcard query that matches all forms of a specific word. For the examples above, you would have to type `show[s,ed,n,ing,]` and `[goose,geese]`. A much easier solution makes use of headword information in the BNC (cf. Chapter 3), by enclosing the search string in curly brackets (`{…}`) similar to the POS abbreviations above:

> `{goose}` → *goose, geese*
>
> `{show}` → *show, shows, showed, shown, showing*

Note that the latter query matches both the verb *to show* and the noun *show*. In the BNC, this is referred to as a headword (similar to the notion of headword or

---

4   For instance, the tag "NN2-VVZ" indicates that the current token could either be a plural noun or a verb in 3rd person singular present, but the tagger considers it more likely to be a noun. If recall is more important for you than precision, you will want to include this tag when searching for nouns, and perhaps also when searching for verbs.

entry in a dictionary)—see 3.5.2. For many purposes, it is desirable to restrict headword matches to a particular grammatical category. One possibility is to add a POS constraint, e.g. {show}_{V}, but there is a simpler alternative. The BNC lemmatization distinguishes between *show* as a verb and *show* as a noun. You can therefore make use of the simplified tags shown in the box above to match a lemma, for example:

> the verb *to show* with {show/VERB} (or the shorthand {show/V})
>
> the noun *show* with {show/SUBST} (or the shorthand {show/N})

Similarly, if you want to isolate the different grammatical realizations of the headword *separate*, you can match

> the adjective *separate* with {separate/ADJ}
>
> the verb *separate* with {separate/VERB}
>
> the rare noun use of *separate* with {separate/SUBST}

If you want to include a modifier like :d in a query item that involves both a word form (or headword) pattern and a POS constraint, it has to be inserted immediately to the left of the underscore separator, and has to be outside the curly brackets in the case of a lemma query. An example is:

> {sautee*}:d_V*

Task:
How many different queries can you come up with that match both forms of the past participle of *to prove* (i.e. *proved* and *proven*)? Try both word form and headword/lemma queries, adding a POS constraint where necessary. How many queries can you find for the past participle of *to be*? Can you match it using POS tags only?

6.8   Matching lexico-grammatical patterns

So far, we have focused on matching single tokens or rigid sequences of tokens. Sometimes, though, it would be useful to allow for some variability. This is especially important when matching whole patterns (or constructions) based on syntactic categories. Our simplistic query _VH* _V?N for perfect tense in the previous section did not find occurrences containing adverbs or negation (*has recently been* or *had not found*). The query _{PREP} _{ART} _{A} _{N} for prepositional phrases requires an article and exactly one adjective in order to match; it finds *in the dark room*, but misses *in the room, in dark rooms, in a very dark room, in the big dark room*, and many other variations. What we want to express in this case is a variable grammatical pattern that might be paraphrased as "a preposition followed by an optional article, any number of adjectives and a noun". *BNCweb*'s Simple Query Syntax borrows the notation of REGULAR EXPRESSIONS (see e.g. Friedl 2006) to formulate such conditions. Regular expression syntax allows you to enclose parts of a phrase query in parentheses, marking them as optional or repeatable, or indicating a set of alternatives. The basic operators are summarized in the table below; note that the ellipsis (...) stands for an arbitrary query expression (covering a single token or multiple tokens) in each case.

Regular expression notation for grammatical patterns:	
(...) ?	part ... is optional
(...) *	zero or more repetitions of ... (optional)
(...) +	one or more repetitions of ... (non-optional)
(... | ... | ...)	match one of the alternatives
(... | ... | ...) *	alternatives combined with repetition (optional)
(... | ... | ...) +	alternatives combined with repetition (non-optional)

Thus, the general pattern for prepositional phrases described by the intuitive paraphrase above can be expressed with the following query (which has been extended to allow for adverbs in between the adjectives).

```
_{PREP} ( _{ART} )? ( _{A} | _{ADV} )* _{N}
```

Consulting the overview of regular expression notation in the box above should help you to understand each part of this query. Firstly, _{PREP} asks for a preposition; then (_{ART})? asks that the preposition is followed by an optional article; (_{A}|_{ADV})* asks for any number of adjectives and/or adverbs; finally, _{N} asks for precisely one noun. This query also returns hits like *by contrast, in other words, on a very cold day*, and *for a fat old gentleman*; but it still does not find examples such as *with the red, blue and yellow boxes*.

In the example above, the regular expression syntax has been separated from the token items for better readability, but parentheses and the vertical bars between alternatives may also be attached to tokens in a "natural" way, i.e. as you would place them in ordinary text:

```
_{PREP} (_{ART})? (_{A}|_{ADV})* _{N}
```

The **REPETITION OPERATORS** ?, * and + must be attached directly to the preceding parenthesis, though, since they would otherwise be interpreted as separate tokens consisting of a single wildcard. Note the different meaning of the metacharacters ?, *, + as wildcards and in regular expression notation, as well as the different ways of specifying alternatives. In particular, if you want to match the noun *can* or the noun *might*, you can either use the token-level syntax for alternatives [can,might]_{N} or the regular expression syntax (can_{N} | might_{N}). If you want to match *into* or *out of*, though, only the regular expression syntax is available: (into | out of).

Regular expression notation also offers a generic repetition operator of the form {n,m}, where n specifies the minimum number of repetitions and m the maximum number of repetitions allowed for the preceding parenthesized block (also called a "group"). For example, a prepositional phrase containing between 3 and 5 adjectives can be matched with the query

    _{PREP} (_{ART})? (_{A}){3,5} _{N}

If n is omitted, a default value of zero is used; if m is omitted, there is no upper limit on the number of repetitions. Thus, the different versions of the generic repetition operator can be paraphrased as follows:

Generic repetition operators in regular expression notation:

{n,m}	between *n* and *m* repetitions	
{,m}	at most *m* repetitions (*m* or fewer)	
{n,}	at least *n* repetitions (*n* or more)	
{0,1}	optional (zero or one), equivalent to:	?
{0,}	zero or more repetitions, equivalent to:	*
{1,}	one or more repetitions, equivalent to:	+

Groups in regular expressions can also contain further nested groups. A more sophisticated version of the previous query allows optional commas or coordinating conjunctions between the adjectives; this matches complex phrases like the example *with the red, blue and yellow boxes* above:

    _{PREP} (_{ART})? _{A} ((\,|and|or)? _{A}){2,4} _{N}

The first adjective has to be matched separately by _{A}. It is followed by a large group that matches 2 to 4 further adjectives. Inside this group, the regular expression (\,|and|or)? allows an optional *or, and* or comma before each adjective. This last example illustrates how *BNCweb*'s Simple Query Syntax is able to express complex lexico-grammatical patterns in a clear and intuitive way.

We now have a useful building block that can be reused and integrated as part of even larger patterns. We can for example (slightly) extend the recall of our query for the perfect (see 6.7) by allowing an optional prepositional phrase to occur between the auxiliary verb *have* and the past participle:

```
_VH* (_{PREP} (_{ART})? _{A} ((\,|and|or)?
   _{A}){2,4} _{N})? _V?N
```

Notice that the optionality of the prepositional phrase is indicated by surrounding it with parentheses and appending the modifier ? to the end of it.

No special syntax is needed to match or skip arbitrary words. The single wildcard + matches any token (consisting of one or more arbitrary characters); * also matches a sequence of zero characters (i.e. nothing at all), hence it stands for an optional token. Returning to an example from the previous section, the query

```
(black*white | black * white)
```

finds *black-and-white* (first alternative) as well as *black and white* (amongst many other strings, second alternative). For convenience, sequences of + and * items can be lumped together to match a certain number of arbitrary tokens. Both + + + * * and +++** match between 3 and 5 arbitrary tokens. A more explicit equivalent form would be (+){3,5}.

Simple queries also allow you to make use of text structure and typographical information provided by the BNC, e.g. sentence boundaries and speaker turns. The original BNC mark-up represents such structures in the form of XML tags like "<s>" (start of s-unit), "</s>" (end of s-unit) or "<u>" (start of a speaker turn). The same notation can be used in Simple queries to match these boundaries. As an example, the query <s> but finds sentences beginning with *but*, and <s> \L:C matches a lowercase word at the start of a sentence. You can use such XML tags anywhere within a query pattern: it {be} <hi> _{Pron} _{N} finds expressions like *it was **your** fault*, where the pronoun (and possibly also the noun) is emphasized in print ("<hi>" stands for "highlighted phrase"). The emphasis will not be shown in the concordances you see on the query results page, but it is visible in the extended context display. Use a pair of start and end tags to match the highlighted region from beginning to end:

```
it {be} <hi> _{PRON} </hi> _{N}
```

finds examples where *only* the pronoun is highlighted (if you omit </hi>, the noun may also be highlighted). Note that your query only has to match all *tokens* between the start and end tag, but not necessarily all XML tags. XML tags have "zero length" and are automatically ignored unless they are explicitly specified in the query.

If you do not wish to impose any restrictions on the material between two XML tags, you have to provide an expression that matches an arbitrary number of arbitrary tokens. For instance, the following query builds a list of all quotations in the BNC:

```
<quote> (+)+ </quote>
```

Note that the + inside the parentheses is a wildcard (which matches an arbitrary token), while the + outside is a regular expression operator (which allows one or more repetitions of the parenthesized group). A detailed description of text structure and typographical mark-up can be found in the *BNC Reference Guide*. The most important XML tags are listed in the box below.

Selection of useful XML tags:	
`<s>` … `</s>`	sentence-like unit
`<p>` … `</p>`	paragraph
`<u>` … `</u>`	speaker turn
`<head>` … `</head>`	heading or caption
`<quote>` … `</quote>`	quotation
`<item>` … `</item>`	list item
`<hi>` … `</hi>`	highlighted text
`<mw>` … `</mw>`	multiword unit

Finally, when writing queries involving optional elements and repetitions, you have to be aware that *BNCweb* uses a form of "shortest match" strategy during query evaluation. This means that once a match has been found, no further (longer) matches are attempted at the same location in the corpus. The most visible consequence is that optional elements at the beginning of a query are included in the match, while those at the end of a query are not. For example, the query

```
(_{ART})? (_{A})* (_{N})+
```

includes the optional determiner and adjectives whenever they are present; but if the noun phrase spans a sequence of two or more nouns (*a warm autumn evening*), only the first noun will be part of the match.

6.9   Proximity queries

In addition to the standard "phrase queries" described in the previous section, *BNCweb* allows you to search for combinations of words that occur near each other (e.g. within five tokens, or within the same sentence). These "proximity queries" are an experimental feature, and their precise functionality might change in future *BNCweb* versions.

Proximity queries always search for single tokens, but they will match only if the token in question is accompanied by a particular word or expression within a specified distance. For example, if you are looking for variations of the idiom *kick the bucket*, you might search for co-occurrences of *kick* and *bucket* in the same sentence with the query

```
kick <<s>> bucket
```

Here `kick` is the target token, and `bucket` a constraint that has to be satisfied by successful matches. The operator `<<s>>` specifies that the constraint has to occur in the same sentence as the target. Note that although this query returns instances of *kick* where there is an instance of *bucket* in the same sentence, only the target token *kick* will be highlighted.

Of course, it would be better to search for all forms of the verb *to kick* and all forms of the noun *bucket* rather than just the specific surface forms *kick* and *bucket*. This can be achieved easily, since proximity queries offer exactly the same functionality for matching individual tokens as phrase queries, including wildcards, parts of speech and headwords/lemmas. A better version of this query is thus:

```
{kick/V} <<s>> {bucket/N}
```

The proximity operator has the general form `<<`*(context)*`>>`, where *(context)* either refers to a level of text structure (s = s-unit, p = paragraph, u = speaker turn, `item` = list item, `text` = BNC file, etc.) or a positive number specifying the distance between the two words, measured in tokens. Thus, `<<s>>` indicates co-occurrence within the same sentence, `<<u>>` within a speaker turn and `<<text>>` within an entire BNC text; `<<5>>` searches the constraint within a range of 5 tokens to the left and right of the target, `<<10>>` within 10 tokens, etc. Keep in mind that these ranges are not automatically limited by sentence boundaries, so the constraint may not always be visible in the results display. For instance, one of the matches for the query `When:C <<3>> question` crosses a sentence boundary: *I formulate a carefully unsurprised* **question**. *'**When** was that?'*. In the results display, only the second sentence, which contains the target, will be shown.

Overview of proximity operators: constraint must be ...

<<s>>	within same sentence as the target
<<u>>	within same speaker turn as the target
<<text>>	within same BNC document as the target
<<*n*>>	within distance of *n* tokens from the target
<<*n*<<	within *n* tokens to the *left* of the target
>>*n*>>	within *n* tokens to the *right* of the target

Numeric contexts can also be one-sided: <<5<< searches within 5 tokens to the *left* of the target and >>5>> to the *right*. The query kick >>5>> bucket finds co-occurrences of the form *kick ... bucket*, while kick <<5<< bucket finds those of the form *bucket ... kick*. It is currently not possible to search for one-sided co-occurrences within text structure regions, i.e. you cannot use <<s<< to find *bucket* in the same sentence as *kick*, but to the left of it.

A target can have multiple constraints, which must all be satisfied. For example,

    {waste/V} <<s>> time <<s>> money

finds sentences containing *waste*, *time* and *money* (of course, it isn't necessarily the time or money that's being wasted). Recall that the result page highlights only instances of the verb *to waste* in these sentences. If you want *time* and *money* to be closer together, say within 3 tokens of each other, you can create a "subquery" where the constraint is enclosed in parentheses:

    {waste/V} <<s>> (time <<3>> money)

BNCweb first evaluates the subquery time <<3>> money; then, only instances of the verb *to waste* that co-occur with a hit of the subquery (in the same sentence) are accepted by the main query. The final result is a list of instances of the verb *to waste* which have been found with *time* and *money*. If the constraint is a fixed phrase, you can use a convenient shorthand notation:

    {waste/V} <<s>> (time and money)

requires *waste* to co-occur with the phrase *time and money*. Of course, you can use wildcards, parts of speech and headwords in each element of the phrase. Note that the shorthand (time and money) is equivalent to the rather clumsy subquery (time >>1>> and >>2>> money). Yet another variant is (time >>1>> (and >>1>> money)).

> **Task:**
> Explain why these last three queries are fully equivalent, i.e. they re-
> turn exactly the same set of hits. Rephrase the query such that *and* is
> highlighted on the result page rather than *time*. How many different,
> but equivalent, ways of writing the new query can you find?

Nested subqueries allow users to write very sophisticated proximity queries.
There is an important limitation, though: it is not possible to mix proximity queries with phrase query syntax. In particular, you cannot include optional tokens,
repetition operators or XML tags in a subquery constraint, even if it is written in
shorthand notation. Queries like `{kick/V}` `<<s>>` `(the` `(_{A})*`
`bucket)` will simply produce a syntax error. You also cannot include proximity constraints in a standard phrase query.

6.10   Matching special characters

Some words in the BNC contain special characters such as accented letters (e.g.
fiancée, déjà vu), Greek letters (e.g. *α-particles*) and various non-alphabetic
symbols (e.g. ♥). Many accented Latin letters that are commonly found in West-
ern European languages can be used directly in *BNCweb* queries: try `fiancée`
or `déjà vu`. The precise range of characters that can be entered directly in
BNCweb Simple queries is known as the "Latin-1 character set"; its formal name
is ISO-8859-1. A complete table of these characters can be found online at
http://en.wikipedia.org/wiki/ISO_8859-1. Remember, however, that words that
can or even should be spelled with an accented letter may be rendered without it
in the corpus.[5] If you want to find all instances of a word that can be spelled
with an accented letter it is usually safer to make use of the modifier `:d` in your
query. This will allow you to retrieve both accented and non-accented instances.
In the case of the French word *école*, for example, you will only find 22 instances if you use the accented letter (`école`) but 74 instances if you search for
`ecole:d`.

If your Web browser does not allow you to enter accents on Latin letters or
if such queries fail for some other reason, you can also enter the accented letters
in a special notation known as "HTML entities". Such entities start with the am-
persand `&`, followed by a descriptive name for the special character and termi-
nated by a semicolon (`;`); examples are `&eacute;` (for *é*) and `&Ocirc;` (for
Ô). For illustration, try `d&eacute;j&agrave; vu`, which should find the

---

5   This could be because the original source did not have the accent, or due to an error when
     the text was converted for inclusion in the corpus.

same matches as the query déjà vu above. All HTML entities for accented letters follow the basic pattern &Xaaaa;, where x is a lowercase or uppercase letter and aaaa stands for the name of an accent. The most frequently used accents are acute (e.g. é), grave (è), circ for circumflex (ô), tilde (ñ) and uml for umlaut (ä). Several common symbols from the Latin-1 character set can also be queried as entities, e.g. £ for £.[6]

Less common accents and other special symbols, including the entire Greek alphabet, can only be queried using HTML entity notation. A complete listing of HTML entities supported by *BNCweb* (outside the Latin-1 character set) is shown in the table in Appendix 4. Using this table you can search for such things as α-particles and also find the single occurrence of ♥ in the BNC, with the query ♥. The entities ‘ and ’ distinguish between opening and closing quotation marks, unlike the more convenient " shorthand.

Note that case-insensitive matching—which is the default mode for Simple queries in *BNCweb*—also works for accented and Greek letters: déjà vu will find both uppercase and lowercase spellings, and δT finds the temperature difference ΔT (with an uppercase delta Δ). However, the modifier :d does not recognize the less common accents listed in Appendix 4.

Please note that in the current *BNCweb* implementation, the notation ? to match single characters (cf. Section 6.4) does *not* in fact match any of the special characters listed in Appendix 4; this is because these characters are represented within *BNCweb* as HTML-entities and would therefore require a match of more than a single character. This caveat does not, however, apply to standard accented letters and Latin-1 symbols, which are stored as single characters. Finally, you may see surprising effects if your searches contain the * or + wildcards. To illustrate this, try running the query *helli* and see if you can explain why it not only matches words like *hellish*, but also something entirely different.

6.11   Exercises

1. *To boldly split*. Traditional prescriptive grammars advise against the use of split infinitives such as the famous *to boldly go*. Use *BNCweb* to find out how far actual usage in Present-day English conforms to this prescription.

    a) Write a query that matches split infinitives, consulting Appendix 2 or the *BNC Reference Guide* to find the appropriate part-of-speech tags. How many split infinitives can you find in the BNC?

---

6   A comprehensive listing of these standard HTML entities can be found online at http://en.wikipedia.org/wiki/List_of_XML_and_HTML_character_entity_references

    b) Compare this result to the number of prescriptively correct infinitives (*boldly to go* or *to go boldly*). Why can't you just search for the pattern *to <infinitive>* as a point of comparison?

    c) Are split infinitives used more often in spoken than in written English?

    d) Can you extend your queries to also find (split) infinitives with complex adverbs, such as *to at least consider* and *to sort of say*?

2. *Who's using the passive?* Let's explore the use of passive voice in different registers. Restrict your searches to specific genres (say, academic writing vs. conversation) as explained in 4.6, and compare the relative frequencies of passive constructions. Is there a difference between male and female speakers, or teenagers and adults, in the spoken part of the BNC? The following steps will help you develop a query that matches a broad range of passives.

    a) First, think of a few examples of passive constructions. The basic pattern is BE + optional adverbials, negative particle, etc. + past participle.

    b) Look up the POS tags for past participles, adverbs, the negative particle, ordinal adverbs, etc. in Appendix 2 or the *BNC Reference Guide*.

    c) Write a first query that allows for an arbitrary number of adverbs etc. between *BE* and the past participle. (You might want to include ambiguity tags for the past participle to achieve good recall.)

    d) Refine the query so that it also matches passive constructions in interrogative clauses, i.e. it must allow a noun phrase between BE and the past participle.

    e) You may have noticed that your query does not find passives involving complex adverbials such as *is in part caused* or *was none the less enjoyed*. Can you explain why these cases are missed? The CQP Query Syntax offers an easy way to match complex adverbials (cf. Chapter 12).

7 Automated analyses of concordance lines—Part I: Distribution and Sorting

7.1 Outline

This is the first of two chapters dealing with automated analyses of concordance lines in *BNCweb*. The following functions will be covered:

- Analyzing the distribution of a query result over the metatextual categories encoded in the BNC
- Sorting a query result
- Obtaining a frequency breakdown of different forms of a query result—or of items found in the immediate context of a query result

The analysis of habitual co-occurrences of words—or, collocations—represents another prominent way of exploring a query result by automatic means. This will be discussed in Chapter 8.

7.2 Distribution

7.2.1 A *lovely* example: distributional facts about the users of *lovely*

Up until now, our description of *BNCweb* has mainly dealt with the different ways in which it is possible to perform searches on the whole BNC or individual sub-sections. As mentioned in Chapter 3, one of the important features of the BNC is that its contents are heavily marked up with metatextual information. In Chapter 4, we demonstrated how the various types of mark-up can be employed to restrict queries to certain sub-parts of the corpus, e.g. by searching only books from the text domain of "Natural and pure sciences" or only utterances produced by female speakers aged 25 to 49. With the help of such restricted searches, the use (and frequency) of a word or a construction can be compared across different contexts (or different kinds of speakers), which can reveal interesting facts about language that could not easily be discovered through general searches over the whole BNC.

One way of doing comparisons of this sort is to perform a series of individual searches—using the same query term, but applying different metatextual restrictions. Furthermore, if you wanted to cross-tabulate your findings for two or more categories (e.g. both age and sex of speakers), you would then have to carry out separate queries for each of the possible combinations. And although some categories have only two values (e.g. "Sex of speaker"), this is not usually the case: for example, the category "Text domain" has nine values and "Genre" has seventy. Needless to say, it can become quite difficult—and tedious!—to keep track of the results if these categories are combined with any of the other metatextual categories available in the BNC (e.g. if you were to combine "Text domain" with "Age of author" (six values), you would end up having to do 54 different queries).

Fortunately, the DISTRIBUTION feature of *BNCweb* can be used to do all of the above types of comparisons and cross-tabulations with just a few mouse-clicks. This is best demonstrated with a simple example, and we'll choose the lexical item *lovely* for this purpose. Before you go on reading, you could, as in previous chapters, ask yourself first what your intuitions tell you about the use of this word. Is it more frequent in written or in spoken language? Who do you think uses it more often in spoken language—men or women? Younger or older speakers? Well, let's have a look.

1. Perform a Simple query for `lovely`; this retrieves 6,028 hits in the whole BNC.

2. In the query result page, choose DISTRIBUTION from the post-query options menu and click [Go!]. This will display a
   page containing an overview of the
   distribution of *lovely* over a number of
   different metatextual categories in the corpus.
   The first of these—"Spoken or Written"—is
   shown in Figure 7.1.

New Query
Thin...
Frequency breakdown
✓ Distribution
Sort
Collocations...
Download...
Categorize...
Save current set of hits...

Your query "lovely" returned 6028 hits in 1253 different texts. The current solution set was found in 1253 texts.

Categories:	General information	Show distribution
Categories (for crosstabs only):	no crosstabs	New Query Go

The following distribution was found:

Spoken or Written:

Category	No. of words	No. of hits	Dispersion (over files)	Frequency per million words
Spoken	10,409,858	2,397	318/908	230.26
Written	87,903,571	3,631	935/3,140	41.31
total	**98,313,429**	**6,028**	**1,253/4,048**	**61.31**

Figure 7.1:   Distribution of *lovely* over spoken and written texts

As you can see, a larger number of instances of *lovely* are found in the written component of the corpus: there are 3,631 hits in written texts vs. 2,397 hits in spoken texts. Remember, however, that raw frequencies have to be normalized when subsets of different sizes are involved—this was discussed at length in 5.3. This is definitely the case here, as is confirmed by the second column of the table: there are only 10.4 million words in the spoken component of the corpus but 87.9 million words in written texts. Therefore, if you want to compare results for the two categories, you will need to look at the relative or normalized frequencies displayed in the rightmost column of the table ("Frequency per million words"). Here, things look very different: with 230 instances per million words, spoken texts contain about 5.5 times as many instances of *lovely* than written texts (approx. 40 instances pmw).

Finally, the table contains a column with the heading "Dispersion (over files)", which displays information about the total number of files in each category as well as the number of files in which *lovely* was actually found. Thus, although there are 908 spoken text files in the BNC, *lovely* is only found in 318 of these. This information constitutes a basic measure of how evenly distributed your query item is, and it can therefore for example help you distinguish specialized vocabulary from items of more general currency. We will return to a more detailed discussion of the usefulness of this feature below.

Your query "lovely" returned 6028 hits in 1253 different texts. The current solution set was found in 1253 texts.

| Categories: | Speaker: Age | ⬍ | Show distribution |
| Categories (for crosstabs only): | no crosstabs | ⬍ | New Query ⬍ Go |

The following distribution was found:

Age:

Category	No. of words	No. of hits	Dispersion (over speakers)	Frequency per million words
60+	1,137,433	528	108/318	464.2
25-34	1,120,516	363	76/351	323.96
15-24	594,400	166	54/302	279.27
45-59	1,638,364	454	97/436	277.11
35-44	1,075,749	271	81/335	251.92
0-14	385,234	80	36/258	207.67
total	**5,951,696**	**1,862**	**452/2,000**	**312.85**

Figure 7.2:   Distribution of *lovely* over "Age of speaker"

At the top of the page, you will find two drop-down menus that let you choose from the complete range of individual metatextual categories that are available for display. Select "Speaker: Age" from the upper of the two menus and then click [Show distribution]. This will display a single frequency table with the different speaker age-bands—cf. Figure 7.2. This table clearly shows that older people appear to favor the use of *lovely*: speakers belonging to the age group 60+ utter this word more than twice as often as the youngest group of speakers (464 pmw vs. 208 pmw). Notice, by the way, that since we are now dealing with a speaker-based distribution, the dispersion information has been changed from the number of texts where *lovely* is found to the number of speakers who use it.

However, the picture is not quite as simple as that: the frequencies in the other age groups don't support the hypothesis that the use of *lovely* is highly influenced by speaker age. Thus, speakers belonging to the second-oldest group (45-59) in fact use this word less often than speakers in their twenties and early thirties.

Your query "lovely" returned 6028 hits in 1253 different texts. The current solution set was found in 1253 texts.

| Categories: | Speaker: Sex | Show distribution |
| Categories (for crosstabs only): | no crosstabs | New Query | Go |

The following distribution was found:

Sex:

Category	No. of words	No. of hits	Dispersion (over speakers)	Frequency per million words
Female	3,290,569	1,428	318/1,360	433.97
Male	4,949,938	665	251/2,448	134.35
total	8,240,507	2,093	569/3,808	253.99

Figure 7.3:   Distribution of *lovely* over male and female speakers[1]

In such situations, it is often a good idea to look at additional metatextual categories that have been marked up in the corpus in order to try and find out whether the observed distribution in one category could in fact be the result of a combination of other factors. To test this, select the option "Speaker sex" instead, and again click on [Show distribution]. The result is shown in Figure 7.3. As you can see, women use *lovely* about three times more frequently than male speakers (434 pmw vs. 134 pmw).

---

[1]   The results in the column "No. of hits" in Figures 7.2 and 7.3 don't add up to the same total. As we have already mentioned before in Chapter 3, this has to do with the fact that there are quite a number of speakers about whom we have only partial information. However, since we are working with normalized frequencies, this is no problem, and we can still directly compare findings from different categories with each other.

If you now want to investigate whether the age of speakers might have a different influence on the use of *lovely* by women and men, you can make use of the cross-tabulation function of the DISTRIBUTION feature. In the lower of the two drop-down menus, select the category "Age of speaker" and click [Show distribution]. The result of this cross-tabulation is shown in Figure 7.4.

Your query "lovely" returned 6028 hits in 1253 different texts. The current solution set was found in 1253 texts.

Categories:	Speaker: Sex		Show distribution
Categories (for crosstabs only):	Speaker: Age		New Query	Go

The following distribution was found:

Age / Sex: Male

	No. of words	No. of hits	Dispersion (over speakers)	Frequency per million words
25-34	549,763	103	25/201	187.35
60+	599,631	112	47/201	186.78
0-14	224,388	40	17/152	178.26
45-59	1,086,180	166	52/303	152.83
35-44	558,419	82	31/190	146.84
15-24	237,033	34	15/143	143.44
total	**3,255,414**	**537**	**187/1,190**	**164.96**

Age / Sex: Female

	No. of words	No. of hits	Dispersion (over speakers)	Frequency per million words
60+	537,802	416	61/117	773.52
45-59	550,563	288	45/132	523.1
25-34	570,544	260	51/149	455.71
15-24	357,367	132	39/159	369.37
35-44	517,330	189	50/145	365.34
0-14	160,846	40	19/106	248.69
total	**2,694,452**	**1,325**	**265/808**	**491.75**

Figure 7.4:   Distribution of *lovely*—cross-tabulation of speaker age and speaker sex

As will immediately become apparent, the two distributions are radically different. For the male speakers in the corpus, age does not appear to be an influential factor at all. Thus, the youngest and the oldest age groups display similar frequencies (178 pmw for speakers aged 0-14 vs. 187 pmw for the oldest male speakers in the BNC); furthermore, the difference between the speakers who use *lovely* most frequently (25-34) and those who use it least frequently (15-24—the next lower age-band) is not very great (187 pmw vs. 143 pmw).

For women, the picture is very different indeed. Not only is there a threefold difference in frequency between the youngest and the oldest female speakers (249 pmw vs. 774 pmw), the second-oldest group of speakers is now found in second place (523 pmw). The remaining age-bands lie between these extremes, but don't display any clear age-related pattern. This suggests that the results shown in Figure 7.4 may again only be part of the whole story, and that other factors may be contributing to the somewhat more frequent use of *lovely* by women who are aged 25-34.

As you will no doubt have realized by now, the DISTRIBUTION feature of *BNCweb* is a powerful tool for discovering interesting correlations between various categories of annotation. It produces descriptive statistics on the fly that would otherwise be very tiresome, and also potentially error-prone, to compile via a long list of individual queries. As a result, there is sometimes a tendency to get carried away by the ease with which often quite fascinating—and intuitively plausible—findings can be made with this feature. It is therefore necessary for us to add a word of caution. The results obtained by the DISTRIBUTION feature are no doubt useful descriptive statistics—but they are really only one part of the whole story. These statistics tell you nothing about the actual use or meaning of a particular word or construction in context. For example, there is no indication of whether one of the age groups uses *lovely* in a sarcastic or ironic way more often than the other groups.

The only way to make sure that you are not missing important aspects of the phenomenon that you are investigating is to look at a sufficient number of uses in context. Fortunately, this is very easy in *BNCweb*: each number in the frequency tables shown in Figures 7.1 to 7.4 represents a link that will display a concordance of the corresponding instances of your query item.

7.2.2   Frequency distribution by genre

Let's extend our understanding of the DISTRIBUTION function by studying another lexical item. Many language teachers have observed that learners have a tendency to overuse the word *because* in their essays instead of using a variety of terms to express causation (e.g. *due to*, *since*, *as*, or even *the reason for this is*, *so*, *therefore*, *hence*), and cite *because* as one among many words that are more spoken than written in flavor. How would you go about checking this hunch that *because* is more often used in spoken than in written genres? And, for that matter, do native-speaker school children also overuse *because* in their essays?

If you are interested in looking at how the usage of a lexical item (or any kind of term or pattern) is patterned or distributed across a variety of spoken and written genres, *BNCweb* offers a genre distribution function that will give you just such a snapshot. The genres here are the 70 spoken and written genres that have been determined for the BNC based on the hand-categorization of the texts by Lee (2001).

For our example here, we will look at the distribution of *because* across the 70 genres in order to get a finer-grained picture of its usage than simply looking at "spoken language" as a whole and "written language" as a whole (because too many disparate genres get lumped together). To begin with, we will need to include variant spellings and spoken forms of *because*. Our first step is therefore to do a Simple query for because|cos|'cos|'cause. (We will treat these variants together even though they show slight differences with respect to their degrees of formality.) You should get 117,335 hits. Next, select DISTRIBUTION from the post-query options menu and press [Go!].

Spoken or Written:				
Category	No. of words	No. of hits	Dispersion (over files)	Frequency per million words
Spoken	10,409,858	38,634	860/908	3711.29
Written	87,903,571	78,701	2,906/3,140	895.31
total	98,313,429	117,335	3,766/4,048	1193.48
Derived text type:				
Category	No. of words	No. of hits	Dispersion (over files)	Frequency per million words
Spoken conversation	4,233,962	18,110	150/153	4277.32
Other spoken material	6,175,896	20,524	710/755	3323.24
Academic prose	15,778,028	14,974	479/497	949.04
Non-academic prose and biography	24,178,674	22,454	737/744	928.67
Newspapers	9,412,174	8,462	421/486	899.05
Fiction and verse	16,143,913	14,409	438/452	892.53
Other published written material	17,924,109	15,052	629/710	839.76
Unpublished written material	4,466,673	3,350	202/251	750
total	98,313,429	117,335	3,766/4,048	1193.48

Figure 7.5:   General distribution information for the query because|cos| 'cos|'cause

The initial distribution results—displayed in Figure 7.5—show us that *because* is generally more common in speech than in writing (in fact, four times as common). This fact has been observed before by researchers such as Beaman (1984) and Tottie (1986), but with the wealth of data and metadata in the BNC we can now get a much more detailed picture of the distributional facts. Under "Derived text type", you can see that conversations and "Other spoken material" (all the other spoken genres lumped together) have the highest frequencies of *because,* followed by the written text types of academic prose, non-academic prose and biographies, newspapers, and fiction/verse. These text categories are still very broad, however, so let's do a more detailed breakdown by genre. From the top-most drop-down menu labeled "Categories", select "Overall: Genre" and press [Show distribution]. The top part of the resulting distribution report is displayed in Figure 7.6.

The following distribution was found:				
Genre:				
Category	No. of words	No. of hits	Dispersion (over files)	Frequency per million words
S:tutorial	144,783	703	18/18	4855.54
S:lect:soc_science	162,030	696	13/13	4295.5
S:conv	4,233,962	18,110	150/153	4277.32
S:demonstratn	32,062	137	6/6	4272.97
S:interview	125,096	525	13/13	4196.78
S:speech:unscripted	469,492	1,839	51/51	3917
S:consult	139,320	544	103/128	3904.68
S:lect:humanities_arts	51,510	199	4/4	3863.33
S:classroom	433,646	1,638	55/58	3777.27
S:sermon	82,775	311	16/16	3757.17
S:unclassified	425,097	1,578	38/44	3712.09
S:meeting	1,391,207	4,999	129/132	3593.28
S:lect:commerce	15,233	51	3/3	3347.99
S:interview:oral_history	822,489	2,734	117/119	3324.06
S:brdcast:discussn	761,595	2,211	53/53	2903.12
S:lect:polit_law_edu	51,407	147	7/7	2859.53
S:lect:nat_science	22,938	60	4/4	2615.75
S:courtroom	129,067	337	13/13	2611.05
S:parliament	97,289	237	6/6	2436.04
W:essay:school	147,736	343	7/7	2321.71
S:speech:scripted	193,020	423	21/25	2191.48

Figure 7.6:   Distribution of the query `because|cos|'cos|'cause` over the category "Genre"

One of the striking things about this distribution is the fact that the written and spoken genres are clearly divided in this table. With just one exception ("Written school essays"), all the spoken genres are at the top while all the written genres are at the bottom. If you scan the "Frequency per million words" column here, you will notice that there are no sharp differences between any two adjacent figures, illustrating the fact that while we often focus on the dichotomy of "spoken" and "written", there is actually a continuum of genres, as shown in this example.

If you examine the genre distribution more carefully, you will note that *because* is used very frequently in spoken instructional or persuasive / argumentative contexts: university tutorials, academic lectures, "live" demonstrations and job interviews. It is also very common in casual conversation. Written genres tend to use *because* comparatively less often, although school essays (at 2,321 pmw) and university essays (at 1,297 pmw), many of which are also argumentative in nature, have quite a high usage, along with parliamentary proceedings, which are really the written records of (argumentative/persuasive) speeches made in parliament ("W:hansard", at 1,570 pmw). We also saw earlier (when looking at "Derived text type") that if we combined the various written academic genres together, academic writing as a whole also uses *because* quite frequently (949 pmw). The differences in the frequency figures between academic writing as a whole and university and school essays seem to suggest that as the genre of writing becomes more formal and professional, the expression of causation or reason becomes lexically more diversified, or that perhaps the meaning gets expressed through syntactic rather than lexical means (this would of course need to be followed up by more detailed study). The detailed genre breakdown thus gives us some clues about the functional reasons for the use of *because* and supports our earlier suspicion that *because* tends to get overused in school essays (even by native speakers), and is associated more with oral than literate genres.

A further example will demonstrate the usefulness of thinking about frequencies across a spectrum of genres rather than between just "spoken" and "written". Let's consider the expression "*so* + adjective" (e.g. *so good, so bad, so important, so close, so easy*). First, do a Simple query for so _AJ*. You should get 32,470 hits. Again, use the post-query options menu to do an initial DISTRIBUTION. You will see that this time there is no clear distinction between the two broad categories "spoken" and "written": 390 pmw versus 323 pmw respectively. Now do a DISTRIBUTION by genre. Figure 7.7 shows the top entries of the resulting distribution table.

This genre breakdown suggests that such "amplifying" expressions tend to be used frequently in the more informal, "involved" or personally charged speech genres (or creative representations of them), where "*so* + adjective" serves as an interactive, rhetorical or suasive device: it is most common in, for instance, drama, fiction, personal letters, school essays, conversation, "live" demonstrations, poetry, sermons, tabloid newspapers. Note that the picture here is not as simple as with *because*: here, spoken and written genres stand interspersed at all points along the genre spectrum, so it cannot really be said that "*so*

+ adjective" is a spoken language feature. Instead, a look at its distribution across genres suggests multiple factors at play.

The following distribution was found:				
Genre:				
Category	No. of words	No. of hits	Dispersion (over files)	Frequency per million words
W:fict:drama	46,094	50	2/2	1084.74
W:fict:prose	16,033,634	11,319	420/431	705.95
W:letters:personal	52,915	37	5/6	699.23
W:essay:school	147,736	86	7/7	582.12
S:conv	4,233,962	2,406	135/153	568.26
S:demonstratn	32,062	17	4/6	530.22
W:fict:poetry	223,683	111	28/30	496.24
S:sermon	82,775	41	14/16	495.32
W:newsp:tabloid	733,066	345	6/6	470.63
S:lect:humanities_arts	51,510	24	4/4	465.93
W:biography	3,556,685	1,640	98/100	461.1
S:lect:polit_law_edu	51,407	23	7/7	447.41
S:consult	139,320	58	31/128	416.31
W:newsp:brdsht_nat:social	82,605	34	17/36	411.6

Figure 7.7:   Distribution of "*so* + adjective" over the genre classification scheme

---

Task:
Do a genre distribution of the usage of the word *absolutely*. What can you observe about the usage and (rhetorical) functions of this word, based on the detailed genre breakdown?

7.2.3   Dispersion & File-frequency extremes: checking the influence of idiosyncratic texts on frequencies

As we mentioned earlier, the dispersion information provided by the DISTRIBUTION feature offers a convenient measure of the general currency of the phenomenon you are investigating. As a case in point, consider a search for the headword ADJECTIVE—that is, the actual word *adjective* (in its singular and plural forms) rather than any word tagged as an adjective. For this purpose, perform a Simple query for {adjective}—this will reveal that there are 999 instances in the whole BNC. The overall frequency of ADJECTIVE is thus about 10.2 instances per million words. Yet how reliable is this frequency information? Are there any contexts (genres, text domains etc.) where the term *adjective(s)* is particularly frequent? Run the DISTRIBUTION feature over the complete set of results, and you will see that this word is indeed very unevenly distributed across the different parts of the corpus. Figure 7.8 shows the distribution of the query term {adjective} over the eight major derived text types of the BNC. Thus, in the 153 texts of the demographically sampled component of the corpus (i.e. spontaneous conversation), not a single instance is found. At the other extreme, we find the category "Academic prose" with a total of 704 instances (44.6 instances pmw).

This is not really surprising; in fact, it seems fitting that the word *adjective* should most frequently occur in texts of an academic nature. Let's now look at the dispersion measure: it reveals that ADJECTIVE occurs in 48 out of a possible 497 texts.

However, we now also need to take account of the overall number of hits involved and compare these figures across the different text types. The ratio of hits to the number of texts in "Academic prose" is almost 15:1 (704 instances in 48 texts), whereas all of the other text types display a much lower ratio (e.g. 35 instances in 28 different "Fiction and verse" files or 17 instances in 14 different "Newspapers" files). But crucially, these figures don't tell us anything about how evenly distributed the individual instances are within the text types concerned.

Derived text type:				
Category	No. of words	No. of hits	Dispersion (over files)	Frequency per million words
Academic prose	15,778,028	704	48/497	44.62
Unpublished written material	4,466,673	51	10/251	11.42
Other published written material	17,924,109	75	31/710	4.18
Other spoken material	6,175,896	25	13/755	4.05
Non-academic prose and biography	24,178,674	92	55/744	3.81
Fiction and verse	16,143,913	35	28/452	2.17
Newspapers	9,412,174	17	14/486	1.81
Spoken conversation	4,233,962	0	0/153	0
total	**98,313,429**	**999**	**199/4,048**	**10.16**

Figure 7.8:   Distribution of ADJECTIVE over the eight derived text types of the BNC

It is therefore worth investigating the distribution of ADJECTIVE still further. One possible option is of course that the term is found particularly frequently in a small number of files—or perhaps even in a single one. This can be tested with the help of an additional option in the DISTRIBUTION feature: in the top drop-down menu of the "Distribution results" page select "File-frequency extremes" and again click [Show distribution]. You will now see two tables: the upper one lists those files where your query item was found most frequently (see Figure 7.9), while the lower table lists those files in the BNC where ADJEC-TIVE was found with the lowest frequency. Note that the lower table does not list texts where your query item was not found at all. As is immediately obvious, there is indeed a single file where ADJECTIVE occurs with a particularly high frequency: the text HPY alone contains 548 instances—or more than half of all 999 instances found in the whole corpus!

Click on the name of the text, and it will become apparent why such an astonishingly large number of instances are found in this text: it contains a sample from a book entitled *The meaning of syntax: a study in the adjectives of English*. Without access to the dispersion measure—and of course the "File-frequency extremes" option of the DISTRIBUTION feature—this skewed distribution caused by a single file might have gone unchecked. This could in turn have led to inaccurate conclusions being drawn about the use of the term *adjective(s)* in Present-day English.

Your query "{adjective}" returned 999 hits in 199 different texts. The current solution set was found in 199 texts.			
Categories:	File-frequency extremes ⬍	Show distribution	
Categories (for crosstabs only):	no crosstabs ⬍	New Query ⬍	Go

It was most frequently found in the following files (only texts with at least three occurrences are considered)			
Name of Text	Number of words	Number of hits	Frequency per million words
HPY	44,522	548	12308.5210
HBX	1,398	4	2861.2300
H0Y	37,290	33	884.9550
HSC	36,617	31	846.6010
EWA	42,284	35	827.7360
CG3	34,474	25	725.1840
K93	38,269	17	444.2230
J40	6,835	3	438.9170
HXG	43,919	13	295.9990

Figure 7.9:   "File-frequency extremes" display for the query {adjective}

In the spoken component of the BNC, a similarly skewed result can occur when a spoken text contains a conversation about a highly specialized topic.

Also, individual speakers may exhibit idiosyncrasies by using a particular feature of language exceptionally often. In order to detect such potentially distorting influences, the DISTRIBUTION feature also offers the option to list "Speaker-frequency extremes", with tables listing speakers who use the query item most frequently and least frequently. Again, the tables do not list those speakers for whom no matches at all were found.

7.3 Sort

7.3.1 Sorting a query result on preceding or following context

In Chapter 1, we investigated the use of *goalless* and found that it is exclusively restricted to the domain of sports—at least in the BNC. As an additional point, we noted that *goalless* is quite often found in combination with *draw*—in fact, more than half of all instances of *goalless* are immediately followed by *draw*. This is particularly obvious when the concordance is displayed in "KWIC" (i.e. "key word in context") view. However, it is quite unusual for a word to have such a strong link with another lexical item. More often, words tend to be found with a whole range of other items, and patterns of co-occurrence are therefore more difficult to detect. This is particularly the case when we are looking at words (or phrases) that are fairly frequent: if you have several thousand concordance lines to look at, it is difficult to keep track of recurring combinations in a reliable way. The SORT feature of *BNCweb* is designed to help you with this type of task. In order to demonstrate the use of this feature, we will look at a pair of near-synonyms: *pretty* and *handsome*. The intuition of many speakers is that *pretty* is typically used to refer to women or girls, while *handsome* is the more appropriate term to use in the context of male referents. We will test whether this is in fact true.

To start this, perform a query for both words—do this in two separate browser windows (or tabs) in order to make it easier to compare query results. For *pretty*, the query retrieves 7,547 hits (in 1,773 different texts), while *handsome* is less frequent: only 1,577 hits (in 700 different texts). In the first 50 hits of *pretty*, we get *pretty moon face*, *pretty lady*, *pretty limbs*, and *pretty woman*. However, we also see *pretty* used as an intensifying adverb: *pretty run down*, *pretty sordid*, *pretty funny*, *pretty bizarre*, etc. Remember that if you place your cursor over the word *pretty* in the concordance lines, a toolbox will pop up showing the immediate context with part-of-speech tags. As you will see, these instances of *pretty* are tagged as AV0 ("general adverb"). In the case of *pretty face* (the seventh hit in the concordance), however, *pretty* is tagged as adjective (AJ0). Since *handsome* is unlikely to be used as an intensifier, a direct comparison of its co-occurrence patterns with *pretty* is problematic. It is therefore necessary to restrict your initial query to *pretty* tagged as an adjective—the query for this is `pretty_AJ0`. If you don't do this, you would not be able to directly compare your findings for the two words.[2] The POS-restricted query only returns 2,613 hits of *pretty* in the whole BNC.

If you now turn to the window of concordance lines for *handsome*, you will again see a variety of uses: *handsome police chief, handsome inn, handsome building* and *handsome boy*. Interestingly, we also find an instance of *handsome woman* on this first page—this is the 12th hit in the concordance. Clearly, a closer look at the co-occurrence patterns of the two words is required to work out a comprehensive description.

The SORT feature offers the option of re-arranging your concordance lines with respect to any position between "5 Left" and "5 Right" from the query result. The default sort position is "1 Right", i.e. the item immediately following the word or phrase matched by your query. Select SORT in the post-query options menu of the two query results and click [Go!]. After a few seconds, you get a concordance of the respective query items sorted alphabetically according to the word that follows the query item (highlighted in boldface). This is shown in Figure 7.10. (The default display format for sorted concordances is "KWIC"-view; however, it is possible to switch to "Sentence view" by clicking on the corresponding button at the top of the page.)

Your query "[word = "pretty" %c & pos = "AJ0" %c]" returned 2613 hits in 891 different texts (98,313,429 wor 26.58 instances per million words), sorted on *position +1* (2613 hits)

| |< | << | >> | >| | Show Page: 1 | | Show Sentence View | | Show in random order |

Sort parameters: Position: 1 Right Tag restriction: no restrictions □ exclude Starting with letter: all

No	Filename		Hits 1 to 7	Page 1 / 374
1	HA2 2904	here much,' said Theodora disingenuously. 'They were both	pretty	**absentee** of late. Ti
2	BPF 1102	Available from all Electrolux retail outlets it costs around £209.99. These	pretty	**accessories** (right) ε
3	HGE 3256	can you believe her, Cochrane? Did she put on her	pretty	**act** for you? Show
4	HAE 4322	when a client mutilates one of her girls. The petite,	pretty	**actress** met Clint 1ε
5	AEA 1179	lust and a sort of snobbism for the theatre in general and	pretty	**actresses** in particul
6	CGM 294	on a dark bob created by George at Paterson S.A. in Edinburgh	Pretty	**adaption** of a class
7	FAE 29	repaired the house, he constructs a vista culminating in a '	pretty	**alcove**' of his own

Figure 7.10:   Query result for `pretty_AJ0`, sorted by following word (cropped view).

---

2   However, the distinction between adjectives and adverbs is a difficult area of tagging, and the error rate produced by automatic taggers may be much higher than the average given for the whole corpus. As a case in point, consider the 38th concordance line:

Rosa glauca has handsome foliage, pretty_**AV0** single flowers and good red hips.

(A0G: 2311)

By excluding instances of *pretty* that are not tagged as adjectives, you therefore somewhat reduce the recall of your query.

Since our investigation is concerned with the type of referent described as *pretty* or *handsome*, we are particularly interested in the nouns that immediately follow these adjectives. We therefore need to apply a filter to the sorted concordance lines. This can be done via the "Tag restriction" drop-down menu just above the concordance lines. Apart from individual tags, a list of higher-level tag groups is available. Select "any noun" and press [Submit]. This reduces the query result to 1,387 hits.[3]

7.3.2   The Frequency breakdown function

In this sorted format, it is of course much easier to detect recurrent word combinations. However, it would still be tedious to navigate through the complete concordance in order to determine which of these combinations is the most frequent one. Fortunately, this can be discovered much more quickly: in the post-query options menu, select "Frequency breakdown" and press [Go!].

There are 580 types and 1387 tokens in your sorted query result

|< << >> >|	Frequency breakdown of tags only ⧫ (Go!)	(Download whole table)
No.	**Lexical item(s)**	**No. of occurrences**	**Percent**

No.	Lexical item(s)	No. of occurrences	Percent
1	girl	87	6.27%
2	face	68	4.9%
3	woman	48	3.46%
4	Polly	39	2.81%
5	girls	35	2.52%
6	village	34	2.45%
7	sight	27	1.95%
8	lady	19	1.37%
9	villages	19	1.37%
10	garden	18	1.3%
11	boy	18	1.3%
12	clothes	13	0.94%
13	dress	13	0.94%
14	Things	13	0.94%
15	dresses	13	0.94%

Figure 7.11:   Frequency breakdown of nouns immediately following the adjective *pretty*

---

3   To look at items starting with a specific letter, use the drop-down menu at the top entitled "Starting with letter". To reverse the part-of-speech filter, activate the check box labelled "exclude". This will display a sorted concordance for all items in the selected position that do not correspond to the chosen tag or set of tags.

This FREQUENCY BREAKDOWN function gives a listing (in descending order) of the different forms found in the previously selected sort position. The result of applying FREQUENCY BREAKDOWN on our concordance of `pretty_AJ0` sorted and filtered by any noun in the position "1 Right" is shown in Figure 7.11. As you can see, the most frequent noun found in the slot immediately following *pretty* is *girl* (6.3% of all instances). Other human referents include the plural form *girls* (2.5%) and *woman* (3.6%)—but interestingly also *boy*.[4] If you wish to save the complete frequency breakdown to your computer, press [Download whole table].

Now perform the same steps for *handsome*. As you will see, the most frequent noun immediately following *handsome* is *man*; in fact, almost every tenth instance of *handsome* is immediately followed by *man*. Other human referents include *prince*, *boy*, *men*, and *husband*. However, *handsome woman* is the third most frequent combination—it occurs 16 times (approximately 2%)—and *handsome girl* is found 6 times. It thus appears that the male/female distinction between *pretty* and *handsome* isn't as clear-cut as might have been presumed.

What we have done so far is only compile descriptive statistics. As we've previously pointed out in this book, we need to go beyond this to arrive at a fully explanatory account—a look at the actual uses of the word combinations is needed. Figure 7.12 displays the first 10 of the 16 instances of *handsome woman* in the BNC.

It appears that in the majority of cases, the women described here are in some way special (although with some of these sentences, we would need to see more context to be sure). For example, in the vicinity of *handsome* we find some additional adjectives used to characterize these women: *ripely*, *fearsome*, *tall*, and in at least a few of the sentences, it is apparent that the women referred to are not very young.[5] Clearly, substituting *pretty* for *handsome* in these sentences would evoke a different set of connotations. It is a similar case with *pretty boy*: the boys referred to are either very young (or perceived to be so), or they are addressed in a belittling or disparaging manner.

On the whole, we have thus confirmed our initial assumptions concerning the gender differences between *pretty* and *handsome*. However, we have also found interesting additional aspects of their usage that may have remained hidden had we not had access to the SORT and FREQUENCY BREAKDOWN features.

---

4   To find out whether singular nouns are, on the whole, more common than plural nouns after pretty, select "Frequency breakdown of tags only" in the drop-down menu of the "Frequency breakdown" page. The results show that singular nouns cover about two thirds of all instances in the "1 Right" position.

5   In fact, the ninth concordance line where the term is described as "patronising", spells this out when it continues as follows:

> What does it mean? It means something like: surprisingly fanciable if it was socially OK to fancy women of that age. (EDJ: 1074-5)

No	Filename	Hits 1 to 16 Page 1 / 1
1	AOD 1344	Marion, a ripely **handsome** woman in her mid-thirties, who had played a season at Stratford-on-Avon and toured as Mrs Tanqueray, was extremely displeased at having to share Jessie, let alone a dressing-room, and particularly with a chit like Bunty; but the Regent was small and naturally the two Star dressing-rooms, 1 and 2, went to Salt and Pepper, that perennial and professionally married pair of comedy-thriller performers whose productions never ran for less than a year — a godsend in a profession where rehearse for three weeks, open and close in two was not unusual.
2	AJR 446	For Pierantozzi, a fearsome if **handsome** woman, has come to Crystal Palace this weekend in order to challenge her youthful rival once more.
3	ANF 49	Gaby, a **handsome** woman of 30, was a very experienced and alluring person, madly in love with Modi.
4	ANF 1014	Nevertheless, she was a **handsome** woman and very competent and Modi persuaded her to pose for him nude.
5	C8D 1000	A **handsome** woman, with a streak of sensuality.
6	C8T 28	He saw a tall, **handsome** woman dressed with careful and expensive informality in a black cashmere sweater with a silk scarf at the throat and fawn trousers.
7	CA6 915	'A very **handsome** woman with a dark skin, West Indian blood, I suspect.
8	CE5 1359	Cowley was met at the front door by an elderly, but still **handsome** woman, dressed in trouser suit and a very westernised poncho.
9	EDJ 1073	She was — is — what people call a **handsome** woman, a phrase which has always struck me as a bit patronising.
10	FPN 865	She is a **handsome** woman, intelligent, articulate and faithful to inflexible socialist principles, which I must confess I have never shared.

Figure 7.12:   The phrase *handsome woman* in the BNC (cropped view)

Nevertheless, it is also necessary to alert readers to some of the limitations of these features. When we compiled a frequency breakdown of nouns that immediately followed *pretty*, we in fact missed quite a few relevant instances. As a case in point, consider sentences (1) to (3):

(1) She is young and *pretty*, and filters her fury through irresistible humour. (A06: 812)

(2) Nevertheless he seemed willing enough to accompany the Finnish detective in the dangerous climb down over the tumbling rocks to where his cousin and his cousin's *pretty*, peroxided fiancée lay. (A0D: 257)

(3) 'Sarah's *pretty*,' said her mother, awarding first prize to her sister. (A0L: 248)

In (1) and (3) *pretty* is used as a predicative adjective, i.e. it is found inside the verb phrase and therefore does not function as a premodifier of the noun. Instead, the noun phrase it belongs to is found in the preceding context (i.e. *she* and *Susan*, respectively). In contrast, *pretty* in (2) is certainly a premodifier, but it is not immediately adjacent to the noun it modifies (*fiancée*) because of the comma—which counts as a token (cf. 3.5.3)—and the second premodifier (*per-oxided*). In order to capture the noun in sentence (2) for the type of statistics presented in the FREQUENCY BREAKDOWN feature, we would therefore have to change the sort position to the third item following *pretty*. This can easily be done via the leftmost drop-down menu on top of the sorted query result (labeled "Sort on:"): change this to "3 Right" and click [Submit]. However, this is hardly an overall improvement: even though this will now retrieve relevant instances like (2) that were previously omitted, it will also select a large number of cases where *pretty* does not modify the noun (e.g. *there is a very **pretty** walk around **Bathford*** or *Mark's **pretty** good at **building**, actually*). Co-occurrence patterns are often quite variable, and a retrieval strategy that relies on fixed distances between items will almost always miss some relevant cases. In Chapter 8, we will introduce the COLLOCATION feature of *BNCweb*, which represents a partial solution to the problem of retrieving constructions of variable form.

> **Tip:**
> Note that you can apply the various features of *BNCweb* iteratively, i.e. it is possible first to use SORT to re-arrange your Query result, then to compile a FREQUENCY BREAKDOWN, and in turn to establish the distribution of—for example—the most frequent item in the list via the DISTRIBUTION feature. As you become more proficient in using *BNCweb*, you will increasingly see ways of combining the different functions of the program in order to home in on specific aspects of the linguistic item you are investigating.

7.3.3   Sorting on the query hit

Apart from sorting on any position between "5 Left" and "5 Right", you also have the option of alphabetically re-ordering the concordance lines on the basis of the query item itself (i.e. the node position). For single words like *pretty* or *handsome*, this is not a meaningful action, as every hit has exactly the same form. However, if your query is made up of any wildcards in the Simple Query Syntax (cf. 6.4), or if your query involved part-of-speech tags (or sequences of these tags) rather than lexical items (cf. 6.7), it may be useful to have the different matched words or phrases sorted alphabetically.

For example, if your query was for *pretty* followed by any noun (i.e. `pretty  _{N}`), sorting on the node position will result in a concordance where all the different noun forms are grouped together in alphabetical order. It is then possible to compile a frequency breakdown of the items in the sorted position—in this case, a frequency breakdown of all the items matched by your query. In fact, because compiling such a frequency breakdown will often be the main reason for sorting a query result, *BNCweb* offers a convenient shortcut: simply select FREQUENCY BREAKDOWN in the post-query options of a Query result page and press [Go!] and you are immediately presented with the corresponding frequency table (i.e. you need not do a SORT first).

7.4   Exercises

1. *Looking at "bad language"*. You may have heard or read complaints from people who are concerned at the amount of swearing nowadays used by an apparently large proportion of the population. Let's use corpus data—and the DISTRIBUTION feature of *BNCweb*—to test the extent to which "bad language" is indeed a prominent characteristic of Present-day English. Apart from general frequencies, we are also particularly interested in finding out who swears, and in what contexts.

   a) First, concentrate on a number of well-known four-letter words to get a general impression of some typical ways of swearing. Look at both spoken and written language, and use the option to cross-tabulate categories (e.g. "Speaker sex" and "Speaker age") to uncover some of the more fine-grained details of what type of speakers are the most prolific swearers. Also, use the "File frequency extremes" and "Speaker frequency extremes" options to determine the "worst" swearers in the corpus.

   In answering this question, you might also want to distinguish between different grammatical functions of four-letter words. For example, some of these words can be used either as intensifiers, as exclamatives, or with a literal reference. Also, when you look at your data, remember to take into account that the precision of your searches may not be 100%, i.e. you may also be retrieving instances of your search items that are not used for the purpose of swearing.

   b) Now think about the recall of your procedure: what percentage of all ways of swearing have you been able to cover with your four-letter words? How can you improve recall? You might for example also want to consider milder forms of swearing or cursing—e.g. by way of euphemisms (e.g. *effing, darn, heck*). Is it possible to retrieve all instances of swearing in the corpus? If not, why is this the case?

c) As an additional point of interest—and you won't need the DISTRIBUTION feature for this—have a closer look at some swearwords that have a clear gender reference. For example, a *bitch* is a 'female dog', and according to dictionaries, the word is used as a derogatory reference to a woman. But how consistent is this link with gender? Can you find instances in the corpus where *bitch* refers to a man? Try a few other swearwords and determine the proportion of instances where the stereotypical gender-link is not upheld.

2. *Verb-complementation of* try. The verb *try* is a transitive verb—i.e. it requires a complement which functions as an object. There are various ways in which this complement can be realized. For example, it can be a noun phrase (e.g. *Try **this trick*** or *She tried **another dealer***), but the object can also take the form of a *to*-infinitive clause (*e.g. I try **to explain that*** or *You should try **to read as much as you can***). An interesting variant of the clausal complementation type is the "*try and* + verb"-construction: *She decided to try **and visit him***. This construction is often referred to as "pseudo-coordination" in grammars (see for example Quirk et al. 1985: 978-9) and is said to be more informal and conversational than the "*try to*"-construction. In this exercise, we'll first look at the complementation patterns of *try* as a whole and then investigate the variation between *try to* and *try and* + verb a little further. For a detailed discussion of this variation (and a comparison between British and American English use) see Hommerberg & Tottie (2007).

a) Do a search of the lemma TRY (i.e. use the query term `{try/V}`) over the whole BNC. Look at the first few pages of the Query result (in random order) and try to—or try and—establish rough proportions of the various complementation patterns of *try*.

b) Next use the SORT feature to sort the concordance by "1 Right" and compile a frequency breakdown for this position. Does the result confirm the proportions you have established in Step a)? If not, this may have to do with the number of instances you have looked at. You might want to re-visit the section on statistical significance in 5.6 to refresh your memory of the issues involved.

c) Now think about the variation between *try to* and *try and* + verb: is the alternation between these two forms possible with all word-forms of *try*? If not, adjust your query accordingly.

d) Finally, use the DISTRIBUTION feature to establish whether there indeed is a difference in use between the two constructions in spoken and written language. To arrive at a more detailed picture of this difference you could also look at the distribution over spoken and written genres.

8 Automated analyses of concordance lines—Part II: Collocations

8.1 Outline

This is the second of two chapters dealing with the automated post-query options available in *BNCweb*. We will cover the following issues:

- A definition of the term "collocation" and the concept of "collocational strength"
- The steps involved in discovering collocations with *BNCweb* (both in the whole corpus and in sub-sections of the BNC)
- An overview and comparison of different measurements of collocational strength

8.2 Introduction

The term COLLOCATION refers to the habitual co-occurrence of two (or more) words. As a typical example, consider *express* and *opinion*. In principle, there is no reason why *express an opinion* should be more acceptable than *say an opinion*—in both cases, we have a verb that has to do with speaking, and *express* and *say* are certainly closely related concepts. Yet only the combination *express (an) opinion* is found in general language use, while *say* (or *tell*) *an opinion* sounds unidiomatic—that is, *say* and *tell* do not collocate well with *opinion;* in other words, they are not (strong) collocates of *opinion.*

But collocations are not simply a matter of distinguishing between idiomatically appropriate and inappropriate expressions. There can be a variety of other kinds of semantic preference. As Stubbs (1995: 25) says, "[...] it is becoming increasingly well documented that words may habitually collocate with other words from a definable semantic set." For example, the verb *commit* commonly occurs with negative concepts such as *offence, crime, murder, breach* and *adultery.* In contrast, it would be odd—or perhaps an ironic use—if somebody were to be described as *committing good works.* This type of collocational preference is widely referred to as "semantic prosody" (Louw 1993, see also Sinclair 1991). Such collocational tendencies can arguably be seen as part of the meaning of a word. A famous example is that of the verb CAUSE. Although in principle there is no reason why one should not speak of something (or somebody) causing *happiness* or *bliss,* in practice CAUSE shows an overwhelming tendency to co-occur with events of a negative or unfortunate nature (e.g. *problems, injury* or *death*). Linguists such as Sinclair, Louw and Stubbs contend that the notion of negativity is thus a major part of the meaning of the verb CAUSE itself.

One consequence of this line of argument is that the study of collocations can reveal subtle differences in meaning between two or more words that are said to be (near) synonyms. For example, one key difference between CAUSE and BRING ABOUT lies in the fact that the latter occurs with both positive and negative as well as neutral events (e.g. *change, downfall, shift* and *peace*).

Mastering the collocational tendencies of English can be a major hurdle for non-native speakers. Even advanced learners who rarely produce grammatical errors will often use combinations that are not fully idiomatic. A big problem facing language teachers and materials developers, meanwhile, is that while native speakers normally do not have any trouble choosing the "right" combinations, they nevertheless often find it difficult to give a detailed listing of all the most common collocates of a word, or rank them in order of frequency and importance for teaching to learners of the language. For example, although native speakers may think of *express* as a common collocate of *opinion*, they will typically not be able to indicate the full range of verbal collocates, nor tell you which ones are the most common. (The answer is: *express, give, voice, state, offer, deliver,* etc.; and, with different meanings, also *form, influence, confirm, ask, revise, change,* etc.) This is where corpus data—and the COLLOCATION feature of *BNCweb*—can provide invaluable input.

8.3   Understanding the concept of collocational strength

In Chapter 7, you learned how to discover patterns of co-occurrence with the SORT and FREQUENCY BREAKDOWN features. As a quick revision exercise, let's do a search of the adjective *dangerous* and use these two *BNCweb* functions to list the most common words that occur immediately to the right. You will find that the most frequent noun in this position is *thing* (51 instances), followed by *situation* (47 instances) *substances* and *place* (both 38 instances). However, these figures are just raw frequencies, and it is important to interpret them with caution. Does this frequency ranking really indicate that the connection between *dangerous* and *thing* is stronger than the one between *dangerous* and *situation*, or between *dangerous* and *substances*? If you have compiled a FREQUENCY BREAKDOWN for all words following *dangerous* rather than just nouns, you will notice that, for example, *dangerous and* (262 instances) and *dangerous in* (72 instances) are even more frequent than *dangerous thing*. Does this mean that *in* is more strongly collocated with *dangerous* than *thing*?

If you think about these questions for a moment, you will certainly realize that you need to take into account the fact that *in* is a much more frequent word than *thing*. For this reason alone, you would *expect* it to occur more often after

dangerous—or indeed after any other adjective. You might have used the following reasoning to come to this conclusion: imagine that the words in the BNC
were all shuffled randomly. How often would you expect to see the combination
dangerous thing in this jumble of words? And how often would you expect to
see *dangerous and, dangerous in* and *dangerous substances*? Clearly, it partly
depends on the frequencies of occurrence of the collocates themselves: *thing* has
33,874 instances in the BNC, while *substances* occurs only 1,329 times; the
words *in* (1,937,819 instances) and *and* (2,616,708 instances) are much more
frequent, and therefore logically have more opportunities to co-occur with *dangerous*.

It is possible to work out the precise *expected frequencies* of these collocates
mathematically, i.e. to calculate how often you would expect to find each combination in a randomly shuffled corpus. For instance, *dangerous thing* in the 97-
million-word BNC has an expected frequency of less than 2 occurrences (1.69,
to be precise), and *dangerous in* is expected to occur 97 times. While *in* is one
of the most frequent collocates of *dangerous,* with 72 observed instances, there
are in fact *fewer* co-occurrences than expected. There is nothing in the BNC to
suggest a habitual collocation of the two words, and the *observed (co-
occurrence) frequency* can be attributed to chance combinations. For *thing,* on
the other hand, we have observed 30 times as many instances as expected (51
vs. 1.69), so it appears to be strongly connected to *dangerous.* We can apply the
same reasoning to the word *substances*: it co-occurs with *dangerous* almost as
often as *thing,* but its individual frequency is much lower (1,329 vs. 33,874). We
might therefore conclude that *substances* is, in a sense, a more common or
"typical" collocate of *dangerous* than *thing.*

The mathematical result for the expected frequency of *dangerous substances*
may be surprising at first sight: 0.07 co-occurrences in the corpus. In other
words, you would not expect to see the combination *dangerous substances* at all
in a randomly shuffled version of the BNC. This situation is quite common,
though, and all but combinations of very frequent words will have expected frequencies less than one (for instance, that of *dangerous liaisons* is less than 0.01).
You can still use such extremely low expected frequencies as a reference point
for interpreting the observed number of co-occurrences: *dangerous substances* is
more than 500 times as frequent as expected (38 vs. 0.07), making it an even
stronger collocation than *dangerous thing.*

In order to measure collocational strength in a principled and reliable way,
linguists and statisticians have developed a whole range of formulae that are all
based on the observed and expected co-occurrence frequencies of words and
word pairs. When you use the COLLOCATION feature of *BNCweb*, a selection of
these so-called "(statistical) association measures" is available for you to choose
from. Furthermore, *BNCweb*'s collocation facility allows you to search for collocates that are not necessarily adjacent to the query item (rather than concen-

trating on neighboring words exclusively, as in our example above). We will now describe the steps in using the COLLOCATION feature, and then return to the issue of how to choose an appropriate association measure for your study.

When *BNCweb* identifies the collocations of a query result, it builds an internal database containing all tokens—i.e. both lexical items and punctuation markers—that are found in the surrounding context of each hit. Once this database has finished compiling, *BNCweb* displays a list of collocates in a table. This list is ranked by the strength of association between the collocate and the NODE, i.e. the word or phrase that was matched by your query. A number of options are then available to manipulate this output according to the task at hand. To illustrate the functionality of the COLLOCATION feature, we will now have a closer look at *dangerous* and its collocates.

8.4   Steps in collocation analysis

In order to find the collocates of *dangerous*, follow these steps:

1. Perform a Simple query for `dangerous`. This will retrieve 5,621 hits from the whole BNC.

2. In the post-query options menu, select "Collocations..." and press [Go!]. This will display a page with the title "BNC collocation settings" (see Figure 8.1). The available options are as follows:

   - **Calculate over sentence boundaries:** If set to "yes", the calculation will include collocations which cut across sentence boundaries (more precisely: s-unit boundaries). In spoken data, this may include items that were uttered by different speakers. Let's accept the default option for this setting, which is "no".

   - **Include lemma information:** If set to "yes", it is possible to group collocations by lemma. However, it is worth noting that grouping different wordforms under one lemma is not always desirable. Many idiomatic phrases (e.g. *He was in stitches* = 'he was laughing'; or *He kicked the bucket* = 'He died') tend to take only one particular word form (cf. **He was in a stitch* or **He kicks the bucket*). Since the inclusion of lemma information considerably increases the disk space used, the default option for this setting is "no". For our analysis of *dangerous*, however, we will change this to "yes".

   - **Maximum window span:** This setting determines the size of the immediate context that is stored by *BNCweb*. Accept the default option of "5", which means that the five items (i.e. words or punctuation marks) to the left and right of the node word *dangerous* will be included in the internal database that is used to generate the collocates. Once the database has finished compiling, any span within this maximum window size can be used as basis for the calculation of collocational strength.

BNC Collocation Settings

Calculate over sentence boundaries:	no ⬦
Include lemma information:	no ✓ yes
Maximum window span:	+/- 5 ⬦

Submit

Figure 8.1:   BNC collocation settings

3. After making the desired adjustments to the collocation settings, press [Submit]. Depending on your browser, *BNCweb* will then either give you feedback about its progress in compiling the collocation database or after a short wait switch to the result page. Even with fairly large query results (e.g. 50,000 or more hits), this process is usually fast.

The result of the collocation analysis is shown in Figure 8.2. The screenshot here is cropped, and shows only the first 10 collocates. The full table in your web browser will display the first 50 collocates of *dangerous*, along with links at the bottom of the screen for paging through the remaining collocates. As the table shows, *potentially* was identified as the strongest collocate of *dangerous*. In the third column, we see that *potentially* occurs a total of 2,422 times in the whole BNC. The expected frequency of the node-collocate pair is shown in the fourth column: if the words in the BNC were randomly shuffled, the two words *dangerous* and *potentially* would not be expected to co-occur even a single time (0.667). In the fifth column, however, we see that *potentially* in fact occurs 154 times in close proximity to *dangerous*. As shown in the sixth column, these 154 instances are distributed over 130 different files, which suggests that we are not dealing with a collocation that is restricted to very specific topic matter. The rightmost column, finally, displays the statistical association score according to which the collocates are ranked. By default, the log-likelihood method is used to compute the scores, but individual users can choose their own default setting (see Chapter 13). For the collocate *potentially*, the log-likelihood score is 1379.9313. Further details on the interpretation of association scores and the different statistical methods available in *BNCweb* are given below (see Section 8.5).

Collocation parameters:

Information:	collocations		Statistics:	Log–likelihood
Collocation window span:	3 Left – 3 Right		Basis:	whole BNC
Freq(node, collocate) at least:	5		Freq(collocate) at least:	5
Filter results by:	Specific collocate:		and/or tag: no restrictions	Submit changed parameters Go!

There are 6956 different types in your collocation database for "[word = "dangerous" %c]". (Your query "dangerous" returned 5621 hits in 1807 different texts)

No.	Word	Total No. in whole BNC	Expected collocate frequency	Observed collocate frequency	In No. of texts	Log-likelihood value
1	potentially	2,422	0.667	154	130	1379.9313
2	most	97,999	27.006	268	202	750.5818
3	very	119,400	32.903	286	218	733.3336
4	be	650,082	179.143	619	470	661.9379
5	more	209,333	57.686	322	257	581.3623
6	is	990,281	272.891	753	515	576.1624
7	too	66,855	18.423	191	153	549.6281
8	a	2,164,238	596.398	1148	748	410.6212
9	driving	6,308	1.738	71	40	389.1837
10	it	1,054,279	290.527	680	494	382.7155

Figure 8.2:   Result of a collocation analysis of *dangerous*

The second and third strongest collocates of *dangerous* are *most* and *very*. Notice that with 97,999 and 119,400 instances, respectively, both words are far more frequent in the corpus than *potentially*, and they also collocate more often with *dangerous*. However, their log-likelihood values are considerably lower— 750 and 733, respectively. This is because unlike ranking by raw frequencies of co-occurrence, the log-likelihood calculation takes into consideration the expected frequency of each combination, based on the overall frequencies of node and collocate.

Above the table of collocates, in a "Collocation parameters" panel, several options are displayed that allow further manipulation of the analysis. In our case, for example, we are particularly interested in **noun** collocates that **follow** *dangerous* rather than precede it; both of these conditions can easily be set with the help of parameters provided.

We will first outline the full set of options and then illustrate how these can effect the collocation analysis of *dangerous*.

- **Information:** There are three options here: "collocations", "collocations on POS-tags" and "collocations on lemma". The first of these is the default setting, while the third option is only displayed if the user has selected to include lemma information in the "BNC collocation settings" page. Choosing "collocations on POS-tags" returns a list of part-of-speech tags as collocates. If "collocations on lemma" is selected, the list of collocates will be lemmas—i.e. the combination of headword and simplified tag (cf. 3.5.2)—instead of word forms.

- **Statistics:** *BNCweb* currently offers a total of six statistical association measures for calculating collocational strength: "Mutual information", "MI3", "Z-score", "T-score", "Log-likelihood" and "Dice coefficient". In addition, users can also choose to rank collocates by raw frequency. A detailed description of these measures and their mathematical background is far beyond the scope of this book. Nevertheless, it is certainly important to understand at least some of their characteristics in order to select a suitable measure and interpret results correctly, so we give a brief overview in Section 8.5 below. Readers are also strongly encouraged to consult the recommended readings listed at the end of this chapter.

- **Collocation window span:** This allows users to control the size of the context used in the collocation analysis. The default window size is "3 Left" to "3 Right", i.e. the three items before the node (both lexical items and punctuation marks) and the three items following the node. The maximal window size available will depend on the choice made previously on the "BNC collocation settings" page. It is possible to select asymmetrical window sizes, i.e. it is not necessary to choose the same number of items on both sides of the node. You can also select only the left or only the right collocates: by selecting e.g. a window of "1 Right" to "3 Right", we can restrict collocates to items that follow the query item.

- **Basis:** This option refers to the internal frequency lists used by *BNCweb* to determine the frequencies of collocates in the appropriate (sub-)corpus. If the search was conducted without any restrictions, "Whole BNC" is the default. If the search was run over the complete written or spoken component, "written texts only" or "spoken texts only", respectively, will automatically be selected. If the search was conducted over a different subsection of the corpus—either via metatextual restrictions or via a user-defined subcorpus (see Chapter 10)—*BNCweb* will make use of a custom-made frequency list and display "subcorpus" in the drop-down menu.

- **Freq(node, collocate) at least:** This option determines how often the node and the collocate have to co-occur in order to be included in the list of collocates. The default value is "5".

- **Freq(collocate) at least:** This option determines how frequent the collocate has to be in the relevant (sub-)corpus in order to be included in the collocations table. The default value is "5".

In addition to these general options, collocates can be filtered in two ways:

- By entering a specific collocate in the text box. This can be useful for finding association values for collocates that do not appear in the top 50 list.

- By selecting a part-of-speech tag or pre-defined set of tags. For example, the display of collocates can be restricted to only include nouns.

The two filtering options can be combined: i.e. it is possible for example to enter the specific collocate *driving* and restrict it to instances where it has been tagged as a singular noun (NN1).

After making the desired changes in the parameters, select "Submit changed parameters" and press [Go!].

Collocation parameters:

Information:	collocations		Statistics:	Log-likelihood
Collocation window span:	1 Right - 3 Right		Basis:	whole BNC
Freq(node, collocate) at least:	5		Freq(collocate) at least:	5
Filter results by:	Specific collocate:		and/or tag: any noun	Submit changed parameters Go!

There are 6956 different types in your collocation database for "[word = "dangerous" %c]". (Your query "dangerous" returned 5621 hits in 1807 different texts)

No.	Word	Total No. in whole BNC	Expected collocate frequency	Observed collocate frequency	In No. of texts	Log-likelihood value
1	substances	1,329	0.173	41	32	368.0714
2	precedent	857	0.112	28	28	254.5931
3	situation	15,705	2.045	51	45	230.4708
4	dogs	4,332	0.564	34	20	212.1815
5	driving	1,343	0.175	26	21	208.9812
6	situations	3,839	0.500	28	21	170.6745
7	thing	33,871	4.411	53	49	166.59
8	liaisons	71	0.009	13	11	165.0278
9	drugs	5,273	0.687	29	21	160.6837
10	chemicals	2,159	0.281	19	18	122.8527

Figure 8.3:   The strongest noun collocates of *dangerous* within the window "1 Right" to "3 Right"

Figure 8.3 displays the modified list of collocates of *dangerous* if only nouns in positions "1 Right" to "3 Right" are considered (only the 10 strongest collocates are shown here). To save the complete collocation table to your hard disk, choose "Download all results" from the drop-down menu at the bottom right of the Collocation parameters and then press [Go!].

If you refer back to the raw frequency ranking provided by the SORT feature, considerable differences emerge. First of all, the frequencies reported for node–

collocate combinations do not fully match the results we got earlier by sorting one position to the right of *dangerous*: while there were 38 instances of *substances* before, we now have 41. One reason, of course, is that the collocation results here capture a range (window span) of positions (here, the following three words) rather than being restricted to a single slot. More importantly, however, the ranking shown in Figure 8.3 is quite different too. Although *thing* co-occurs 53 times with *dangerous*, it is only ranked seventh with respect to its collocational strength. On the other hand, *substances*, which was ranked third in terms of absolute frequencies, now appears in first position. And *precedent*, which only collocates 28 times with *dangerous* is found in second position.

If you enter a specific collocate in the collocation parameters, a different page will be displayed. For example, enter *mind* and press [Go!]. As shown in Figure 8.4, this will produce a table with collocability values for the collocation "*dangerous* + *mind*", using all seven association measures, based on the window span selected. The log-likelihood value, for example, is very low (0.6011), suggesting that "*dangerous* + *mind*" is not a strong collocation in the BNC. In fact, *dangerous* and *mind* only co-occur a total of four times in the corpus. The lower part of the page consists of a table which displays the distribution of *mind* for each position within the selected window span. The information is given both in raw frequencies and in percentages.[1]

Collocation information for the node "[word = "dangerous" %c]" and "mind" with tag restriction *any noun* (20,296 occurrences in whole BNC)			
Type of Statistics	**Value** (for window span 1 to 3)		
Mutual information	0.5978		
MI3	4.5978		
Z-score	0.5271		
T-score	0.6784		
Log-likelihood	0.6011		
Dice coefficient	0.0003		
Within the window 1 to 3, *mind* with tag restriction *any noun* occurs 4 times in 4 different files (expected frequency: 2.643)			
Distance	**No. of Occurrences**	**In No. of Files**	**Percent**
1	2	2	*50%*
2	0	0	*0%*
3	2	2	*50%*
Total	**4**		*100%*

Figure 8.4:   Detailed information for the collocation *dangerous* and *mind*

---

1   The same type of information is also displayed if you click on the links in the second column of the collocation table (cf. Figure 8.3). In this way, it is easy to determine the distribution of a collocate in the different positions of the chosen window span.

As in the case of the DISTRIBUTION feature, the statistics provided by the COL-LOCATION feature of *BNCweb* are only one side of the coin. Subtle shades of meaning—e.g. straightforward vs. ironic uses of a collocation—may only emerge when the larger context of the collocation is consulted. To facilitate such detailed or manual investigations, the collocation tables always contain links to the corresponding concordance lines. For example, to display a concordance of the 41 collocations of *dangerous* and *substances*, click on the relevant link in the fifth column of the table ("Observed collocate frequency") displayed in Figure 8.3. As shown in Figure 8.5, the collocate *substances* is conveniently high-lighted in boldface in the concordance lines.

A similar link to the display of concordance lines is also available from the detailed overview for a single collocate (cf. Figure 8.4). In this case, however, clicking on any of the links in the first column will only display concordance lines that correspond to collocates found in that particular position in the win-dow span. Again, the relevant collocate is highlighted in boldface.

Your query "dangerous" returned 5621 hits in 1807 different texts (98,313,429 words [4,048 texts]; frequency: 57.17 instances per million words), collocating with *substances* with tag restriction *any noun* (41 hits)		
I< << >> >I (Show Page) 1 (Show KWIC View) (Show in random order) New Query [≑] (Go!)		
No	**Filename**	**Hits 1 to 41 Page 1 / 1**
1	A1T 233	Because Britain has been covered, during the last few weeks, with record levels of toxic and other <u>dangerous</u> **substances**.
2	A3B 14	Yet the applied energy, constant movement of people, heavy loads and handling of what are sometimes the most <u>dangerous</u> **substances** imaginable make many industrial environments intrinsically dangerous.
3	A8X 409	'Policing the most indentified <u>dangerous</u> **substances** would no longer be independent of government control — they will be controlled by government,' he said.
4	A9F 146	Microwave cooking creates potentially <u>dangerous</u> **substances** in baby milk which may damage the brain, liver and kidneys, doctors said.
5	A9F 522	MICROWAVE cooking creates potentially <u>dangerous</u> **substances** in baby milk which may damage the brain, liver and kidneys, doctors said yesterday.
6	AAC 271	The conditions are designed to prevent or minimise the release of the most <u>dangerous</u> polluting **substances**.
7	ALW 747	The report of a five-year study into the risks of transporting <u>dangerous</u> **substances** by rail and road has been published by the Health and Safety Commission (HSC).

Figure 8.5:   A concordance of the collocation *dangerous* and *substances*

Another important reason for looking at concordance lines for individual collo-cations is that it can also reveal whether the node and the collocate actually "be-long together", so to speak. As a case in point, consider the two instances of *dangerous* and *mind* in which the collocate *mind* is found in position "3 Right", i.e. with two intervening items—they are shown in (1) and (2). In contrast, (3) is one of the two sentences where *dangerous* and *mind* are immediately adjacent.

(1) When she arrived in Paris in May 1914, she was in a **dangerous** *frame of*
     mind, footloose, resentful and spoiling for adventure. (ANF: 147)

(2) British seamen in the US deserted in droves, alarming the new British gov-
     ernment and bringing about a revived dialogue [...] on the **dangerous** *state*
     of **mind** of seamen who were incensed by the conviction that they were
     constantly subject to neglect, mishandling and coercion. (FES: 1361)

(3) According to the Mail on Sunday, John Major is telling friends that Blair is
     'the most formidable debater and has the quickest and most **dangerous**
     mind' on the Opposition benches. (K52: 4043)

In (1) and (2), *dangerous* does not premodify *mind*. Instead, the noun collocates
of *dangerous* are *frame* and *state*, respectively, and the meaning conveyed is
very different from the *dangerous mind* in (3). Since the calculation of collocational strength is purely based on positional criteria—i.e. is the item within the
window span or not?—it cannot take structural characteristics and grammatical
boundaries into consideration. The larger the window span is, the greater is the
likelihood of structurally different combinations being included in the analysis.
Conversely, if a smaller window span is chosen, a proportion of relevant collocates might be missed. A closer look at the context of individual collocations
will thus help in evaluating the reliability of your findings.

Task:
Have a look at some words from the same semantic field as *danger-*
ous: for example *unsafe, hazardous, risky* and *perilous*. How close in
meaning are they to each other? In other words, how synonymous are
they? In what contexts can they be used interchangeably? As suggested in 8.2, differences in collocates are likely to reflect subtle differences in meaning (e.g. differences in connotations). Investigate the
level of synonymy of these adjectives using the COLLOCATION feature,
again restricting your analysis to noun collocations within the window
from "1 Right" to "3 Right".

8.5   Which association measure should I use?

One of the questions you might now have is: which of the different association
measures in *BNCweb* is the "best" one? Unfortunately, there is no simple answer
to this question. All of the formulae have their strengths and drawbacks, and different linguistic questions may call for different measures of collocational
strength. In this section, we outline the most important characteristics of each

measure so that you can make an informed choice. In general, you should ideally never rely on a single association measure, but consider rankings for two or
three different measures that highlight different aspects of collocability.

What is it that makes some of the words that co-occur with the node habitual
and linguistically relevant collocates? If you think back to our initial example
for the node *dangerous*, you will find three quantitative properties that might intuitively play a role in defining collocational strength:

1. The **frequency** of co-occurrence: Frequent combinations will sound familiar and plausible when you read them (this has been demonstrated by
   the psycholinguistic experiments of Lapata, McDonald and Keller 1999),
   but they are typically not the most characteristic collocates of the node
   word that come to mind, especially if the "expected co-occurrence frequency" of the combination is also relatively high.

2. The **significance** of co-occurrence: A pair of words can only be considered a potentially meaningful collocation if the combination is statistically
   significant, i.e. if the words co-occur more often than would be expected
   in a randomly shuffled corpus (or, in statistical terms, if their "observed
   frequency" is higher than their "expected frequency"). Random variation
   also needs to be taken into account, especially for low expected frequencies (cf. the remarks on statistical tests in Chapter 5): a single co-
   occurrence of a word pair (observed frequency = 1) that has an expected
   frequency of 0.1 is clearly not sufficient to establish the words as a habitual collocation, even though they co-occur ten times as often as expected,
   because any single event could be a mere coincidence. Statistical measures can be used to determine whether the available evidence is mathematically significant in such cases.

3. Using a term from mathematical statistics, **effect size**—defined here as the
   ratio between observed and expected frequency—determines how "characteristic" a collocate is for the node. A frequent combination such as
   "*dangerous* + *and*" (1,685 co-occurrences within a window of 3 words)
   can be highly significant even though it is not much more frequent than
   expected (about 900 co-occurrences). In fact, *and* figures prominently in
   the list of collocates for *dangerous* ranked by the log-likelihood measure.
   It is intuitively clear that such combinations are not very characteristic for
   the node because effect size is relatively small: the most typical collocates
   will co-occur ten or fifty times as often as expected.

Some collocates satisfy all three criteria and form very strong collocations: they
co-occur frequently, significantly more often than expected, and their effect size
is large. Likewise, some words do not meet any of the conditions: their observed

co-occurrence frequency is very low, while their expected frequency is much higher.

Unfortunately, there are usually rather few such clear-cut cases on which all measures tend to agree. Most intuitively relevant collocates meet only two of the three criteria, and a key difference between association measures is how much weight they put on each condition. Some permissive measures might even rank words highly that satisfy only a single criterion (one example is the mutual information measure, as we shall see below).

We can now categorize the different association measures available in *BNCweb* with respect to the three criteria of collocational strength:

- A pure measure of **frequency** is the ranking by **co-occurrence frequency**. This is offered by *BNCweb* as an alternative to the other association measures which are statistically more complex.

- **Log-likelihood** is a measure of **significance**, based on a particular statistical hypothesis test.

- **Effect size** is characterized most clearly by **mutual information**, which is calculated from the ratio between observed and expected frequency.

- The remaining formulae can be seen as hybrid measures that do not focus on a single criterion: **T-score** is a hybrid between frequency and significance; **Z-score** is a hybrid between effect size and significance; both **MI3** and **Dice** balance frequency and effect size, but do so in diametrically opposed ways.[2]

Implementation note (for statistically minded experts only)

The association measures listed above are implemented in *BNCweb* as described by Evert (in press), using the observed and expected frequencies for surface co-occurrence. For computational reasons, an approximation has had to be used that does not take overlaps between collocational spans into account. It may therefore happen in very rare cases that a collocate is reported to have a higher co-occurrence frequency than its overall number of instances in the corpus. As long as the default frequency thresholds are applied, the effect of this on collocation lists generated by *BNCweb* will be negligible.

---

2   If you already know Z-score and T-score as measures of statistical significance from a statistics textbook, it may come as a surprised to see them described as "hybrid" measures here. When applied to co-occurrence data, these formulae give entirely different results from proper hypothesis tests, so they cannot be seen as significance measures in this context.

> There are two small modifications of the equations given for association measures in Evert (in press). For the Z-score measure, Yates' continuity correction has been applied to improve its accuracy for low-frequency data (cf. Evert in press, Section 5.2, where Yates' correction is described for the chi-squared measure only). The Dice measure has been modified in order to correct for different window sizes. Mathematically speaking, the modified equation computes the harmonic mean of the probability that an instance of the node co-occurs with the collocate (ignoring multiple instances in the same window) and the probability that an instance of the collocate co-occurs with the node.
>
> In all cases, one-sided versions of the measures were used so that word pairs with negative association (i.e. where the observed co-occurrence frequency is lower than expected) cannot achieve high scores. For log-likelihood, mutual information, Z-score and T-score, the corresponding association scores will be negative.

Especially for the description of hybrid measures, it is useful to distinguish between frequent collocates (for which the expected frequency is greater than 1, rare collocates (words with few occurrences in the BNC, resulting in an expected frequency far below 1) and intermediate collocates (words in an intermediate frequency range for which the expected frequency is close to 1 or slightly lower). Note that these adjectives refer to the "expected frequency" of node-collocate pairs (which depends on the overall frequency of the respective collocate as a separate word) rather than to high or low "observed co-occurrence frequency". We now turn to a brief discussion of each measure, illustrated with collocations for the node *dangerous*.

Ranking by **co-occurrence frequency** focuses solely on the frequency criterion, and typically lists very frequent function words and punctuation symbols as collocates. Most of these combinations—as shown in Figure 8.6—are not very significant, and some (e.g. "*dangerous + the*") co-occur even less often than expected in a randomly shuffled corpus. To that extent, this is only a rough and ready method for identifying linguistically meaningful collocates.

The **log-likelihood** measure, which is the default choice used by *BNCweb*, is a pure measure of significance. It will assign high scores neither to chance combinations involving very common words and punctuation symbols (despite their high co-occurrence frequency), nor to combinations involving very rare words that co-occur just once or twice (even though their expected frequency may be far less than 1). As Figure 8.7 illustrates, log-likelihood is still biased towards high-frequency collocations. This is not surprising: the more often two words co-occur in the corpus, the more evidence for a habitual collocation they provide and the more significant they become (given that observed frequency is higher than expected frequency). As a result, the combination "*dangerous + and*" with 1,264 co-occurrences can be found at rank 12, although it is not much more frequent than expected (about 900 co-occurrences). A rare or intermediate collocate, on the other hand, has to exceed the expected co-occurrence frequency by a large factor in order to achieve a high log-likelihood score.

Collocation parameters:

Information:	collocations	Statistics:	Rank by frequency
Collocation window span:	1 Right - 3 Right	Basis:	whole BNC
Freq(node, collocate) at least:	5	Freq(collocate) at least:	5
Filter results by:	Specific collocate:	and/or tag: no restrictions	Submit changed parameters Go!

There are 6956 different types in your collocation database for "[word = "dangerous" %c]". (Your query "dangerous" returned 5621 hits in 1807 different texts)

No.	Word	Total No. in whole BNC	Expected collocate frequency	Observed collocate frequency	In No. of texts
1	.	4,713,133	613.788	1582	894
2	,	5,014,383	653.019	957	650
3	to	2,593,729	337.779	567	437
4	and	2,616,708	340.772	522	402
5	the	6,041,234	786.745	494	389
6	;	751,071	97.811	338	247
7	in	1,937,819	252.361	297	245
8	of	3,042,376	396.206	256	222

Figure 8.6:   Collocates of *dangerous*: ranking by frequency

Collocation parameters:

Information:	collocations	Statistics:	Log-likelihood
Collocation window span:	1 Right - 3 Right	Basis:	whole BNC
Freq(node, collocate) at least:	5	Freq(collocate) at least:	5
Filter results by:	Specific collocate:	and/or tag: no restrictions	Submit changed parameters Go!

There are 6956 different types in your collocation database for "[word = "dangerous" %c]". (Your query "dangerous" returned 5621 hits in 1807 different texts)

No.	Word	Total No. in whole BNC	Expected collocate frequency	Observed collocate frequency	In No. of texts	Log-likelihood value
1	.	4,713,133	613.788	1582	894	1128.0789
2	driving	6,308	0.821	70	40	485.0519
3	substances	1,329	0.173	41	32	368.0714
4	;	751,071	97.811	338	247	361.9438
5	than	144,567	18.827	124	110	257.9702
6	precedent	857	0.112	28	28	254.5931
7	situation	15,705	2.045	51	45	230.4708
8	dogs	4,340	0.565	34	20	212.0576

Figure 8.7:   Collocates of *dangerous*: ranking by log-likelihood value

What this means is that the log-likelihood measure ignores the criterion of effect size, especially for frequent collocates. **Mutual information** (often abbreviated **MI**) very effectively filters out trivial (though statistically significant) co-occurrences with highly frequent words (such as *and* and *it*), but its inordinate emphasis on effect size leads to an often disastrous low-frequency bias. For an impressive demonstration of this bias, set the threshold on "Freq(node, collo-cate)" to 1—see Figure 8.8.

Collocation parameters:

Information:	collocations		Statistics:	Mutual information
Collocation window span:	1 Right – 3 Right		Basis:	whole BNC
Freq(node, collocate) at least:	1		Freq(collocate) at least:	5
Filter results by:	Specific collocate:		and/or tag: no restrictions	Submit changed parameters Go!

There are 6956 different types in your collocation database for "[word = "dangerous" %c]". (Your query "dangerous" returned 5621 hits in 1807 different texts)

No.	Word	Total No. in whole BNC	Expected collocate frequency	Observed collocate frequency	In No. of texts	Mutual information value
1	cherkasov	5	0.001	1	1	10.5847
2	everyfing	5	0.001	1	1	10.5847
3	icefalls	5	0.001	1	1	10.5847
4	knee-capping	5	0.001	1	1	10.5847
5	sorceries	5	0.001	1	1	10.5847
6	ta'kwanya	5	0.001	1	1	10.5847
7	water-horse	5	0.001	1	1	10.5847
8	liaisons	73	0.010	13	11	10.4173

Figure 8.8:   Collocates of *dangerous*: ranking by mutual information value ("Freq(node, collocate)" at least 1)

As you can see, nearly all of the highest-ranked collocates co-occur just once with *dangerous*; they are simply the rarest words allowed by the threshold on "Freq(collocate)". Mutual information is only useful in combination with high frequency thresholds—"Freq(node, collocate)" should be at least 10—and will then often highlight conspicuous and intuitively appealing collocations involv-ing words of intermediate frequency (cf. Figure 8.9).[3]

The three "pure" measures of frequency, significance and effect size that we have looked at so far have clear strengths in identifying a particular aspect of collocability, but they also have serious drawbacks. Therefore, you might some-

---

3   Many of these collocates are the "clear-cut cases" that achieve high scores from (nearly) all association measures. While this preference for intuitive and mostly undisputed collo-cations has made MI a very popular measure (especially among lexicographers), you should not be tempted to rely on MI alone. Otherwise, you might miss many important collocates that are less clear-cut but still habitual combinations and linguistically relevant.

times want to use hybrid measures, which give a more balanced view under certain circumstances.

Collocation parameters:

Information:	collocations ▣			Statistics:	Mutual information ▣
Collocation window span:	1 Right ▣ - 3 Right ▣			Basis:	whole BNC ▣
Freq(node, collocate) at least:	10 ▣			Freq(collocate) at least:	5 ▣
Filter results by:	Specific collocate:			and/or tag: no restrictions ▣	Submit changed parameters ▣ Go!

There are 6956 different types in your collocation database for "[word = "dangerous" %c]". (Your query "dangerous" returned 5621 hits in 1807 different texts)

No.	Word	Total No. in whole BNC	Expected collocate frequency	Observed collocate frequency	In No. of texts	Mutual information value
1	liaisons	73	0.010	13	11	10.4173
2	precedent	857	0.112	28	28	7.9709
3	substances	1,329	0.173	41	32	7.8881
4	junctions	610	0.079	10	5	6.9759
5	driving	6,308	0.821	70	40	6.413
6	chemicals	2,159	0.281	19	18	6.0784
7	dogs	4,340	0.565	34	20	5.9106
8	situations	3,839	0.500	28	21	5.8075

Figure 8.9:   Collocates of *dangerous*: ranking by Mutual Information value ("Freq(node, collocate)" and "Freq(node)" at least 10)

The **T-score** measure is an interesting alternative to explicit frequency thresholds. For rare collocates (up to an expected frequency of roughly one co-occurrence), it behaves like a simple frequency ranking. For frequent collocates, it behaves more like a significance measure and ensures that the observed co-occurrence frequency is higher than the expected frequency. The resulting lists of collocates are often very similar to those of log-likelihood, but show an even stronger high-frequency bias. This property may be desirable if the node itself is rare (i.e. occurs substantially less than 1,000 times).

Z-score is a kind of compromise measure that takes into account both effect size (for rare collocates) and significance (for frequent collocates).[4] It is a well-balanced measure that puts more weight on effect size than log-likelihood for frequent collocates. It focuses not so exclusively on effect size as MI for rare collocates. Indeed, Figure 8.10 shows some collocates from the MI list (with frequency thresholds) as well as some collocates from the log-likelihood list. If very rare collocates are allowed, the Z-score measure, like MI, suffers from a low-frequency bias that assigns high scores to single co-occurrences, but the default frequency threshold of 5 is usually sufficient to avoid this problem.

---

4   *BNCweb* applies Yates' correction to the Z-score measure to improve its scores, especially for low-frequency nodes.

Collocation parameters:					
Information:	collocations ⬍		Statistics:	Z-score ⬍	
Collocation window span:	1 Right ⬍ – 3 Right ⬍		Basis:	whole BNC ⬍	
Freq(node, collocate) at least:	5 ⬍		Freq(collocate) at least:	5 ⬍	
Filter results by:	Specific collocate:		and/or tag: no restrictions ⬍	Submit changed parameters ⬍	Go!

There are 6956 different types in your collocation database for "[word = "dangerous" %c]". (Your query "dangerous" returned 5621 hits in 1807 different texts)

No.	Word	Total No. in whole BNC	Expected collocate frequency	Observed collocate frequency	In No. of texts	Z-score value
1	liaisons	73	0.010	13	11	128.1044
2	substances	1,329	0.173	41	32	96.9345
3	precedent	857	0.112	28	28	81.9826
4	driving	6,308	0.821	70	40	75.7741
5	dogs	4,340	0.565	34	20	43.8083
6	.	4,713,133	613.788	1582	894	39.0604
7	situations	3,839	0.500	28	21	38.1857
8	generalise	117	0.015	5	3	36.3323
9	chemicals	2,159	0.281	19	18	34.359
10	situation	15,705	2.045	51	45	33.8815

Figure 8.10:   Collocates of *dangerous*: ranking by Z-score value

MI3 is a heuristic variation of the mutual information measure, intended to reduce its strong low-frequency bias, and has been successfully used for the automatic identification of terminological multiword expressions. Mathematically, it gives greater weighting to effect size for rare collocates (but less so than MI), while co-occurrence frequency is emphasized for frequent collocates. As a result, collocation lists generated by the MI3 measure often contain chance combinations involving very frequent words and punctuation symbols, even if they co-occur less often than expected. MI3 can be useful in combination with a part-of-speech filter, but even then tends to display a high-frequency bias and as such is not recommended for general collocation analyses.

Finally, the **Dice coefficient** is also a hybrid measure that takes into account both effect-size and frequency, but takes an opposite approach to MI3 and is much more extreme than other hybrid measures. It switches from a pure frequency measure (as is the case with the T-score and the frequency ranking methods) for rare collocates to a pure effect-size measure (like Mutual Information) for frequent collocates, and this switch is abrupt, with no in-between measures. One curious property of Dice is that the switching point does not depend on expected frequency (as it does for most other hybrid measures), but rather on the frequency of the node itself. The transition occurs roughly for collocates that are ten times more frequent than the node (depending on window size). Empirically, Dice rankings are often quite similar to those obtained by the Z-score method, but show neither a low-frequency nor a high-frequency bias (even without thresholds).

Collocation parameters:

Information:	collocations ⊟		Statistics:	Dice coefficient ⊟
Collocation window span:	1 Right ⊟ – 3 Right ⊟		Basis:	whole BNC ⊟
Freq(node, collocate) at least:	1 ⊟		Freq(collocate) at least:	1 ⊟
Filter results by:	Specific collocate: ▢		and/or tag: no restrictions ⊟	Submit changed parameters ⊟ Go!

There are 6956 different types in your collocation database for "[word = "dangerous" %c]". (Your query "dangerous" returned 5621 hits in 1807 different texts)

No.	Word	Total No. in whole BNC	Expected collocate frequency	Observed collocate frequency	In No. of texts	Dice coefficient value
1	substances	1,329	0.173	41	32	0.0118
2	driving	6,308	0.821	70	40	0.0116
3	precedent	857	0.112	28	28	0.0087
4	dogs	4,340	0.565	34	20	0.0068
5	situations	3,839	0.500	28	21	0.0059
6	drugs	5,285	0.688	29	21	0.0053
7	chemicals	2,159	0.281	19	18	0.0049
8	situation	15,705	2.045	51	45	0.0048

Figure 8.11:   Collocates of *dangerous*: ranking by modified Dice coefficient value ("Freq(node, collocate)" and "Freq(node)" at least 1)

To summarize, log-likelihood and mutual information are rather "extreme" measures. They each focus exclusively on a different aspect of collocational strength, which leads to problematic side-effects: a high-frequency bias for log-likelihood and a low-frequency bias for MI. Z-score strikes a balance between these two extremes. The Dice coefficient shows a similar balancing behavior, but switches more abruptly from an extreme focus on frequency to an equally extreme focus on effect size. As a result, it tends to prefer collocates in a relatively narrow frequency band close to the frequency of the node (cf. the screenshot above). Dice can be a useful measure for certain applications, but its rankings have to be interpreted carefully. MI3 and T-score have been included in *BNCweb* because they enjoy some popularity in the literature, but they cannot be recommended for general collocation studies.

It is important to keep in mind that there is no one "correct" or "best" association measure. You should always consider multiple rankings in your discussion of a collocation analysis—we recommend log-likelihood, MI, Z-score, and possibly Dice. Also keep an eye on the number of texts in which a collocation is found. One of the most prominent collocates of the noun (lemma) *bucket* is the noun (lemma) *record*, but all 42 co-occurrences stem from a single computer science text about the *bucket brigade algorithm*.

As a final warning, we urge you to resist the temptation to directly compare association scores for different types of phenomena. You will often want to make such comparisons, for example by asking whether *hot* is a stronger collocate of *tea* (log-likelihood value 434.2453) than *cold* is of *beer* (log-likelihood value 92.93). Similarly, you might want to compare collocations in different

sub-sections of the BNC ("Is *dangerous thing* more strongly collocated in spoken than in written English?"). Of course, these are perfectly valid questions.
Unfortunately, there is no common scale for association scores, and all measures
are sensitive to a wide range of influences, including random variation, corpus
size, frequency of the node and window size. The precise mathematics of these
effects are not yet well understood, and there are therefore no statistical tests
that will allow you to make a sound comparison of association scores.

8.6   Calculating collocations in sub-sections of the BNC

As we mentioned above, the calculation of accurate association measures involves the frequencies of both node and collocate in the corpus. For the whole
BNC as well as its written and spoken components, *BNCweb* comes with precompiled frequency lists. However, if your search is restricted in any other
way—be it via one of the metatextual restrictions or via a user-defined subcorpus (cf. Chapter 10)—the corresponding frequency lists (for both word forms
and lemma forms) first have to be compiled. If the amount of text searched is
small (i.e. less than 20 million words), this is done automatically without further
intervention from the user. A corresponding note will be displayed on the "BNC
collocation settings" page, and a slight delay in the presentation of the collocation table may be experienced. In the case of larger sections of the corpus, however, the compilation of frequency lists will take longer—depending on the
speed of the server, up to several minutes—and this action therefore first has to
be explicitly invoked by the user. In such cases, the "BNC collocation settings"
page will contain an additional row, offering the user a choice between existing
frequency lists and the option to compile accurate frequency information for the
sub-part of the BNC (see Figure 8.12). Once the frequency list has been compiled, it will remain available for further collocation analyses in the same sub-
part of the corpus through the cache system of *BNCweb* (cf. Chapter 13).

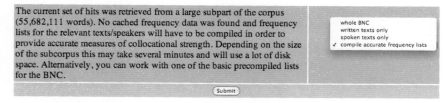

The current set of hits was retrieved from a large subpart of the corpus
(55,682,111 words). No cached frequency data was found and frequency
lists for the relevant texts/speakers will have to be compiled in order to
provide accurate measures of collocational strength. Depending on the size
of the subcorpus this may take several minutes and will use a lot of disk
space. Alternatively, you can work with one of the basic precompiled lists
for the BNC.

- whole BNC
- written texts only
- spoken texts only
- ✓ compile accurate frequency lists

Submit

Figure 8.12:   Additional row in the "BNC Collocation Settings" page after a
search in a large sub-part of the corpus

8.7   Further reading

Stubbs (1995) presents a very accessible description of MI and T-score, including a step-by-step explanation of the formulae used, as well as an introduction to the concept of "semantic prosody" (see 8.2 and the exercise below). If you want to find out more about collocations than this chapter could cover—including a more detailed description of the different ways in which collocational strength is calculated—Evert (in press) is a good place to start. Online information on association measures can also be found at http://www.collocations.de/AM/.

8.8   Exercises

1. *Collocations: semantic preference.* The verb *tumble* is roughly synonymous with *fall* and *collapse*, but can a collocation analysis help to tease these verbs apart? Are you aware of any differences in the range of things that can *tumble*, *fall* and *collapse*? Let's start by identifying the main grammatical subjects of tumble. We'll use the COLLOCATIONS function of *BNCweb*, and observe the effect of adjusting the various settings on the contents, length and order of the list of collocates.

   - First do a lemma search for *tumble*. After selecting "Collocations..." in the post-query options menu, select "yes" for the option to include lemma information on the "BNC Collocations settings" page.

   - On the "Collocation parameters" page, next to "Information" select "collocations on lemma" (which will allow us to collapse all kinds of noun, e.g. singular vs. plural, common vs. proper) and press [Go!].

   - Since we want to concentrate here on grammatical subjects of the respective verbs, we suggest adjusting the options so as to find nouns immediately in front of the query item: set "Collocation window span" to "1 Left – 1 Left", and change "and/or lemma class:" to "SUBST" (i.e. nouns). For the moment, set "Statistics" to "Log likelihood", accept all other default parameters and press [Go!] again.

   - Read through the list of collocates *BNCweb* returns:

     a) How many items are there in the list using these settings? Are you surprised by this finding?

     b) What kinds of things *tumble* – see if you can organize the items into semantic groups: e.g. *share*, *profit* and *price* could be classed as 'financial'.

     c) In what genres or text types do the various collocates occur? Take *hair*, for instance: is it restricted to a particular genre or genres?

To find out, click on the number of hits for *hair*, and do a distribution analysis. You could also check the dispersion value within a particular genre – for example, is *hair* + *tumble* restricted to one or two texts only, or quite evenly dispersed?

d) Now let's see the effect of altering the collocation settings. Change "Freq(node, collocate) at least:" to 3, and "Freq(collocate) at least:" to 3. Do the extra items you obtain fit within the semantic groupings you identified earlier? What additional semantic categories seem to be needed? As before, identify the genres and text types that each collocate of *tumble* is distributed across.

e) What effect on the contents and ordering of the collocate list is produced by changing "Statistics" from "Log likelihood" to "Mutual information"? "Z-score"? "T-score"?

f) Do you notice any preferences for singular vs. plural nouns in subject position? Tip: change the setting for "Information:" from "collocations on lemma" to "collocations" or "collocations on POS-tags".

g) Change "Collocation window span" to "5 Left – 1 Left". What additional entries now appear in the list? Are any of these entries not valid examples of subject + verb *tumble*, e.g. because either they or *tumble* itself has been assigned an incorrect POS-tag?

• Now repeat the above steps for *fall* and *collapse*. What can you now say about the semantic range of noun collocates for the respective verbs? Can you suggest any explanations for these differences?

• Consult one or two dictionaries to see if the differences you have found are described (or at least reflected in the selection of senses) in the entries for *tumble*, *fall* and *collapse*. What information do the dictionaries give that you hadn't found yourself?

2. *Collocations: semantic prosody.* Explore the semantic prosody of some pairs—or groups—of near-synonyms. (Again, it might be a useful exercise to try and use your intuition first to think up some possible answers before testing them through the *BNCweb* Collocation feature.) A famous example is the verb *cause* (see Stubbs 1995 and discussion here in Section 8.2) and synonyms such as *bring about* and *stimulate*. The following set of emphasizing adjectives is given to get you started:

absolute	*outright*	*pure*	*true*
complete	*perfect*	*real*	*utter*
entire	*positive*	*total*	

9 "Adding value" to a concordance using customized annotations

9.1 Outline

This chapter explores how to extend your analysis of a concordance by manually adding linguistic information to the hits of a concordance. It thus provides a contrast to the automated methods of data analysis highlighted in Chapter 7 and Chapter 8.

We first describe the motivation for manual annotation, and how it can be applied using *BNCweb*'s CATEGORIZE HITS function. We then explain how to obtain and present frequencies for data that have been categorized. Finally we describe two alternative methods of annotating concordance data using *BNCweb* in conjunction with external software:

- DOWNLOAD the current set of hits to an external database for further analysis
- reimport an analyzed database into *BNCweb*

9.2 Introduction: why annotate your concordance data?

In previous chapters we looked at the standard facilities provided in *BNCweb* for exploring the data retrieved by a concordance query: displaying the hits of a concordance, sorting the hits, extracting collocations, and showing frequency distributions across text-types and speaker-types. We saw that these functions can provide valuable insights into patterns of usage of the linguistic item(s) you are focusing on.

However, there are times when even these functions are insufficient to show the most relevant patterns among the query results. One recurrent problem is that of precision, or rather imprecision (see 5.5). That is, the software sometimes returns examples that don't match what you set out to find—e.g., a query looking for *cool* as an expression of approval or admiration (as in *That is such a cool movie* [KPP 907]) is liable to bring up cases of *cool* referring to temperature (as in ...*such an easy walk on such a cool day* [CDX 1784]). Similarly, among the results of a query for the modal auxiliary *can* (see 6.7), occasionally you will find examples of the noun use, designating a metal container. There is thus often a need to weed out intended examples from different types of "noise".

A second problem you may have noticed is that important aspects of the behavior of a linguistic expression do not always jump out at you from the concordance. Even after you have discarded unwanted cases, and applied tools such as collocations and distributions, it is still possible for trends in the functions and behavior of a query item to go undetected. To uncover them, it's usually necessary first to read the concordance lines (or a sample of them) closely, and to annotate them—that is, to add some labels or notes describing any relevant (or potentially relevant) features. So, in the case of *can*, for instance, you might want not only to discard the instances where it represents a metal object, but also to label the meaning of *can* as one of permission (e.g. *Can we start eating yet?*), ability (*Can you swim?*), or possibility (*It can get hot in here.*).

Annotations of this kind generally have to be done by hand.[1] This may seem a laborious and time-consuming business, but it's still a much more efficient way of finding patterns in your data than using pencil and paper.

There are three main approaches available for manually categorizing and analyzing concordance hits:

a) annotating them within *BNCweb*, using the CATEGORIZE HITS function

b) downloading (or exporting) the set of concordance lines from the corpus tool to your local computer system, and from there importing them into a database program for analysis

c) annotating the categories in a database, as in (b), but additionally reimporting selected hits *back* into *BNCweb*.

Each of these approaches will be demonstrated in this chapter. We also review some of the advantages and disadvantages of each method, to help you choose the appropriate one for different types of analysis.

Naturally, once you have carried out a manual analysis, it is important to be able to present and interpret your results. Our discussion therefore includes some suggestions for presenting quantitative findings based on the frequencies of categories set up by the user.

9.3   Annotation within *BNCweb*: using the "Categorize hits" function

We will illustrate the use of manual categorization first with *BNCweb*'s CATEGORIZE HITS function, taking the expression *you know* as our example. One

---

1   Manual annotation is to be distinguished from automatic annotation, which is the labelling of features in the text by software, often as an auxiliary process in the compilation of a corpus. In the case of the BNC, wordclass tags and lemmas were added by the CLAWS annotation program (see Chapter 3). Naturally the two kinds of annotation can go in hand in hand. You may wish to use the wordclass tags provided in the BNC to retrieve instances of a grammatical construction (e.g. the passive), then manually annotate the resulting data to remove errors and mark the functions of the passive.

very important use of *you know*, especially in spoken language, is as a discourse marker: e.g. *he was very good <pause> you know, he was quiet and peaceful.* (KCN 6395)

Of course, *you know* is also often used as an ordinary sequence of the personal pronoun *you* and the lexical verb *know*, as in as in *Do you know Karen?* (JA9 996) and *Choose people you know well and trust...*(A01 423). Unfortunately, the grammatical tagging provided with the BNC does not distinguish the lexical from the discoursal uses, so if we are only interested in where *you know* functions as a discourse marker, we will need to differentiate the two uses by hand-coding the concordance lines.

9.3.1   Setting up a category for analysis

Before you start coding your concordance hits, *BNCweb* asks you to define your categories—i.e. to choose a name for each category that the search word/expression may assume in the corpus. To do this:

1. Run a query for the pattern you know. For this worked example, we suggest searching only the spoken texts.

2. Many queries on the BNC produce a query result that is too large for you to go through manually—as is the case for *you know* with its 30,829 instances in spoken texts. Two options are helpful in this type of situation:

   a. Randomly reducing the hits to a manageable number with the THIN feature—available from the post-query options menu. You may choose between a number (e.g. 1000) or a percentage (e.g. 10%).

   b. SHOW IN RANDOM ORDER, which retains the full set of instances but displays them randomly.

   In most instances, random order without thinning is preferable (see the Tip box in Section 9.3.2). Accordingly, in the *BNCweb* Query result window, select [Show in random order][2], then press [Go!].

3. Next, from the post-query functions menu select "Categorize hits..." and press [Go!].

4. On the next page, enter a name for the feature you want to categorize. We'll call the set of categories you_know, and specify the categories this pattern may have as discoursal and lexical—see Figure 9.1.

   Note that category names and value names can be up to 50 characters long, but they may only contain letters of the alphabet, numbers, and the

---

2   It is also possible to select "Show in random order" as the default display order of concordances under USER SETTINGS (see Chapter 13).

underscore character ("_"). You may enter up to six values. By default, the values "unclear" and "other" are added to the values you have chosen.

5. The "Default category?" checkbox is available for cases where you expect most of the hits to belong to one particular category. We recommend that when using CATEGORIZE HITS for the first time, you do not make use of this functionality.

   Checking this option next to one of the categories will automatically set all hits to that value. This then means that you only have to mark exceptional cases by hand, thus potentially saving you considerable time. On the other hand, selecting this option will mean that you would then need to read and verify the categorization of the complete set of concordance lines.

6. Click [Submit].

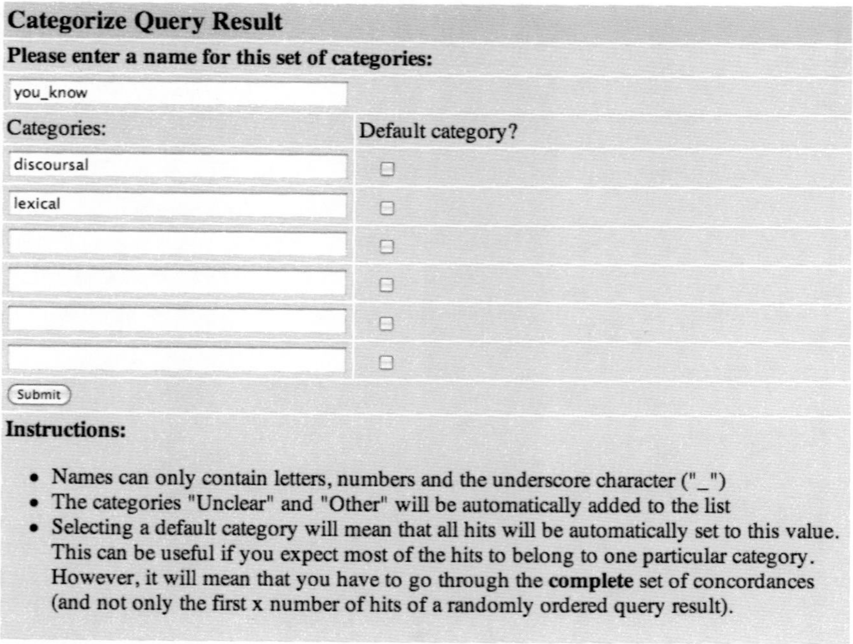

Categorize Query Result

Please enter a name for this set of categories:

| you_know |

Categories:	Default category?
discoursal	☐
lexical	☐
	☐
	☐
	☐
	☐

(Submit)

Instructions:

- Names can only contain letters, numbers and the underscore character ("_")
- The categories "Unclear" and "Other" will be automatically added to the list
- Selecting a default category will mean that all hits will be automatically set to this value. This can be useful if you expect most of the hits to belong to one particular category. However, it will mean that you have to go through the **complete** set of concordances (and not only the first x number of hits of a randomly ordered query result).

Figure 9.1:   Defining a set of categories for annotation, by entering a name and relevant values

9.3.2   Categorizing concordance hits

You are now in "Categorization mode": your query result will reappear, but showing a column of drop-down menus to the right of the concordance lines, in which you can assign a category value to each example: see Figure 9.2. The choice of value will depend on the context in which the query item is used. One example of *you know* in this screenshot is clearly lexical (no. 7), while the majority are clearly discourse markers (e.g. nos. 2 and 8). There is also one case where it is difficult to decide on the appropriate value (no. 1).

Your query "[word = "you" %c] [word = "know" %c]" in spoken texts returned 30829 hits in 813 different texts (10,409,858 words [908 texts]; frequency: 2961.52 instances per million words) (displayed in random order)

|< << >> >| (Show Page:) 1   (Show KWIC View)

No	Filename	Hits 1 to 50 Page 1 / 617	Categories
1	KD0 5073	I don't think [unclear] you know.	unclear
2	JJL 646	I really, I really get the impression that there's, there's [unclear] , it's incredibly sort of nobody really knows what to do, you know, there's this big turbulent thing just happening [pause] and people are very confused about the whole thing because the M-- May the fourth directive isn't particularly er it didn't give anybody an absolute guideline, guide to erm what to do.	discoursal
3	FUT 561	Th-- the legal documents you know th-- going back to the cooker.	discoursal
4	KB8 6052	But I read [pause] you know when you make your coffee in it	✓ discoursal / lexical / other / unclear
5	KB1 4034	That reminds me, I've got that box and all, the [pause] you know when you took that bo-- that [pause] box of Twix back [pause] that time [pause] what do you do when you take them back?	
6	JND 102	[unclear] yeah but you know [pause dur="26"]	discoursal
7	KBX 164	Er Nepal from Nepal, Nepal they're speak Fin language, do you know that?	lexical
8	J8B 871	yes and that, that in a way leads me on to the next party, if we're gonna have an agreement between this group or, you know, the other group	discoursal

Figure 9.2:   The CATEGORIZE HITS feature of *BNCweb* at work

Tip:
Recall that when exploring a concordance in depth, it is generally a good idea to rearrange the initial query result into a random order—otherwise you run the risk that the first instances of your query result will give you a skewed impression of the phenomenon under investigation (cf. 4.4.3). In the context of categorizing hits, random ordering has a further advantage. As mentioned above, many query results will be too large for a complete manual analysis. One option is to randomly THIN the query result to a manageable size (e.g. 500 hits). However, the disadvantage of this option is that you need to make up your mind before you start categorizing how many hits you would need to analyze to answer your research question.

If your estimate is not accurate, you may end up with too much work on your hands: even though you might find that you already have a sufficient number of categorized hits, you still have to go through the rest of your sample to avoid ending up with a skewed set. Even worse, if it turns out that the random subset you have selected is not large enough, you will not be able to add extra random hits to your data—and if you look at a second set of random hits separately, there might be overlap with your first one.

If, instead, you choose to work with a randomly ordered version of the full query result, you can stop at any time when you feel that you have a sufficient number of categorized hits: whatever the number of examples you have, it will always be a random selection of the full set. The only thing to observe is that your categorized hits need to be consecutive (i.e. in a "single block"). If you were to analyze non-consecutive instances (e.g. because you only choose the ones that are easy to categorize) this would again result in a potentially serious skewing of the result.

Now, to categorize your concordance data:

1. In the column labeled "Categories", select the appropriate category in the drop-down menu.

   If you need more context to decide on the appropriate value, simply click on the link to the query item (e.g. *you know*) in the concordance column. If you are still unsure, select "unclear".[3]

2. Continue doing this for subsequent concordance lines.

3. When you reach the end of a page, you can continue working through the data by selecting "Save categorization values for this page!", then clicking [Go!]. This will display the next page of concordance lines.

4. Whenever you want to pause or stop categorizing the data—say if you want to get an early idea of the most recurrent patterns—select "Save values and leave categorization mode", then click [Go!].

Be sure to save before leaving categorization mode, otherwise your changes and additions on the last page you edited will be lost.

---

3   Having "unclear" as a default option is convenient for dealing with indeterminate cases. Very often it simply isn't clear whether *you know* is being used as a discourse marker or as a pronoun plus verb combination.

When you leave categorization mode, you will be taken to a list of your categorized queries. This list is also available via the main navigation panel of *BNCweb*. As shown in Figure 9.3, the list displays a variety of information about your categorized queries, including the categories that you have chosen for classification, the total number of hits in your query, and the number of hits that have already been categorized (also as percentage of the whole). You can return to categorization mode by clicking on the name of the categorized query.

BNC*web* (CQP-Edition)

Categorized queries

No.	Name of set	Categories	No. of hits	Completed	Date	Action
1	you_know	discoursal, lexical, other, unclear	30829	1000 (3.24%)	26.03.2008 13:47:54	✓ Add categories / Separate categories / Delete complete set (Go)

Figure 9.3:   List of categorized queries

If for some reason you wish to delete a categorized query, this can be done via the corresponding drop-down menu in the "Action" column of the list. Since this action is irreversible (and could potentially delete weeks of manual work) you are asked to confirm your choice before proceeding. The remaining two actions available via the drop-down menu ("Add categories" and "Separate categories") will be presented below.

9.3.3   Analyzing data categorized in *BNCweb*

When you have finished categorizing your data (or a substantial part of it), you can use *BNCweb* to explore the characteristics of the feature(s) you are most interested in. In the example above, this would most likely be cases where *you know* functions as a discourse marker. You might ask yourself, for example, which spoken genres show the highest frequency of this use—more informal ones such as face-to-face conversation, or more structured activities such as classroom lessons and public talks? What are the main collocations of *you know* as a discourse marker?

To examine the relevant examples, you first need to separate the data you have analyzed into their respective categories. You will then be able to apply the standard functions of *BNCweb*—distributional statistics, collocations, sorting, etc.—to just this set of data.

1. After selecting "Save values and leave categorization mode" and clicking [Go!], you should see a table listing the query you just categorized (and any other data you may have categorized previously).

2. In the line containing the query you just categorized, select "Separate categories" in the drop-down menu and press [Go] (see Figure 9.3 above). The categories will now appear individually—e.g. one called "you_know_discoursal", one called "you_know_lexical"—in a table of SAVED QUERIES (rather than CATEGORIZED QUERIES) as shown below. They are thus treated in the same way as any query that has been saved for further reuse.

10	you_know_discoursal	759	10.05.2008 16:08:43	Rename Delete
11	you_know_lexical	164	10.05.2008 16:08:43	Rename Delete
12	you_know_unclear	77	10.05.2008 16:08:43	Rename Delete

3. Click on one of the category names (e.g. "you_know_discoursal") to view the query result of just that type.

4. As with any query result, you will see frequency information and a concordance, which you can analyze by simply browsing through it, or by choosing a standard *BNCweb* function (e.g. COLLOCATIONS) from the post-query functions menu. So, with *you know*, for example, you would now be able to obtain collocations, distributions and so on of just the cases coded as discourse markers.

You can also re-apply the CATEGORIZE HITS function to your selected data, and thus identify subcategories of usage. For example, you could indicate which cases of the discourse marker *you know* occur in initial position in the clause (e.g. ***You know****, I mean that that goes beyond parties!* [FLE 146]); which in medial position (e.g. *as soon as you explain why,* ***you know****, it's been accepted.* [H49 634]); and which in final position (e.g. *they were sort of long since run out,* ***you know****.* [G4T 386]).

Note:
If you select "Separate categories" again, then any saved queries that you "separated" earlier will be overwritten. If for any reason you wish to keep the original version, make sure to rename the query first. To do this, return to the SAVED QUERIES table (off the main navigation panel) and click "Rename": this will take you to the "Saved Queries Administration Page" where you enter a new name into the box, then press [Submit].

9.3.4 Re-editing your annotations

Resuming categorization: Because concordances can run into thousands of hits, it often isn't feasible to finish categorizing your data in a single session. You can, however, easily resume categorizing at a later date, by doing the following:

1. In the main navigation panel, select CATEGORIZED QUERIES. This will show a table of category sets you have previously applied, e.g. the set "you_know".

2. Under the column headed "Name of set", click on one of the category set names (e.g. "you_know"). This will return you to categorization mode on the first page of the relevant query result data.

Adding categories: Suppose that you decide to use an additional category to the ones you're already using. For example, you might decide that *you know* in *you know what I mean* forms part of a distinctive idiom, separate from the other uses. Or you might be categorizing a concordance of the verb *give* according to its meanings/uses, and suddenly realize that you had overlooked cases like *He gave it a push* and *I gave it some thought* (a category called "expanded predicate" in some grammar books). You can easily set up the new category (e.g. "exp_pred") via the "Add categories" action. Note that this procedure can be used to extend the number of categories beyond the default maximum of six.

Deleting categories: Note that once you've created a category you can't delete it from the list of options. This isn't usually a problem, however: you can simply ignore the category in your analysis, or use the CATEGORIZE HITS function again to reassign any cases you no longer wish to use.

9.3.5 Advantages and disadvantages of categorizing queries within *BNCweb*

There are a number of advantages, as well as a few drawbacks, in categorizing your data using *BNCweb*'s CATEGORIZE HITS function. Being aware of the pros and cons of this method should help you to decide whether it is appropriate for your needs, or whether you should consider alternative methods.

One clear advantage of categorizing a query result within *BNCweb* is that the larger context of the concordance hits is immediately accessible. You can use the context to check—or modify—the decisions you make about assigning examples to one category or another (e.g. lexical vs. discoursal use of *you know*). You also get a better sense of how the example fits within the structure of paragraphs, speaker turns, and so on of the text in which it originally appeared.

A further benefit is that once the data has been manually categorized (and you have run SEPARATE CATEGORIES), you can apply any or all of *BNCweb*'s post-query functions—e.g. COLLOCATIONS, DISTRIBUTION, SORT—to any category. To take our working example once more, you can find out the collocations and preferred genres of *you know* specifically where it functions as a discourse marker.

Further, there is the time-saving aspect: having everything available in *BNCweb* means that you only need to use one piece of software to code and analyze your data.

Among the disadvantages of this approach is the fact that you can only work on one annotation category at a time. Suppose you are interested in ditransitive verbs such as *give*, and want to code examples in BNC as (a) taking an indirect object (e.g. *Susan gave him a tie*) or as taking a prepositional object (*Susan gave a tie to him*); and (b) as passivizable or not (*A book was given to him* is OK, but *A push was given to him* would be less acceptable to most people). You could not combine these analyses into one set of data in which one minute you can select (say) passivizable indirect objects, and the next minute non-passivizable prepositional objects and non-passivizable indirect objects.[4]

There is also a minor inconvenience in that annotations must belong to one of the categories you have set in advance. Furthermore, the format of category names is rather constrained (see 9.3.1) and you cannot therefore insert spontaneous, free-form notes, such as "Good example for my presentation" and "Category X chosen here because...".

A more serious limitation is that the CATEGORIZE HITS function in *BNCweb* lacks some very useful data analysis functions such as are generally to be found in database software, e.g. the availability of multiple fields of categories, and advanced filtering possibilities. However, this shortcoming can largely be overcome by combining *BNCweb* with database software, harnessing the advantages of each. We illustrate this second main approach to categorizing concordance data in Section 9.5, with an optional further step in Section 9.6. But first, let's see how we can summarize the findings of a categorized query.

9.4   Summarizing and presenting results of customized annotations

Once you have finished manually annotating your concordance lines, you will then typically want to summarize and compare the findings across different sub-

---

4   The only workaround is to annotate one of the categories (e.g. the ability to take an indirect object) first, then separate the categories, and code the resulting sets according to one of the other categories.

parts of your data. For example, if you are investigating the use of *you know* as a discourse marker, you may want to use your annotated data to answer such questions as: Are there differences in usage that can be explained by (or at least correlated with)

- the social class of the speakers?
- the age or sex of the speakers?
- the context and setting of the conversation?

For this purpose, you would want to find out whether the cases of *you know* that you categorized as discourse markers—and only those!—are particularly frequent or infrequent in certain categories (or combinations of categories). Unfortunately, this is not an entirely straightforward process. Remember that the direct comparison of raw frequencies is only possible when the different sections of the corpus are the same size (cf. Chapter 5). As soon as this is not the case, you'll need to calculate normalized frequencies. In addition, you may only have worked with a (random) subset of your initial query: this will introduce an additional need to adjust your figures.

Let's look at a sample analysis in more detail to illustrate how this is done in practice. We'll assume that you have been investigating the phrase *you know* in the spoken component of the BNC. This search retrieved 30,289 hits in 813 different texts, or almost 3,000 instances per million words. Not surprisingly, you were not able to manually work your way through the complete set of data—instead, let's say you displayed your query result in random order and annotated the first 1,000 instances. Of these, 759 turned out to be clear cases of discourse markers, 361 of which were found in the demographically sampled part (DS) and 398 in the context-governed part (CG) of the corpus. You further discovered that 246 of these were spoken by women and 332 by men. (Remember that we don't have information about all speakers in the corpus and that your data will therefore often not be complete for all of your matches.) Finally, you looked at the sex of the speakers in the two spoken sub-parts and determined that there are 176 female vs. 134 male occurrences in DS but 70 female vs. 198 male occurrences in CG. Even though we really only have two categories with two values each (male vs. female and DS vs. CG), this is already quite a complex picture. Just imagine what would happen if we were to add "Age of speaker" with its six age bands to the analysis.

As a first step, it is generally helpful to look at your results in table form. As you can see, things already look much neater in Table 9.1. However, what can you really say about the frequency of the discourse marker *you know* on the basis of this table? At first sight it seems that women use the discourse marker *you know* more often than men in DS (178 vs. 134), but much less often in CG (70 vs. 198). But before you can safely say this, remember that you first need to normalize your frequency data (cf. 5.3). Second, since you have only looked at a random subset of your data, it is also necessary to multiply the relative frequencies by an appropriate factor.

Table 9.1: Raw frequencies of the discourse marker *you know*—male and female use in the demographically sampled and context-governed parts of the BNC

	Demographically sampled (DS)	Context-governed (CG)	Total
Male	134	198	332
Female	176	70	246
Unknown	51	130	181
Total	361	398	759

In order to calculate relative frequencies, you will need to determine the number of words from which each cell in the table was sampled—for example, if you know the number of words spoken by men in the demographically sampled part, you can calculate how many instances of the discourse marker *you know* they have uttered per million words. To recap, the formula is:

$$\text{Frequency pmw} = \frac{\text{number of instances}}{\text{number of words}} \times 1{,}000{,}000$$

But how do you find out the word count for each cell? The quickest way to get a word count is do a standard query in Spoken or Written texts, and select the relevant text or speaker restrictions. You can enter anything in the "Query term" box—or even leave it blank—and click [Start query]. In the title bar of the query result you will then see the number of words that were searched.[5] For male speakers in DS, this figure is 1,454,344 words, while female speakers in DS utter a total of 2,264,094 words. If you use this information to calculate

---

5 Alternatively, you can use David Lee's *Excel* spreadsheet BNC Index (available at http://clix.to/davidlee00), which allows you to apply filters to the metatextual categories listed for the complete set of BNC texts. After the filters have been applied, you can copy the column of word totals into a separate spreadsheet and add up the numbers to get the total number of words for that set of files.

normalized frequencies, you can see that women in fact use the discourse marker less frequently than men, namely 77.7 pmw (i.e. 176 ÷ 2,264,094 × 1,000,000) as opposed to 92.1 pmw (i.e. 134 ÷ 1,454,344 × 1,000,000).

Table 9.2:   Frequencies per million words of the discourse marker *you know*— male and female use in the demographically sampled and context-governed parts of the BNC—frequencies pmw

	Demographically sampled (pmw)	Context-governed (pmw)	Total (pmw)
Male	92.1	56.6	67.1
Female	77.7	68.2	74.8
Unknown	99.0	78.6	83.4
Total	85.3	64.4	72.9

As you can see in Table 9.2, the differences between male and female usage of the discourse marker *you know* are less pronounced than the raw frequencies initially suggested. Furthermore, the data presented in Table 9.1 above was clearly misleading: whereas women in fact use the discourse marker *you know* less often than men in spontaneous conversations (DS), the opposite is the case in the context-governed part of the BNC (68.2 pmw for female speakers vs. 56.6 pmw for male speakers).

Tip:
It is quite tedious to determine the total number of words for each cell via individual queries, particularly when categories with more than two possible values (e.g. "Age of speaker" with its six possible values) are involved. In these cases, the DISTRIBUTION feature of *BNCweb* can be employed to arrive at word counts more quickly: first perform a search in the whole demographically sampled part, then do a distribution analysis, selecting "Speaker: Age" as the category. This will display all six word counts in one go (although not necessarily in the desired order). Note that *BNCweb* does not give you information about word counts for the value "unknown"—e.g. the number of words uttered by speakers whose age is not known. In these cases, you will have to subtract the sum of all known cells from the total number of words in the category.

We now have just one step to go. Remember that you did not look at all 30,289 instances but only at the first 1,000 hits (in random order). In order to present realistic frequency information, you therefore have to multiply your figures by the relevant "thinning factor": the full query result is just over 30 times larger than the 1,000 instances on which your results are based. So, if you found 759 discourse markers in the 1,000 instances you categorized, you would expect— by extrapolation—to find 122,989 discourse markers (i.e. 759 × 30.289) in the full set. Since the thinning factor applies equally to all cells, we simply have to multiply all raw and normalized frequencies by 30.289. The result of this is shown in Table 9.3.

Table 9.3:   Raw frequency (n) and frequency per million words (pmw) for the discourse marker *you know*—male and female use in the demographically sampled and context-governed parts of the BNC (extrapolated from a random subset of 1,000 instances)

	Demographically sampled		Context-governed		Total	
	n	pmw	n	pmw	n	pmw
Male	4,059	2,791	5,997	1,716	10,056	2,031
Female	5,331	2,355	2,120	2,065	7,451	2,264
Unknown	1,544	3,000	3,938	2,381	5,482	2,527
Total	10,934	2,582	12,055	1,952	22,989	2,208

9.5   Exporting a *BNCweb* query result to an external database

So far we have relied totally on *BNCweb* to insert our annotation categories. We now look at the main alternative method, namely database programs—which we extend here to include spreadsheet software such as Microsoft *Excel*. Database software offers a high degree of flexibility and functionality in the ways you can categorize, retrieve and analyze your linguistic data. For example, you can include as many annotation categories as you wish, selectively retrieve data by using filters, and incorporate comments about your examples in free-form notes.

The database approach, as we call it, has four main steps:

a) download the concordance from *BNCweb*

b) import the concordance into a database

c) annotate the database

d) analyze the database

There is an enormous choice of database software available. However, we illustrate steps b) to d) using just one package, Microsoft *Excel*. Although *Excel* is better known as a spreadsheet package, designed for numerical analysis, its database functions are adequate for many kinds of linguistic processing—and it has the advantage of familiarity to many users.[6] At the end of this section we summarize the main strengths and weaknesses of the database approach, just as we have done for the *BNCweb*-only approach presented in the previous section.

9.5.1   Downloading from *BNCweb*

The first step is to save the concordance to your local computer system. After selecting "Download" in the post-query options menu, you will be presented with a list of options for setting the format and types of information you want to save together with your concordance. As well as the concordance data, text ID and the sentence number, you can choose to save information about the source of each citation: for example, the gender of the speaker (if it's from a spoken text) or author (if it's a written text), the genre of the text, and its publication date.

The data is exported as a plain text file with a tab between each column of information. This format is recognized by practically all database and spreadsheet packages.

Download steps:

1. In the *BNCweb* Query result page, select "Download..." from the post-query options menu and press [Go!].

2. The download form that appears may look daunting at first—if you are in doubt about any of the options, simply accept the defaults until you become more familiar with them.

   In the top half of the form (cf. Figure 9.4) you can choose the platform on which you expect to use the data (e.g. Windows, Unix), and how you would like the concordance data to be formatted: e.g. how much context, and whether to include codes or full names for metatextual categories (i.e.

---

6   When you use *BNCweb*, you will also see an occasional reference to *FileMaker Pro*, which is an advanced relational database application (e.g. when you use the DOWNLOAD feature, there will be a link to an import template for *FileMaker*). However, given that only a small proportion of our readers will have access to *FileMaker*, we have opted to focus here on the much more widely used Microsoft *Excel*.

speaker and text type categories). The drop-down menu "Write information about order of categories at the beginning of file" has three options:
the default is that no such information is included in the download. If you
select "yes" you can choose between a format suitable for *Excel* and other
database applications ("Yes—as a header row") and a format suitable for
paper print-out ("Yes—printer-friendly version"). The option "Include
corpus positions" determines whether the internal codes used by *BNCweb*
to refer to individual words in the corpus are downloaded as well. Including these CORPUS POSITIONS is essential if you wish to reimport any
downloaded concordance lines into *BNCweb* (see 9.6).

3. Choose a name for the file you are downloading, or accept the default
   name (which is your *BNCweb* username).

Download concordance	
Output format options	
Choose operating system on which you will be working with the file:	UNIX (incl. OS X)
Print codes (numbers) or full values for metatextual categories:*	full values
Mark query result in sentence (format: <<< result >>>):	yes
Size of context:	1 <s>-unit
Download both tagged and untagged version of your results:*	yes
Write information about order of categories at the beginning of file:*	no
Format of output: KWIC or list:*	List
Include corpus positions (required for re-import)*	Yes
Include URL to context display*	Yes
Enter name for the downloaded file:	shcorp

Figure 9.4:   Options for exporting a concordance from *BNCweb*, upper half
                of window

4. In the bottom half of the form (cf. Figure 9.5), choose the text category
   and speaker/author information you want stored with your concordance.

5. When working with spoken texts, bear in mind that "Speaker information"
   is generally more informative than "Respondent information". As discussed in Chapter 3, "Respondent" merely refers to the person responsible

for collecting the recording, who will be only one of several speakers within the BNC file.

6. You can reset to the default values at any time by clicking [Clear form].

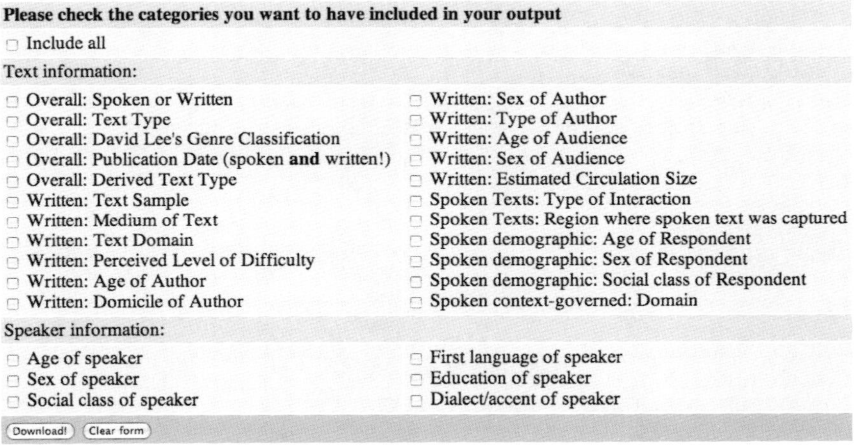

Please check the categories you want to have included in your output

☐ Include all

Text information:

☐ Overall: Spoken or Written
☐ Overall: Text Type
☐ Overall: David Lee's Genre Classification
☐ Overall: Publication Date (spoken **and** written!)
☐ Overall: Derived Text Type
☐ Written: Text Sample
☐ Written: Medium of Text
☐ Written: Text Domain
☐ Written: Perceived Level of Difficulty
☐ Written: Age of Author
☐ Written: Domicile of Author

☐ Written: Sex of Author
☐ Written: Type of Author
☐ Written: Age of Audience
☐ Written: Sex of Audience
☐ Written: Estimated Circulation Size
☐ Spoken Texts: Type of Interaction
☐ Spoken Texts: Region where spoken text was captured
☐ Spoken demographic: Age of Respondent
☐ Spoken demographic: Sex of Respondent
☐ Spoken demographic: Social class of Respondent
☐ Spoken context-governed: Domain

Speaker information:

☐ Age of speaker
☐ Sex of speaker
☐ Social class of speaker

☐ First language of speaker
☐ Education of speaker
☐ Dialect/accent of speaker

(Download!) (Clear form)

Figure 9.5:   Options for exporting a concordance from *BNCweb*, lower half of window

7. When you click [Download!], save the file to your local computer system just as you would normally from any web site. You can also choose to change the name of the file at this point as well.

9.5.2   Importing into database software

When imported into the database or spreadsheet software, the concordance lines and their associated categories become a set of "records" which you can filter, sort, add notes to, print, etc. Once you have the file open in your database software, you can refine the formatting of the file further.

Note that the instructions we give here for importing and working with the data refer to *Excel*. Instructions may differ slightly depending on the software and version you are running. We advise you to consult your database or spreadsheet software manual if you need more detailed help. The following are the steps for computers running Windows with *Excel 2003*:

1. Open *Excel* (or other database software)

2. Select "File > Open".

3. Select the folder where you previously saved the file, if necessary, set the file type to "All Files *.*", select the filename and then click [Open].

4. Follow the steps of the "Text Import Wizard": it is usually enough to click [Finish]. As you become more proficient, you may wish to adjust certain options, such as "Data format".

The resulting spreadsheet is displayed in Figure 9.6.[7] Note that this spreadsheet has been tidied up to improve readability (see Tip box below).

A	B	C	D	E	F	G	H	I	J
Num	Text	S-unit	Speaker-ID	Sentence	Spoken or	Genre	Age	Sex	Social Clas
1	FL7	279	FL7PSUNK	I can walk out or [unclear] , and get erm , <<< you know >>> tonnes of any any shop I can get pornography that tells me that , or tell any man who chooses to buy that magazine that 's it okay to take a women even if she says no .	Spoken	S:brdcast:	Unknown	Unknown	Unknown
2	FLE	146	FLEPS001	<<< You know >>> , I mean that that goes beyond parties !	Spoken	S:brdcast:	Unknown	Unknown	Unknown
3	FRH	2599		‘ It 's a meaningless gesture , <<< you know >>> .	Written	W:fict:pros	n/a	n/a	n/a
4	FY8	701	PS25M	you know , because they do n't know what their right are with And you know , I think places like the law centre , which fight for the rights of people in [gap:name] , <<< you know >>> to develop that that kind of service for people .	Spoken	S:interview	Unknown	Unknown	Unknown
5	G5J	507	PS2B2	I mean w with stamps at least you can look at them and <<< you know >>> go over them	Spoken	S:interview	45-59	Female	Unknown
6	HGK	3718		‘ Do <<< you know >>> how you are looking at me ? ’ he asked fiercely , but as she only shook her head he tilted her face and searched frustratedly for her mouth , crushing her against him .	Written	W:fict:pros	n/a	n/a	n/a
7	HTH	164		‘ Do <<< you know >>> how big space is ? ’ it said .	Written	W:fict:pros	n/a	n/a	n/a
8	HUX	103	HUXPS001	Yes definitely I mean I do n't think we ever dreamt in our wildest dreams I think really it was maybe chance thing f fate or whatever <<< you know >>> .	Spoken	S:interview	Unknown	Unknown	Unknown

Figure 9.6:   *Excel* spreadsheet containing concordance data and metatextual categories

---

7   Another method is to drag and drop the file from its folder into the database software:

- Open *Excel* (or other database software)
- Open your file manager program (but not at full screen size)
- Drag the file from the file manager program into *Excel*

Alternatively, right-click the file in a file manager program:

- Open your file manager program
- Right-click the file in the file manager program, choose "Open with...", then *Excel*

Tips for tidying up a concordance in *Excel*:

- Reduce the width of columns containing a lot of empty space (click on the letter name: A or B or C etc. at the top of the spreadsheet, and drag the column divider to the left).

- Reformat the column containing the concordance. You will probably want to widen this first, by dragging the column divider to the right. You can also make the concordance easier to read by selecting that column again, then selecting "Format > Cells > Alignment" and check the Wrap text box. Click [OK].

- You can "freeze" the header row (see 9.5.1, step 2), so that it stays visible even when you scroll down several pages through the concordance: select the row below the header row, then click "Window > Freeze panes".

9.5.3   Annotating the database

You are now in a position to add your own qualitative coding to each concordance line record.

1. Immediately to the right of the concordance column, insert a new column. Let's label it "Function".

2. Now read the first example and code it according to the function of *you know*; e.g. put "disc" (or "d") if it functions as a discourse marker, "lex" (or "l") if it's a lexical use, "unclear" (or "u") if it's unclear—just as you would when using the CATEGORIZE HITS feature in *BNCweb* (see 9.3.2).

3. If you need to check the larger context of a given example, you can simply copy and paste the web address from the database back into *BNCweb*. The example will be displayed through the BROWSE A TEXT facility of *BNCweb*. Note that *BNCweb* addresses will only be visible in the database if you responded "Yes" to the question "Include URL to context display?" when you downloaded the query result.

4. Proceed in the same way for subsequent examples in the database. (You can pause and resume coding at any time.)

   You can add as many extra columns, or fields, for annotation categories as you wish. Simply repeat the above steps for a new category. If you are coding "Position", for example, you can mark the position of *you know* in the clause as initial, medial or final (cf. 9.3.3 above).

9.5.4   Analyzing the database

Once you have a sufficient number of examples analyzed, you can check to see if patterns are emerging. To illustrate this, we will focus on the filter function of *Excel* (a similar function is available in most database programs).

To filter your database in *Excel*, first select "Data > Filter > Autofilter" (or in *Excel 2007*: "Data > Filter"). You will see that each column heading is now a drop-down menu (indicated by a button with one or two arrows, depending on your operating system). The fields are now ready for filtering. To retrieve the discourse marker cases, click on the drop-down menu in the "Function" field and select "disc".[8] The arrow (or arrows) on the button should change from black to blue, and in the bottom left-hand corner of your screen, the number of matching records should be displayed.

You can filter more than one field at a time. To retrieve occurrences of the discourse marker produced by speakers aged 25-34, first make sure that the above filter for "disc" is already activated, then click on the drop-down menu for the column headed "Age", and select "25-34"—this is shown in Figure 9.7.

D	E	F	G	H	I	J	K
Speaker-I	Sentence	Function	Position	Spoken or	Genre	Age	Sex
FL7PSUNK	I can walk out or [unclear] , and get erm , <<< you know >>> tonnes of any any shop I can get pornography that tells me that , or tell any man who chooses to buy that magazine that 's it okay to take a women even if she says no .	d	m	Spoken	S:brdcast:discussn	Sort Ascending / Sort Descending / ✓ (Show All) / (Show Top 10...) / (Custom Filter...) / 0-14 / 25-34	own
FLEPS001	<<< You know >>> , I mean that that goes beyond parties !	d	i	Spoken	S:brdcast:discussn	35-44 / 45-59 / n/a / Unknown	own
	‘ It 's a meaningless gesture , <<< you know >>> .	d	e	Written	W:fict:prose	n/a	n/a
PS25M	you know , because they do n't know what their right are with And you know , I think places like the law centre , which fight for the rights of people in [gap:name] , <<< you know >>> to develop that that kind of service for people .	d	m	Spoken	S:interview:oral_his	Unknown	Unknown
PS2B2	I mean w with stamps at least you can look at them and <<< you know >>> go over them	d	m	Spoken	S:interview	45-59	Female

Figure 9.7:   Analyzing a concordance in *Excel* using filters

You can add an indefinite number of filters. You could, if you wished, filter the above data further for cases by female speakers in (say) interviews. (Naturally, the more filters you apply, the fewer examples you will retrieve.)

---

8   You can also select multiple values by clicking on the drop-down menu and selecting "(Custom...)". In *Excel 2007*: use the check-boxes to select the value(s) you require.

To restore any field to its original, pre-filtered state, click on the drop-down menu for that field again, and select "All". To put *all* the fields back to their pre-filtered state (i.e. to remove all filters), select "Data > Filter > Autofilter" again.

9.5.5   Advantages and disadvantages of the database approach

The database approach offers considerable flexibility in entering and retrieving your manual annotations: we compare it here with the CATEGORIZE HITS function of *BNCweb*:

- It allows you to include multiple levels of annotation (CATEGORIZE HITS in *BNCweb* offers only one).

- Both programs allow the context of any concordance hit to be consulted, but with CATEGORIZE HITS the context is always immediately accessible. When using a database, this option is potentially more restricted.[9]

- The number of categories you may have in each category set is not limited, and it is possible to work with several categories at the same time. CATEGORIZE HITS in *BNCweb* only offers a single set of categories.

- Database programs offer a variety of methods for retrieving, sorting, and performing calculations on data from your annotation categories.

The main drawback of the database approach is that the categorized version of the concordance is no longer accessible from within *BNCweb*. As a result, your data cannot be subjected to post-query functions such as COLLOCATIONS, DISTRIBUTION, etc. With CATEGORIZE HITS, this problem doesn't arise. However, a partial solution to this disadvantage is described in the following section.

9.6   Reimporting an analyzed database into *BNCweb*

Although *BNCweb* does not allow you to bring all of the data analyzed in a database back into the program itself, it does allow you to reimport a *selected* set of annotated records. All that is needed for reimport is the set of corpus positions of the relevant examples in the BNC, so that *BNCweb* can locate them. This requires that you have selected "yes" in the relevant option at the time of downloading the concordance (see 9.5.1).

---

9   Provided that you have exported the web address for each concordance line via DOWNLOAD, you can retrieve the example in its larger context by manually copying the link into your browser. However, some advanced database applications—e.g. recent versions of *FileMaker*—have the option of displaying web pages within the tool itself.

Suppose that you have used *Excel*, or equivalent database software, to categorize a *BNCweb* concordance containing *you know*. You have marked all the functions of *you know* in the examples, and the position in the clause in the case of discourse marker uses. Let's suppose you want to find out which genres and types of speaker use the discourse marker *you know* in final position the most.

1. First, filter the database on the "Function" field (selecting discourse markers) and then on "Position" (selecting "end" position) (see 9.5.4 above).

2. Then, from the filtered results, copy and paste the two columns that contain "corpus positions" into a new text file using any text editor (e.g. *Notepad,* for Windows users) and save as "Text only". Each column should consist only of a string of numbers. If you also copy across the top row with the headings (known as header row), these will be ignored.

3. Now return to *BNCweb*, and click on UPLOAD EXTERNAL DATA FILE in the main navigation panel.

4. Click [Browse…] and locate the text file you have just saved. Also enter a name for *BNCweb* to use for the newly uploaded dataset (see Figure 9.8).

BNC*web* (CQP-Edition)

Upload external data file

Select file for upload:	(Choose File) ⊕ you_know_database.txt
Enter a name for the new saved query:	[ ]
	(Upload file)

Figure 9.8:   Uploading an external data file to *BNCweb*

---

5. *BNCweb* treats the data you have just reimported as a new "Saved query" (and lists it in under SAVED QUERIES, available from the main navigation panel). You can now access the relevant examples and process them just like any other concordance data stored in *BNCweb*.

6. To see, for example, whether speaker age is related to frequency of use of the discourse marker *you know* in final position:

   • Click on the query name on the SAVED QUERIES page. This reopens the concordance view of the data.

   • In the post-query options menu, select DISTRIBUTION and click [Go!].

- On the next page, select "Speaker: Age" in the upper of the two drop-down menus, then click [Show distribution].

Of course, you can also apply any of the other post-query functions of *BNCweb* to the dataset that you uploaded: COLLOCATIONS, SORT, FREQUENCY BREAKDOWN, THIN and even CATEGORIZE HITS, if you so wish!

The procedure just described is only a partial solution to the problem identified at the end of 9.5.5. You still cannot reimport into *BNCweb*—in one go—all of the annotated data contained in your database. So, even though you may have coded all the functions and clause positions of the set of *you know* examples, you will not be able to analyze within *BNCweb* the various configurations of these categories. Only one set of category filters at a time is supported.

9.7   Further reading

For an introduction to the characteristics of discourse markers such as *you know*, *I mean*, *like* etc., see for instance (Schiffrin 1987) or Stenström (1994). For further discussion on manual annotation of concordances (including an overview of existing literature and software solutions), see Smith et al. (2008).

9.8   Exercises

1. Literally *again*. Returning to the question of the use of *literally* from Chapter 4, compare how the word is used in different types of spoken language.

    a) First run a query for *literally* in the spoken, demographically sampled part of the BNC. Then using either the CATEGORIZE HITS function or the database method, annotate the examples (there should be 94 of them in total) as either "literal" or "nonliteral". How many nonliteral examples did you find, and what is their frequency pmw?

    b) Now do the same analysis for the spoken context governed part of the corpus, and compare the two sets of results. In which part is the nonliteral use more frequent?

    Similarly, you could compare the usage of *literally* across written genres, such as advertising, tabloid newspapers and religion.

    If any one genre has more hits than you have time to read through, put the concordance into random order; after you finish categorizing the hits, work out the projected frequency per million words of nonliteral *literally*, using the method outlined in section 9.8.

    For any examples where you think the speaker or writer is using *literally* nonliterally, you may wish also to annotate any effects you think he or she might be intending, such as to be humorous, or to impress. If you are using the database method, simply add an extra column and call it 'effect'. If you are using *BNCweb*'s CATEGORIZE HITS function, you will first need to select "Separate categories" before proceeding to annotate the nonliteral set according to intended effects in a new categorized query.

2. *Verb + adjective with positive and negative associations.* Some verbs, such as *become, get, go, grow, prove, come, turn, turn out/end up/wind up* can describe a change in state when they are followed by an adjective, e.g. *grow old, prove fatal, turn out fine* etc. (In grammar books they are sometimes called "resulting copular verbs"). On the surface these verbs seem similar to one another, but in fact there are some interesting differences with regard to meaning, collocational preferences and register distributions. Using *BNCweb*, try to find out which "verb + adjective" combinations have a clearly positive or negative association.

Before searching in *BNCweb*, can you say anything intuitively about the differences between the above-listed verbs (imagine you are explaining this to learners of English)? E.g. do you think that each "verb + adjective" combination typically describes a positive or negative outcome? What sort of states might the adjective describe: emotions? colors? Does the verb usually take a human or a non-human subject? Are there any other differences?

Let's focus here on testing whether "verb + adjective" typically describes a positive or negative result. Your first consideration is: what is the best way to perform a search for one of these verbs followed by an adjective? (Turn back to 3.5.1 for a quick refresher on POS-tags—including simplified tags— but remember that there are usually a number of ways for performing searches using *BNCweb*, and depending on what you're looking for, some may be more useful than others.)

a) Start looking at the adjectives used with GO. Decide what query to enter to find all the forms of GO (*go, goes, went, going, gone*) followed by an adjective.

b) After running the query for "GO + adjective", arrange the concordance in random order, and then use the CATEGORIZE HITS function to mark the adjectives as positive or negative in attitude. (Recall that you can use the categories "other" and "unclear", if appropriate.)

c) Which adjectives have a clear positive or negative association?

d) Are there any adjectives that are more difficult to categorize?

Now do the same analysis for adjectives with COME, and compare the results. Repeat for the other verbs in turn. Which verbs have the clearest pattern of positive or negative associations?

10   Creating and using subcorpora

10.1   Outline

In Chapter 4, we showed how the metatextual information already provided in the BNC can be used to restrict queries to subsections of the corpus. In this chapter, we focus on designing and analyzing a set of texts that meet criteria of your own choosing—i.e. a SUBCORPUS (plural form: "subcorpora"). We'll cover the following points:

- Reasons for creating a subcorpus
- Ways of making a subcorpus
- Using a subcorpus to restrict your queries
- Modifying the contents of a subcorpus

10.2   Introduction: why create subcorpora?

Let's imagine that your interest is in investigating language use in a specific area such as "Applied science," or even a narrower field such as "Travel writing". The BNC makes it possible to explore such areas because it is a large general reference corpus, containing a wide array of texts. In Chapter 4, we looked at how we can use the metatextual mark-up in the BNC texts to select subsections of the corpus for your queries: instead of using the standard query box, you can click on WRITTEN TEXTS or SPOKEN TEXTS (on the main navigation panel) and check some boxes to restrict your query to particular texts that meet your criteria. Using this method is good for single, one-off queries. However, if you wanted to do additional queries on the same set of texts at a later date, you would then need to go back and check those same boxes again. In this chapter, you will learn how to make more lasting and reusable selections of texts that you can name and go back to whenever you wish. We refer to selections of this kind as subcorpora.

While "Applied science" is a pre-defined category in the BNC, "Travel writing" isn't. In other words, you can't simply fill in a set of check boxes in *BNCweb* to search only within the relevant travel texts. The flexibility to design such a set of texts is provided through the SUBCORPUS feature.

You can define (or "compile") a new subcorpus by several different methods:

- Written metatextual categories
- Spoken metatextual categories
- Genre labels
- Keyword/title scan
- Manual entry of text IDs
- Manual entry of speaker IDs

In the following two subsections, we will use the first method as a way of illustrating the creation of a subcorpus, and next show how to use it to restrict a query. In Sections 10.4.1 to 10.4.5, each of the remaining methods of designing subcorpora will then be described in detail.

10.3   Basic steps for creating and using a subcorpus

10.3.1   Defining a new subcorpus via Written metatextual categories

Creating a subcorpus using written metatextual categories is simple. The page is essentially the same as that for running a restricted query on a subsection of written texts. The only difference is that there is no "Query term" box at the top (because you are not running a linguistic search), and the button now says [Get text IDs], because the idea is to get a list of all the BNC files that match the metatextual criteria chosen.

Suppose you wanted to create a subcorpus of academic journal articles. These texts are all to be found within the written academic genres in the BNC, i.e. texts whose genre classification code starts with "W:ac". But besides journal articles, written academic genres include textbooks and unpublished dissertations. To find journal articles only, do the following:

1. Click on MAKE/EDIT SUBCOPORA on the main navigation panel.

2. Select WRITTEN METATEXTUAL CATEGORIES from the drop-down menu and press [Go].

3. Under "Medium of Text", select "Periodical", and under "Genre", select all boxes whose labels start with "W:ac"—i.e. the first six options in the Genre section (see Figure 10.1).

4. Press [Get text IDs]. You will see that there are 153 files (totaling about 2.7 million words) of academic journal articles in the BNC (see Figure 10.2).

Medium of Text:	Genre (description of codes):
☐ Book	☑ W:ac:humanities_arts
☑ Periodical	☑ W:ac:medicine
☐ Miscellaneous: published	☑ W:ac:nat_science
☐ Miscellaneous: unpublished	☑ W:ac:polit_law_edu
☐ To-be-spoken	☑ W:ac:soc_science
	☑ W:ac:tech_engin

Figure 10.1:   Selections for creating a subcorpus of "Academic Journal articles"

Your query returned 153 files with a total of 2,696,318 words.

|< << >> >| (Show Page:) 1   (New Query ⬦) (Go!)   (New subcorpus ⬦) (Add) include all ☐

No	Filename	Hits 1 to 50 Page 1 / 4	
1	A6G	Twentieth century British history. Sample containing about 43756 words from a periodical (domain: social science) - 44,075 w-units, 1,609 s-units	☐
2	A6U	Oxford Art Journal. Sample containing about 26310 words from a periodical (domain: arts) - 26,548 w-units, 1,082 s-units	☐
3	ALM	British journal of social work. Sample containing about 31815 words from a periodical (domain: social science) - 31,872 w-units, 1,421 s-units	☐
4	ALN	British journal of social work. Sample containing about 23152 words from a periodical (domain: social science) - 23,159 w-units, 908 s-units	☐
5	ALP	British journal of social work. Sample containing about 25204 words from a periodical (domain: social science) - 25,277 w-units, 1,078 s-units	☐
6	APE	Parliamentary affairs. Sample containing about 36270 words from a periodical (domain: social science) - 36,442 w-units, 1,436 s-units	☐
7	ARD	Screen. Sample containing about 24424 words from a periodical (domain: arts) - 24,560 w-units, 815 s-units	☐

Figure 10.2:   List of academic journal articles, ready for selection and inclusion in a new subcorpus

5. If you want all of the 153 returned texts to be included in a subcorpus, simply select the checkbox "include all" and press [Add]. You will then be taken to a screen that asks you to name your subcorpus (cf. Figure 10.3). Let's give it the name "W_Acad_Journals".

Subcorpus Administration Page

Please enter a name for your new subcorpus:

W_Acad_Journals	(Submit name)

Figure 10.3:   Selecting a name for your subcorpus.

After pressing [Submit name], you should receive a confirmation that your sub-corpus has been successfully saved. As shown in Figure 10.4, *BNCweb* will also display some information about the size of the saved subcorpus (both the number of texts and an exact word count).

Subcorpus Administration Page
Your subcorpus *W_Acad_Journals* has been saved.
It contains **153** texts with a total of **2,696,318** words.
New Query   Go!

Figure 10.4:   Confirmation display after saving a subcorpus

Tip:
It is a good idea to include "S" or "W" at the front of the genre label and to make your labels "hierarchical" (highest-level category first)—it will help you recognize and understand them later: we could, for example, have another subcorpus labeled "S_Acad_Lectures" for spoken university lectures. Note also that names for subcorpora are case-insensitive and that they can only contain letters, numbers and the underscore character ("_"). Hyphens, spaces or other characters or symbols are not allowed.

10.3.2   Running a query on your subcorpus

Now that you have defined the subcorpus, you can use it to restrict your future queries. The procedure is the same as running a query over the whole BNC—with a simple addition:

1. Enter your query term in the box on the STANDARD QUERY page.
2. In the drop-down menu for "Restriction" select the name of the subcorpus you just created. Notice that *BNCweb* conveniently indicates the size and the number of texts your subcorpus contains.
3. Press [Start query].

Figure 10.5 exemplifies the application of a user-defined subcorpus via the "Restriction" option on the STANDARD QUERY page. By selecting "Subcorpus: W_Acad_Journals", the search for the noun lemma STUDY (by means of the

Simple query `{study/N}`) will be limited to the 153 files of academic journals in the corpus.

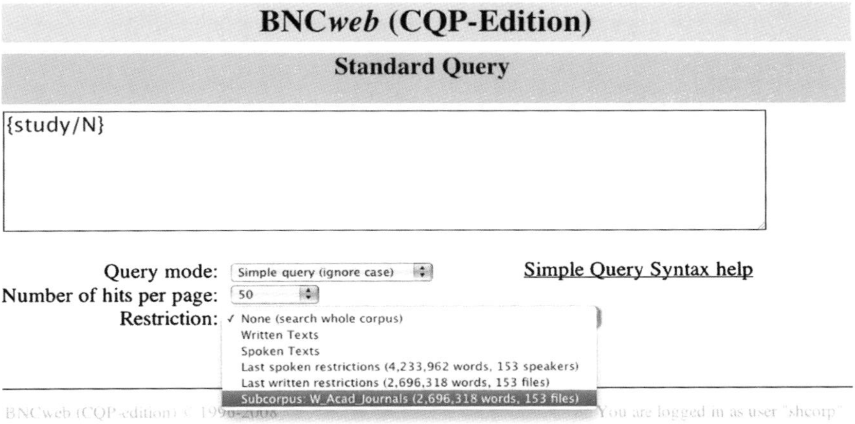

Figure 10.5: Searching for the noun *study* in academic journals

The result of this search is displayed in Figure 10.6. Perhaps not surprisingly, we find that the noun STUDY is used quite frequently in this genre: the search retrieves 5,471 hits in this relatively small sub-section of the corpus. This is equivalent to a normalized frequency of 2,029 instances pmw.

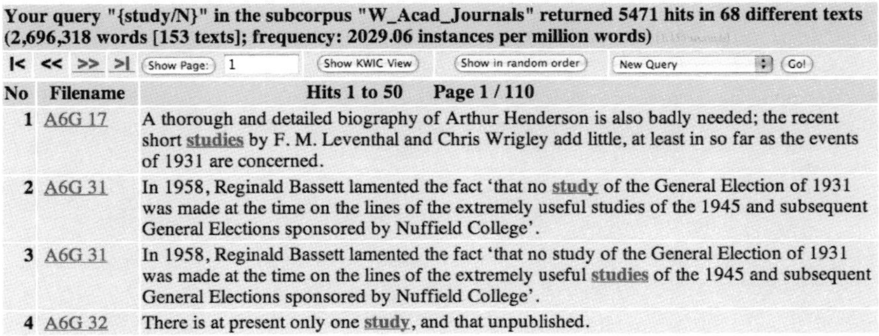

Your query "{study/N}" in the subcorpus "W_Acad_Journals" returned 5471 hits in 68 different texts (2,696,318 words [153 texts]; frequency: 2029.06 instances per million words)

|< << >> >| Show Page: 1 | Show KWIC View | Show in random order | New Query | Go!

No	Filename	Hits 1 to 50 Page 1 / 110
1	A6G 17	A thorough and detailed biography of Arthur Henderson is also badly needed; the recent short **studies** by F. M. Leventhal and Chris Wrigley add little, at least in so far as the events of 1931 are concerned.
2	A6G 31	In 1958, Reginald Bassett lamented the fact 'that no **study** of the General Election of 1931 was made at the time on the lines of the extremely useful studies of the 1945 and subsequent General Elections sponsored by Nuffield College'.
3	A6G 31	In 1958, Reginald Bassett lamented the fact 'that no study of the General Election of 1931 was made at the time on the lines of the extremely useful **studies** of the 1945 and subsequent General Elections sponsored by Nuffield College'.
4	A6G 32	There is at present only one **study**, and that unpublished.

Figure 10.6: Query result of a search for the noun lemma STUDY in the subcorpus "W_Acad_Journals"

If you want to see how this frequency compares to the use of the noun STUDY in the whole written component of the BNC, simply make the appropriate change in the "Restrictions" menu (i.e. select "Written texts") and re-run your query. By doing so, you will be able to confirm that STUDY is indeed very characteristic of academic journals. In written texts as a whole (which of course include the texts from academic journals), the overall frequency is much lower, at just 362 instances pmw. In Chapter 11, we will demonstrate the use of the KEYWORDS feature of *BNCweb*, which allows you to detect such domain- or genre-specific words in an automated way.

Task:
Create a subcorpus of spoken university lectures (calling it "S_lectures") and use it to compare the frequencies—and use—of the noun lemma STUDY in your two subcorpora. Then jot down a number of other words that you would expect to be frequent in these two genres and test whether your intuitions can be confirmed. You might also want to use the functions introduced in previous chapters (e.g. COLLOCATIONS, SORT) to determine whether the usage of your words differs in the two subcorpora in any interesting ways.

10.4   More on methods for creating subcorpora

10.4.1   Selecting a narrower range of texts for a subcorpus

In Section 10.3.1, we chose the simplest way of selecting texts for a subcorpus in that we included all texts that matched the categories we considered to represent academic journals (see Figure 10.1). If you are researching a specific discipline (e.g. only medical journal articles) you might instead only wish to select individual entries from the list of texts. To do this:

1. Follow the first two steps described in Section 10.3.1—i.e. select the appropriate categories and press [Get text IDs].

2. Instead of selecting "Include all", choose texts individually and click [Add]. Then give your subcorpus a name and save it.

If the list of texts runs over more than one page:

3. Use the [Back] button of your browser to return to the display of files and use the arrow link at the top of the list to navigate to the second page. Again, make your selection of texts. Note that it is also possible to select

all texts on a page by checking the "include all files on this page" box at the bottom of the page.

4. Select the name of the subcorpus you previously created in the drop-down menu at the top of the file-list and press [Add]. This will add your selection of texts to the existing subcorpus.

5. Repeat this procedure until you have gone through the complete list of texts.

By default, *BNCweb* displays 50 hits per page; however, a larger value can be selected in a drop-down menu on the WRITTEN RESTRICTIONS or SPOKEN RESTRICTIONS page.

The following sections review some alternative methods of creating subcorpora.

10.4.2   Defining a new subcorpus via Spoken metatextual categories

Creating a subcorpus using spoken metatextual categories is essentially the same process as for written metatexual categories. However, if you select any of the boxes under the heading "Speaker Restrictions", what you get is a subcorpus of actual utterances/speech by people matching your criteria, rather than a subcorpus consisting of entire files (which is what you get when selecting written texts, or when selecting spoken texts on the basis of file-level criteria such as "interaction type", "genre" or respondent characteristics). If you mix file-level and speaker-level criteria, the result will be speaker IDs rather than text IDs. The following examples should make this clear.

Suppose you are interested in the speech of the "younger generation" of female speakers of British English (i.e. those within a range of 20 years, from 25-44). You can create a subcorpus for this group of speakers by doing the following:

1. Click on MAKE/EDIT SUBCOPORA on the main navigation panel, select "Spoken metatextual categories" from the drop-down menu and press [Go].

2. At the next screen, under "Speaker Restriction: Age:" select the age ranges "25-34" and "35-44". Also select "Female" for "Sex" (see Figure 10.7) and press [Get text IDs/speaker IDs]. The result of this action is displayed in Figure 10.8. This list is slightly different from the one that you retrieved for written texts in Section 10.3.1 above: it shows individual speaker IDs rather than text IDs. This is because we have made a speaker-

based restriction, so all word counts and searches are now in reference to the utterances made by the chosen speakers, instead of entire files.

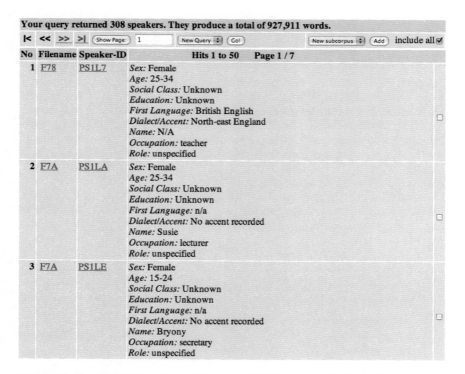

Figure 10.7:   Selections to retrieve a list of female speakers aged 25-44

Figure 10.8:   List of female speakers aged 25-44, ready for inclusion in a new subcorpus

3. Now follow the same steps as given in Section 10.3.1 for written texts (i.e. tick "include all" and add all the speakers to a new subcorpus, or select individual speakers to include).

You are now in a position to do analyses of the language of young female speakers.

> **Tip:**
> If you click on WRITTEN RESTRICTIONS or SPOKEN RESTRICTIONS on the main navigation panel of *BNCweb* (as if you were doing a search on specific subsets of the spoken or written component of the BNC), you can leave the "Query term" box empty and only select metatextual categories. The query result will be then a list of text (or speaker) IDs, which can be used to create a subcorpus in the same way as in the instructions given above.

Note that we said above that we are interested in the language of younger female speakers of British English (rather than any other variety of English). In fact, there is a category called "First language" in the BNC which we could have used in step 3 above to restrict your queries specifically to "British English". However, we would then have got very few matches: just 104 speakers who produce a total of 180,281 words. As discussed in Chapter 3 (Section 3.4), for many speakers we actually do not have information for all possible categories. In fact, out of the 10.4 million words of speech in the BNC World Edition, only around 3 million were spoken by a person whose first language was officially recorded as being British English. For practical purposes, however, we can quite safely assume that the vast majority of the unknowns are actually British English speakers. Whether or not you tick the box for "First language: British English" is therefore a matter of how strict you want to be, and how much (or, rather, little!) data you want to work with.

10.4.3   Defining a new subcorpus via Genre labels

On the MAKE/EDIT SUBCORPORA page, the third option on the drop-down list is for you to define a new corpus via the genre labels in the texts. The full genre classification scheme is found in Appendix 1. This method of creating a subcorpus is recommended only in certain cases, as illustrated below. Usually, it is easier to simply tick the boxes for the genres that you want on the spoken or written metatextual categories pages (as discussed in the previous two sections). The genre labels in the BNC are hierarchical (with higher-level or more general categories always coming first in the label), and it is this aspect that makes creating a subcorpus via the "Genre labels" method worth exploring if you are aiming at one of the categories that are repeated and want to avoid having to tick too many boxes.

For example, if you are interested in examining the language of newspapers, and are not particularly concerned about the topic (sports, science, politics, or fashion) or the different types of newspaper (tabloid, regional paper or national broadsheet), then there are eight different subcategories of national broadsheet newspaper texts in the BNC that you would need to select individually if you were to create a subcorpus through the WRITTEN RESTRICTIONS page (i.e. eight boxes to tick). Using the "Genre labels" method, you would only need to select the string "brdsht_nat" and all the relevant files will be selected (see Fig 10.9). After you click [Submit], a list of 340 texts is returned. To create a subcorpus from these texts, follow the same procedure as outlined in Section 10.3.1 above.

Figure 10.9:   Creating a subcorpus of all national broadsheet newspaper texts via the "Genre labels" method

Other cases where using genre labels to define your subcorpus would be faster include the following:

- All academic texts: 6 subcategories ➜ select "ac"
- All non-academic texts: 6 subcategories ➜ select "non_ac"
- All lectures (spoken): 5 subcategories ➜ select "lect"
- Domain or topic-based texts, such as "all written texts related to politics, law or education (both academic and non-academic)" ➜ select "polit_law_edu"; optionally, also select "S" or "W" from the second or third column.

The last example above illustrates the role of the other two columns joined by the word "AND" in Figure 10.9 (all three columns contain the same set of labels). If only "polit_law_edu" were selected in the first column, the resulting list of files would include both spoken and written texts that relate to politics, law or education. If you want only the written texts, then selecting "W" in the second or third column will apply the additional restriction.

10.4.4   Defining a new subcorpus via Keyword/title scan

Although the BNC texts have been classified according to domain, genre, time period, medium, and so forth, these classifications may still be too broad for your purposes. For example, lots of different topics and fields of study are included under "Humanities and the arts". If your research needs are very specific and require you to zoom in on a very particular set of texts, you may find it useful to use the KEYWORD/TITLE SCAN facility to find texts by entering in key topic words relating to the content that you are interested in. This method, like the "Genre labels" method, is flexible in the sense that it allows you to cut across boundaries easily (e.g. spoken versus written, academic or non-academic). There are two fields you can search by:

1. **Keywords**: terms used to summarize the content of corpus texts. There are two types of keywords in the BNC: one type—the default—consists in the content descriptors provided by library cataloguers (the type called "COPAC"). Alternatively, you can use the (less detailed) descriptions given by BNC compilers (the type called "Descriptive keywords—BNC1 release").

2. **Titles:** the titles given in the headers of BNC files. For written texts, these titles are usually the name of the document from which a text was taken (e.g. "Art criticism: a user's guide"). For spoken texts, the title is a de-

scriptive name reflecting the topic area and/or speech event (e.g. "Careers Service: meeting").

COPAC is the joint academic library catalogue from which the keywords were manually extracted (see Lee 2001 for details). Note that not all published texts have COPAC keywords associated with them (and there are no COPAC entries for the non-published written texts and the spoken texts). Thus, if you want be thorough in your topic-based searches, it is probably a good idea to do two separate searches using both the keyword and the title fields.

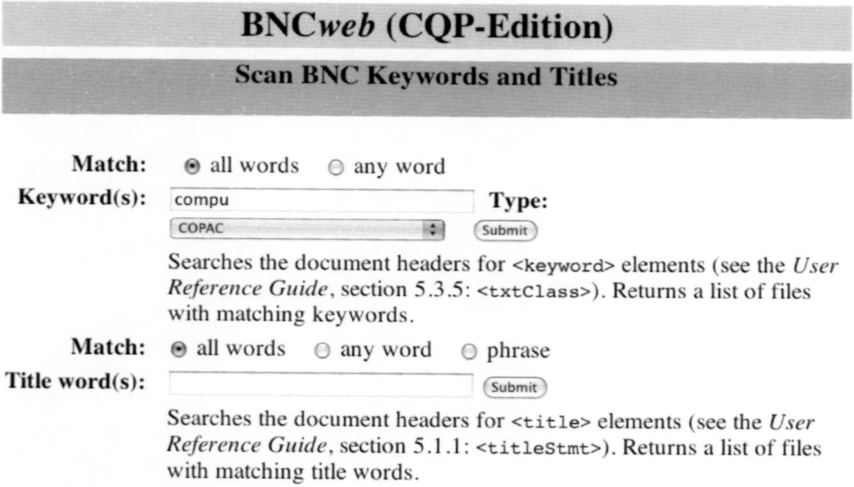

BNC*web* (CQP-Edition)

Scan BNC Keywords and Titles

Match: ⦿ all words   ○ any word
Keyword(s): `compu`   **Type:**
`COPAC` (Submit)

Searches the document headers for <keyword> elements (see the *User Reference Guide*, section 5.3.5: <txtClass>). Returns a list of files with matching keywords.

Match: ⦿ all words   ○ any word   ○ phrase
Title word(s): (Submit)

Searches the document headers for <title> elements (see the *User Reference Guide*, section 5.1.1: <titleStmt>). Returns a list of files with matching title words.

Figure 10.10: Searching for term `compu` to find texts about computing, using the COPAC keyword search option

If, for example, you wish to study the collocates of some words used in the field of computing and do not have any preference as to genre or whether the usage is spoken or written, you could enter `compu` (to match words such as *computer(s)*, and *computing*) as a search term for the keyword search first, and then complement this by a search for title words. Figures 10.10 and 10.11 show the search for `compu` in the keyword field and the resulting list of files.

As with the other modes of subcorpus definition, you can browse through the list to make sure these are all texts that you want. If they are, then just include all of them (scroll to the bottom, tick "include all files" and click [Add]). For this example, we will call the new subcorpus "Computing_texts".

BNC Keyword Information	
For the keyword 'compu', the following 13 texts were found:	

Text	Keyword(s)	Include in subcorpus
AC9	Archaeology, Use of, Science Computer science - Historiography Physical sciences - Historiography Archaeology - Scientific techniques Archaeology - Methodology Archaeometry - London British Museum. Department of Scientific Research British Museum. Department of Conservation	☐
B1G	Geography - Methodology - Addresses, essays, lectures Geography. Use of, Computers Geographic information systems. Geography - Computer programs Geographical information systems	☐
B26	Microsoft Word for Windows (Computer program) Word processing	☐
EUS	Electronic digital computers - Design and construction Computer architecture	☐
FA4	Electronic publishing - Great Britain Publishing. Use of, Computers	☐

Figure 10.11: Query result of a search for texts about computing, using the COPAC keyword search

On the confirmation page, select "Scan keywords/titles" in the drop-down menu and press [Go]. This time, enter compu in the "Title word(s)" field and press [Submit]. You will see a list of 75 files that match this title field search. (Note that two of the files, H61 and JP6, are spoken transcripts—respectively recordings of a computer advice session and a lecture on computing.) This time, instead of adding to a "New subcorpus", you will want to add the 75 files to the previously created subcorpus "Compu_texts", which you can select from the drop-down menu (as shown in Figure 10.12).

You need not worry about duplication: although some files in this list were also in the earlier list obtained by scanning the COPAC keywords field, *BNCweb* will add only new files to an existing subcorpus.

HR3	Computer applications in geography. Sample containing about 40789 words from a book (domain: applied science)	☐
HSY	CompuAdd. The catalogue. Sample containing about 2752 words of miscellanea (domain: applied science)	☐
HWF	Lifespan computer manuals. Sample containing about 211748 words of unpublished miscellanea (domain: applied science)	☐
HXD	Introduction to computer law. Sample containing about 44481 words from a book (domain: social science)	☐
JP6	Computers lecture. Sample containing about 5342 words speech recorded in educational context	☐
JXK	The microcomputer, the school librarian, and the teacher. Sample containing about 34637 words from a book (domain: applied science)	☐

Choose subcorpus:　[Computing_texts ▼]　(Add)　　　　　　　　　　　　　　　☑ include all files

Figure 10.12:　Adding files to an existing subcorpus

10.4.5　Defining a new subcorpus via manual entry of text IDs or speaker IDs

The last method of creating a subcorpus is designed to give you maximum flexibility: you can directly enter a list of text IDs or speaker IDs. This method is useful if you already have a list of files or speakers that you want to include.

Tip:
You may have a pre-defined list of text IDs to include in a subcorpus as a result of previous research or through using the complementary BNC Index spreadsheet (download it from http://clix.to/davidlee00). One of the things that the BNC Index allows (that *BNCweb* does not) is the ability to search by the full bibliographic record, including authors' names and publisher. The BNC Index also has fuller, more detailed titles for a lot of files: the subtitles of many books are not included in the BNC headers, and are therefore not searchable under *BNCweb*. These subtitles and other bibliographical details often serve to disambiguate and fully describe the content of the texts, and so if you are making a careful selection, you may find it fruitful to first use the BNC Index (rather than *BNCweb* itself) to make your selection of individual files.

For example, if your interest is in texts about music, a search of titles and subtitles using the BNC Index will give you 20 text IDs for music-related files, out of which only 5 match your criteria of "academic works on music"—you can tell this from the bibliographical information (including the name of the publisher), as shown in Table 10.1.

Table 10.1 Bibliographic information for five music texts

Text ID	Bibliographic information
FB3	Studying popular music. Middleton, R. Milton Keynes: Open Univ Press, 1993, pp. 3-83. 1223 s-units.
GUH	The concise Oxford history of music. Abraham, Gerald. Oxford: OUP, 1985, pp. 201-327. 1129 s-units.
GVJ	Musical composition. Brindle, Reginald Smith. Oxford: OUP, 1986, pp. 7-147. 1765 s-units.
GWM	Early Music. Oxford: OUP, 1993, pp. 29-120. 1164 s-units.
J1A	Early Music. Oxford: OUP, 1993, pp. ??. 1638 s-units.

This set of 5 text IDs can then be entered directly into *BNCweb* to form a subcorpus as follows:

1. Click on MAKE/EDIT SUBCOPORA on the main navigation panel, select "Manual entry of text IDs" from the drop-down menu and press [Go].
2. On the "Subcorpus Administration Page" enter the text IDs and give your new subcorpus a name, as shown in Figure 10.13.

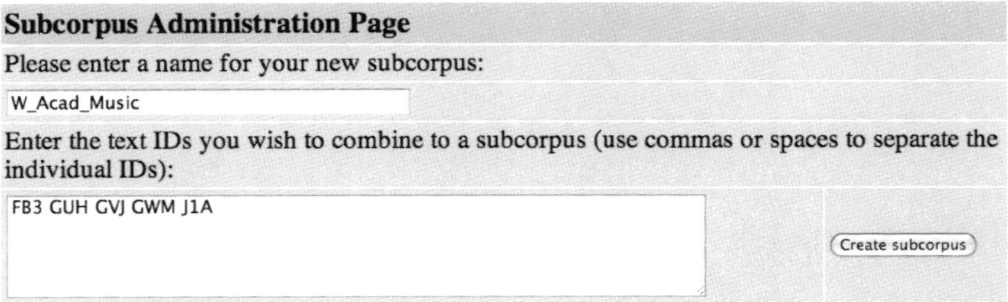

Subcorpus Administration Page

Please enter a name for your new subcorpus:

W_Acad_Music

Enter the text IDs you wish to combine to a subcorpus (use commas or spaces to separate the individual IDs):

FB3 GUH GVJ GWM J1A

Create subcorpus

Figure 10.13: Defining a new subcorpus via manual entry of text IDs

3. Press [Create subcorpus] and *BNCweb* will tell you that you have created
   a subcorpus of 5 texts with a total of 185,886 words.

Creating a subcorpus by "Manual entry of speaker IDs" is a similar procedure. If
you already know in advance which speakers you want to use to constitute a
subcorpus, then this facility of *BNCweb* can be used to enter those speaker IDs
directly.

Tip:

On the main navigation panel of *BNCweb*, you will also see the menu
options SCAN KEYWORDS/TITLES and EXPLORE GENRE LABELS. These
work in the same way to create subcorpora, as described in this chapter (i.e. you do not need to click on MAKE/EDIT SUBCORPORA first, but
can click on these links directly). These two functions are included on
the main navigation panel because users may want to gain additional
information about the BNC texts without necessarily intending to create subcorpora.

10.4.6   Modifying your subcorpora

If you have previously defined subcorpora, they will be listed in the MAKE/EDIT
SUBCORPORA page as shown in Figure 10.14.

BNC*web* (CQP-Edition)

Define new subcorpus via: [Written metatextual categories ▾] (Go)

User-defined Subcorpora

Name of subcorpus	No. of texts/speakers	No. of words	Frequency list	Action	
Computing_texts	82 texts	1,260,122	Compile	Delete	Copy
last_spoken	308 speakers	927,911	n/a	Delete	Copy
last_written	153 texts	2,696,318	n/a	Delete	Copy
W_Acad_Journals	153 texts	2,696,318	Available	Delete	Copy

Figure 10.14: The MAKE/EDIT SUBCORPORA page, showing previously defined
                    subcorpora

A subcorpus can be deleted by clicking on the word "Delete" in the fifth column ("Action"). This action cannot be undone. The functionality of the fourth column—labeled "Frequency list"—will be explained in Chapter 11.

Clicking on the name of a subcorpus will produce a list of the files it contains. From here, it is possible to delete or add individual files, as shown by the checked files in Figure 10.15.

Subcorpus Administration Page

Your subcorpus *W_Acad_Journals* consists of 153 texts with a total of 2,696,318 words.

|< << >> >| [Add files to subcorpus ⬦] (Go!)   (Delete marked files)

No	Text	Title	No. of words	Delete
1	A6G	Twentieth century British history. Sample containing about 43756 words from a periodical (domain: social science)	44,075	☑
2	A6U	Oxford Art Journal. Sample containing about 26310 words from a periodical (domain: arts)	26,548	☐
3	ALM	British journal of social work. Sample containing about 31815 words from a periodical (domain: social science)	31,872	☑
4	ALN	British journal of social work. Sample containing about 23152 words from a periodical (domain: social science)	23,159	☑

Figure 10.15: Marking files for deletion from a subcorpus

The action "Copy" shown in the rightmost column of Figure 10.14 allows you to create a copy of an existing corpus. This is useful when you want to create a new subcorpus that is a subset or an expansion of an existing one. The copied subcorpus can have files added to or subtracted from it, without affecting the original subcorpus. The "Copy" function is the only way to rename a subcorpus: make a copy of it first, at which point you will be asked what name to give to it.

10.5   Saving time by using subcorpora

We have already shown how using subcorpora can save you from having to enter the same selection of metatextual restrictions repeatedly. *BNCweb* has another somewhat hidden feature which takes this approach one step further. As you saw in Figure 10.14 (in Section 10.4.6 above), the list of subcorpora also includes "last_written" and "last_spoken". These two subcorpora are special in that they are not fixed, but are constantly updated whenever you make queries using WRITTEN RESTRICTIONS or SPOKEN RESTRICTIONS: they always consist of the set of texts or speaker IDs that were matched by your last search. For example, if your last search was restricted to female speakers in the age range of "25-44", then "last_spoken" will automatically be set to contain all speaker IDs that correspond to this selection. However, as soon as you perform a different query with another set of spoken text selections, the subcorpus will be automatically re-defined to reflect your new selection.

This functionality is useful if you need to perform multiple searches over the same set of texts (or speakers) but do not wish to create a permanent subcorpus (for example, because you think that it is unlikely that you will need to perform similar searches in the future). Rather than require you to repeatedly select the relevant set of texts or speakers on the WRITTEN RESTRICTIONS or SPOKEN RESTRICTIONS query pages, *BNCweb* will store your selection after the first query and make it available for subsequent queries from the drop-down menu on the standard query page. If at some stage you decide that you wish to save your temporary subcorpus for future use, you can do this by copying "last_written" or "last_spoken" and giving it a name of your choice.

10.6   Exercises

1. *Different kinds of subcorpora.* In order to further practice the different ways of creating subcorpora, experiment with compiling subcorpora as follows:

   a) define a subcorpus of teen fiction (novels)

   b) define a subcorpus of broadcast speech (radio or television talk shows, discussions, etc.)

   c) define a subcorpus of texts (written or spoken) that are about Northern Ireland

2. *Are collocations different in different genres?* The following exercise will illustrate the usefulness of having pre-defined subcorpora, as it will involve multiple searches in a number of subcorpora. Let us narrow down our research question a little: Are the collocates of *factor, issue, concept* and *problem* different in the subcorpora conversations (S_conv), lectures (S_lectures), general written academic language (W_acad), and all spoken texts (S_all)?

   a) If you haven't done so already, create the first three subcorpora mentioned above. (The subcorpus of "all spoken texts" doesn't need to be created because it's pre-defined in *BNCweb*.)

   b) For each of the subcorpora, generate a list of "1 Left" adjectival collocates (with a frequency of 5 or more) for the words *factor, issue, concept* and *problem*. What do you notice about the number of collocates obtained from each subcorpus?

11 Keywords and frequency lists

11.1 Outline

This chapter describes the following two functions of *BNCweb*:

- Finding keywords in different parts of the BNC
- Compiling frequency lists of words and headwords/lemmas

11.2 Introduction

As we have seen throughout this book, corpus-linguistic methodology centers on an analysis of the frequency of features you can observe in your data. In Chapter 4, for example, we compared the frequencies of a word like *wicked* in various sub-sections of the corpus and tried to draw conclusions about its use in contemporary British English from the patterns we observed. Sometimes it is also useful to look at the corpus (or a subcorpus) as a whole and determine some of its salient characteristics without taking a word or other linguistic expression as the starting point.

One such method is to produce lists of "keywords"—i.e. words which occur with significantly greater frequency in one part of the corpus than another. Another method is the compilation of frequency lists of words in a subcorpus of your choice (or, in fact, in the whole BNC). Both functions can help you discover particular lexical (and lexico-grammatical) characteristics of subparts of the corpus; they may therefore alert you to linguistic items that would be worthy of further investigation.

11.3 The Keywords function

11.3.1 About keywords

In Chapter 10, we made use of the SUBCORPUS feature to explore the frequency and use of the noun *study* in academic journals. A comparison of these findings with a search over the written component of the corpus revealed that this noun is—not surprisingly—very typical of academic journals. However, imagine that you were given the task of listing other nouns that show a similarly strong preference to occur in academic journals. Although you may be able to come up with a few further nouns where you can observe clear differences in frequency, it is highly likely that you would miss quite a number of others. This task of detecting particularly typical words for subsections of the BNC can be accomplished automatically—and reliably—with the KEYWORDS feature in *BNCweb*.

In corpus-based linguistics, "keywords" for a (sub)corpus are words which are more frequent or infrequent in a particular "study corpus" when compared against a "reference corpus". These words are considered "key" when the difference in textual frequencies is determined to be statistically significant—in other words, if we can say with a sufficient degree of confidence that the observed difference is not due to chance (cf. 5.6). Both positive keywords—i.e. words used relatively more often in the study corpus—and negative keywords—i.e. words used relatively less often in the study corpus—can be useful in the analysis and characterization of genres.

> Notice that the "Keywords" referred to here are different from what was described under "Defining a new subcorpus via Keyword/title scan" (Section 10.4.4). Those were library catalogue keywords—words that were used by librarians to describe the contents of published books.

11.3.2   Producing keyword lists

To produce a list of keywords, we need one frequency list for the study corpus and one for the reference corpus. As a general guideline, it is a good idea for your reference corpus to be at least five times bigger than your study corpus (Berber-Sardinha 2000).

In the following example, we will compare spoken university lectures with written academic journal articles (the latter is more than eight times larger than the former, so it qualifies as an adequate reference corpus).

Stage A: Preparatory Steps

1. First, ensure that the subcorpora for both "academic journals" and "university lectures" have been defined—if so, they will be listed on the MAKE/EDIT SUBCORPORA page (see Chapter 10, Figure 10.14).

2. Also check on the same page whether frequency data for these subcorpora are available. This is indicated in the fourth column of the table. If frequency lists for both subcorpora are listed as being "Available", go to stage B.

3. If a link labeled "Compile" is found for either of the subcorpora, click the link. After a short while, the list of subcorpora will refresh, with the frequency list marked as "Available".

Stage B: Finding Keywords

4. Click on KEYWORDS in the main navigation panel of *BNCweb*.

5. Choose "S_lectures" from the drop-down menu entitled "Select frequency list 1".

6. For the second frequency list, select "W_Acad_Journals".

7. In the section "Compare", choose "Word + POS-tag combinations" (this way, *kind* as a noun—which is very common in academic speech—will be distinguished from *kind* as an adjective). Figure 11.1 shows these selections.

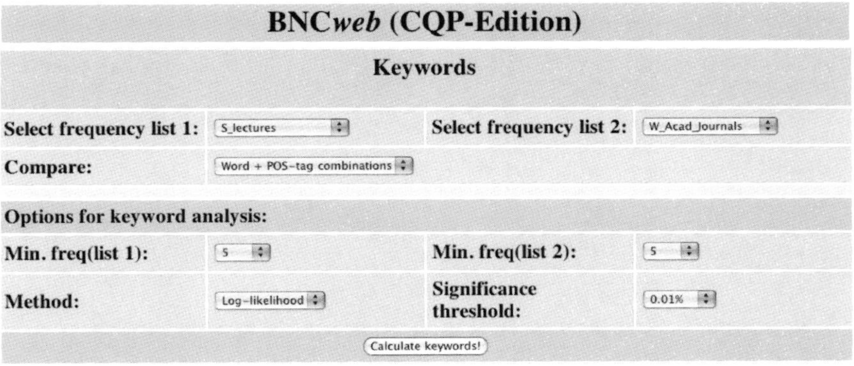

BNC*web* (CQP-Edition)

Keywords

Select frequency list 1:	S_lectures	**Select frequency list 2:**	W_Acad_Journals
Compare:	Word + POS-tag combinations		

Options for keyword analysis:

Min. freq(list 1):	5	**Min. freq(list 2):**	5
Method:	Log–likelihood	**Significance threshold:**	0.01%

Calculate keywords!

Figure 11.1:   Options available in the KEYWORDS feature (upper part of page)

8. For the other parameters on the page, accept the defaults.

9. Finally, press [Calculate keywords!] to compare academic lectures with academic journal articles. The result of this comparison is shown in Figure 11.2.

Keywords in *BNCweb* are ordered according to the *absolute* log-likelihood value (LL-value) in the last column: i.e. the positive and negative signs are disregarded in the ranking, and only the numerical values matter. The meanings of "positive keywords" and "negative keywords" can be explained as follows: a "positive" keyword is one that is significantly more common in subcorpus 1 (in this example, "S_lectures"), while a "negative" keyword is one that is relatively rare ("negatively frequent") in subcorpus 1, compared to subcorpus 2 (here, "W_Acad_Journals"). Or, you could simply think of negative keywords as those that are significantly more common in subcorpus 2.

Keywords for 'S_lectures' and 'W_Acad_Journals'

|< << >> [New Keyword calculation ◆] [Go!]

No.	Word	Frequency in 'S_lectures'	Frequency in 'W_Acad_Journals'	+/-	LL-value
1	you_PNP	6,720	594	+	26907.43
2	's_VBZ	3,596	330	+	14340.71
3	i_PNP	4,908	4,249	+	10821.76
4	n't_XX0	2,218	207	+	8828.96
5	it_PNP	6,076	14,375	+	6096.67
6	're_VBB	1,198	30	+	5233.54
7	've_VHB	1,033	24	+	4526.34
8	that_DT0	2,941	4,632	+	4386.43
9	so_AV0	2,267	2,677	+	4171.38
10	know_VVB	1,046	128	+	4028.41
11	what_DTQ	1,928	2,013	+	3830.28
12	?_PUN	1,629	1,393	+	3614.81
13	,_PUN	20,873	117,031	+	3498.74
14	right_AV0	780	57	+	3182.68
15	got_VVN	640	27	+	2722.77

Figure 11.2:   Keywords for the comparison between "S_lectures" and "W_Acad_Journals"

Note that *BNCweb* shades the cells to make it clear in which subcorpus a word is more common. In Figure 11.2, you can see that all the cells under the "Frequency in S_lectures" column are in slightly darker grey, indicating that these words are all those that characterize academic lectures, relative to academic journal articles. If you study these keywords, they all seem to make sense because *you, 's, I, n't, it, 're, 've* and so forth are characteristic of speaking rather than writing (in academic journals, the reader (*you*) is usually not directly addressed, the writer (*I*) is usually backgrounded, and contractions (*'s, n't, 're', 've*) are generally dispreferred). Other interesting keywords indicating the interactivity of spoken discourse are the question mark (number 12 on the list) and the word *right* tagged as adverb (number 14). Note that the latter item includes—and in fact predominantly consists of—its use as a discourse marker.

Figure 11.3 displays some of the items found further down the list. The column "Frequency in 'W_Acad_Journals'" now has some shaded cells, showing that keywords nos. 33 (*the*), 34 (opening quote mark), 44 (*of*), 45 (closing quote mark) and 46 (colon) are more common in journal articles than in lectures. The second-last column also shows a 'minus' sign, meaning that these words are 'negatively common' in lectures. If you click on the forward arrow at the top to see the next page of keywords, you will see more negative keywords such as *by, in* and *with*. Again, these keyword results make sense, and, importantly, give empirical confirmation to our intuitions: *the, of* and the prepositions *by, in* and *with* are all associated with noun phrases (confirming the "nouny" style of academic writing), while the punctuation marks are, of course, those of written texts rather than spoken transcripts.

28	mean_VVB	649	298	+	1867.96
29	yes_ITJ	453	39	+	1818.89
30	about_PRP	1,149	1,715	+	1788.73
31	kind_NN1	594	311	+	1632.76
32	now_AV0	928	1,178	+	1626.84
33	the_AT0	14,740	182,632	-	1563.75
34	'_PUQ	28	8,194	-	1487.24
35	thing_NN1	415	100	+	1422.6
36	something_PNI	492	231	+	1405.47
37	well_AV0	968	1,575	+	1405.47
38	your_DPS	528	304	+	1400.03
39	actually_AV0	475	210	+	1384.39
40	really_AV0	417	138	+	1324.28
41	do_VDI	644	637	+	1320.42
42	oh_ITJ	337	37	+	1316.17
43	mm_ITJ	362	65	+	1314.18
44	of_PRF	8,936	116,150	-	1272.59
45	'_PUQ	28	6,881	-	1219.38
46	:_PUN	5	6,016	-	1214.13
47	like_PRP	587	628	+	1149.23
48	ca_VM0	291	31	+	1140.73
49	get_VVI	356	140	+	1076.41
50	get_VVB	276	32	+	1070.52

Figure 11.3:   Keywords   for   the   comparison   between   "S_lectures"   and "W_Acad_Journals"—lower part of first page

One additional observation that could be made when comparing the keywords of the two subcorpora is that nearly all the items in the list are function words, and correspondingly that there is a sparsity of lexical content words (e.g. *research, argue, social*). This can probably be explained by a tendency for the subject matter of the respective text types to overlap to a considerable extent.

11.3.3   Interpreting and adjusting keyword list settings

In Section 11.3.2, we asked you to accept the default keyword list settings. Let us now review each setting, and the effect any changes will have.

- **Minimum frequencies**: The parameters "Min. freq(list 1)" and "Min. freq(list 2)" set the minimum frequencies of items in each list that will be considered in the creation of keyword lists. The default frequency for both is "5", i.e. any item occurring fewer than five times will be ignored. This is a reasonable number that weeds out less common words that would otherwise give a skewed picture of the vocabulary of the subcorpora. (For smaller or more specialized subcorpora, however, you may want to experiment with frequencies lower than 5 if the results do not show interesting words that you know are characteristic of that genre.)

- **Method:** This refers to the method used for the calculation of what are called "keyness values": the higher the value, the more significant the difference between frequencies in the two subcorpora. *BNCweb* offers two methods: either the chi-squared or the log-likelihood method. The latter method is more accurate for this type of application (Rayson, Berridge & Francis, 2004) and is therefore selected as the default.

- **Statistics threshold:** This parameter sets a cut-off point for the display of keywords. For example, "0.1%" means that the probability that the observed difference in frequency is purely due to chance is 0.1% or lower. Any items on the list that have a higher probability than the selected threshold will not be displayed.[1]

It is, of course, best to obtain significance at the most stringent level, the 0.1% level ($p < 0.001$). This would mean that there is only a 0.1% probability that the difference between the two subcorpora is due to chance alone—thus suggesting that the observed differences have to do with the nature of the two subcorpora rather than with random variation. By default, *BNCweb* chooses the 0.1% significance threshold, and, in practice, this level is not difficult to achieve.

---

1   The log-likelihood and chi-squared methods are related, and therefore share the same critical values. Table 11.1 lists these values for statistical significance at various levels.

Table 11.1: Keyness values and levels of significance:

Critical Value	Implies the difference is significant at the
3.841	5% level; $p < 0.05$
6.635	1% level; $p < 0.01$
10.827	0.1% level; $p < 0.001$

This is for a 2x2 contingency table, so the degree of freedom = 1.

11.3.4   Finding items contained in only one frequency list

What we have covered so far applies to items that appear in both frequency lists; words that occur in only one of the lists will not be displayed. You would therefore miss any word that is very frequent in one list, and hence very typical of either your study corpus or the reference corpus, but that is not found at all in the other list. The reason for excluding such words is that log-likelihood values cannot be calculated if one of the values is zero.

BNCweb therefore provides the option of generating a list of words that occur in only one of the two subcorpora. To do this:

1. Go back to the KEYWORDS page with the help of the "back" button of your browser.
2. Use the drop-down menu in the lower part of this page (see Figure 11.4) to choose either "Frequency list 1" (the words that are unique to subcorpus 1) or "Frequency list 2" (the words unique to subcorpus 2).
3. Press [Compare lists!]. (Remember that these are not keyword lists—just frequency listings of unique words.)

Options for comparing frequency lists:

Display words that only occur in: [Frequency list 1 ◆]

[Compare lists!]

Figure 11.4:   Options available in the KEYWORDS feature (lower part of page)

Figure 11.5 displays a list of word–tag combinations that are found only in spoken lectures. Not surprisingly, the filled pause *erm* tops the list with over 3,000 instances, followed by *[unclear]*, i.e. passages of speech that could not be properly deciphered and were therefore left untranscribed. Many of the other items of the list are also clearly features of spoken language.

It is important to point out here that *BNCweb* does not generate "Key keywords". These are well-dispersed keywords, or keywords that are key in many different texts, rather than just clumped in a few. (The calculation of key keywords is a feature of *Wordsmith* tools— see Scott 1997 for a detailed discussion.) Therefore, treat your keywords with caution. If you have any reason to suspect that a particular keyword comes from just a handful of texts, click on the frequency count for the word to generate a concordance. The top of the concordance results page will always indicate how many different texts the word was

found in, and this can be used to gauge how "clumpy" or well-dispersed that
particular keyword is.

No.	Word	Frequency in 'S_lectures'	Frequency in 'W_Acad_Journals'
1	erm_UNC	3,103	0
2	[unclear]_UNC	2,348	0
3	okay_AV0	554	0
4	na_TO0	249	0
5	gon_VVG	214	0
6	alright_AV0	121	0
7	y'know_VVB-NN1	105	0
8	i_UNC	95	0
9	mhm_ITJ	87	0
10	y'know_NN1-VVB	79	0
11	w_UNC	58	0
12	superego_NN1	53	0
13	okay_AJ0	51	0
14	an_UNC	48	0
15	y'know_NN1	47	0
16	stuff_NN1-VVB	43	0
17	wh_UNC	42	0
18	y_UNC	37	0
19	handout_NN1	34	0
20	hello_ITJ	34	0

Items which only occur in 'S_lectures'

Figure 11.5:   Word–tag combinations that are exclusively found in the spoken
lectures subcorpus

11.4   The Frequency lists function

The FREQUENCY LISTS function allows you to list frequencies for words and
headwords—with the option of specifying their part of speech (e.g. to match
lemmas). Such lists are useful for detecting potentially salient linguistic items
within the corpus (or sub-parts of the corpus) which you can then analyze more
closely with the help of the other functions of *BNCweb*. Frequency lists can be
generated for the whole BNC, the spoken component of the BNC, the written
component of the BNC, and for any subcorpus that you define (cf. Chapter 10).

Before you can do frequency listings for a subcorpus, *BNCweb* first needs to
build an internal frequency database. As mentioned in Section 11.3.2, you can
do this from the MAKE/EDIT SUBCORPORA page, making sure that each subcorpus

for which you want to see word frequencies is marked as "Available". You can then compile a frequency list as follows:

1. In the main navigation panel, click on FREQUENCY LISTS. The page will refresh and show two panels of options for creating frequency lists (see Figure 11.6)

2. Choose to create either word-based (on the left) or headword-based (on the right) frequency lists; for further discussion of these options, see the more detailed description below.

3. Click the appropriate [Show list] button.

BNC*web* (CQP-Edition)

BNC Frequency Lists

Word frequencies		Headword or lemma frequencies	
Choose one or several POS-tags:	no restrictions any verb any noun any adjective any adverb any article any prepositio	Choose one or more simplified tags:	no restriction ADJ ADV ART CONJ INTERJ PREP
Word pattern:	starting with	Word pattern:	starting with
Range of texts:	Whole BNC	Range of texts:	Whole BNC
Range of frequency (optional):	from to	Range of frequency (optional):	from to
Show individual tag frequencies:	no	Show individual tag frequencies:	no
Type of ordering:	descending	Type of ordering:	descending
Number of items shown per page:	50	Number of items shown per page:	50
(Show list) (Reset)		(Show list) (Reset)	

Figure 11.6:   The options of the FREQUENCY LIST feature

You can set the following options for compiling frequency lists:

- **Choose one or several POS-tags:** Your selection restricts the display of the frequency list to certain parts of speech. You can choose between simplified tags such as "any verb" (cf. Chapter 3) or specific part-of-speech tags such as "VVD" (past tense lexical verb). Note that ambiguity tags (cf. 3.5.1) are listed separately towards the bottom of the list. For lemma frequency lists, only the 11 simplified tags are available. It is possible to select several POS-tags or simplified tags (the procedure for discontinuous selections varies according to operating system).

- **Word pattern:** This option allows you to limit the entries on the frequency list to items that match a particular pattern. You can further determine whether the pattern match applies to the start or the end of the word. If you select the option "containing", the match can be anywhere— i.e. also at the start or the end of the word. For example, you could select words "ending with t", and choose a part-of-speech restriction of "VVD" to retrieve past-tense verbs (e.g. *went, felt*).

- **Range of texts:** Choose the part of the corpus for which frequency lists are to be displayed. This drop-down menu will list any subcorpus for which frequency data is available (see Section 11.3.2).

- **Range of frequency:** Allows you to set minimum and maximum cut-off points for your frequency list (e.g. "from 5 to 100").

- **Show individual tag frequencies:** This option determines whether or not the items in your frequency list will be disambiguated by part of speech (so that, for example, *love* as verb would be counted and listed separately from *love* as a noun).

- **Type of ordering:** Allows you to choose between "descending" and "ascending" order of frequency.

- **Number of items per page:** The maximum number is 1000.

If you make no changes to the default settings, a frequency list of the whole BNC will be displayed. Figure 11.7 shows a frequency list of the subcorpus "W_Acad_Journals" that we created in Chapter 10. You can download the whole frequency list by selecting the appropriate option in the drop-down menu above the list and pressing [Go!].

There are several interesting things about the list displayed in Figure 11.7. First, it may seem unremarkable that *the* is no. 1 on the list, but, this is actually a characteristic feature of only the written genres of English. For spontaneous spoken genres—which have been classified with the genre label "S_conv"—the most frequent words actually tend to be the pronouns *I, you* and *it*. (You could try and see for yourself by compiling a frequency list for "S_conv" in a second browser window or tab.) The next two (alphabetic) words are also quite characteristic of formal written prose: *of* is no. 3 (or no. 2, if you discount the comma), and *in* is no. 6, but they would be nos. 21 and 27 respectively on a frequency list for spontaneous conversations. This is because *of* and *in*, being prepositions, are linked to noun phrases, and academic texts are well-known for being heavily nominalized in style. Another characteristic word is the preposition *by*, which is ranked 17th for academic journals, but 194th for spoken conversations. This dramatic difference again demonstrates how useful frequency lists can be in characterizing genres.

No.	Word	Tag	Frequency
Words in subcorpus "W_Acad_Journals"			
I< << >> [New Frequency List] (Go!)			
1	the	AT0	182632
2	,	PUN	117031
3	of	PRF	116150
4	.	PUN	102211
5	and	CJC	70184
6	in	PRP	68117
7	a	AT0	47086
8	)	PUR	34870
9	(	PUL	34775
10	to	TO0	34594
11	to	PRP	31612
12	is	VBZ	28919
13	with	PRP	25381
14	for	PRP	25161
15	was	VBD	24312
16	that	CJT	22003
17	by	PRP	20662
18	be	VBI	18823
19	were	VBD	15907
20	not	XX0	15069

Figure 11.7:   Frequency list of the subcorpus "W_Acad_Journals"

Now, if you scroll down the list, the 30th most frequent "word + tag" combinations (not shown in Figure 11.7) in this subcorpus of academic journal articles is *patients*. This will seem rather odd, until you realize that almost 50% of texts in this subcorpus are medical texts: journal articles from the *British Medical Journal, The Lancet* or the *Journal of Gastroenterology and Hepatology*. This serves as a warning that the genre-based subcorpora in the BNC are all post-compilation ones: they may not be balanced or representative because they were not used in the designing of the composition of the BNC. The genre labels were added *post hoc*, as descriptive labels of what is available, added *post hoc*, as descriptive labels of what is available, rather than as selectional criteria. As a possible workaround for this bias, you can use the functionality of the SUBCORPUS FEATURE to select only a restricted number of texts from each journal or discipline (see 10.4.1).

11.5   Exercises

1. *Advertising vocabulary.* If you were interested in exploring words that are very characteristic of print advertisements, how would you go about this? What would you compare the print advertisements against?

2. *Arts-specific newspaper vocabulary.* The genre label "W:newsp:brdsht_nat: arts" corresponds to broadsheet national newspaper articles on the arts (cultural material). To find out what is distinctive about these articles compared to newspaper reportage (i.e. home and foreign news reports), do a keywords analysis of "W:newsp:brdsht_nat:arts" against a reference (sub)corpus of all national and regional broadsheet newspaper reportage (i.e. "W:newsp: brdsht_nat:report" + "W:newsp:other:report"; you can name this reference corpus "W_newsp_all_reports"). For the keywords analysis, choose the option for comparing "Word + POS-tag combinations", and use the default settings for the remaining options (i.e. the statistical settings).

   a) Do you notice anything interesting about the positive keywords (i.e. those that are characteristic of the arts section)? Do they give you a very good idea of the different fields or disciplines covered by the term "the arts"?

   b) What about the negative keywords? Can you suggest why these are distinctive of newspaper reports?

   c) Now study keyword number 80 ("last_ORD"). What could account for this being a keyword in newspaper reports? Can you recall which *BNCweb* functions (and steps) you could use to investigate the collocates of this word? What do these collocates tell you about some of the commonly used phrases involving "last"?

12   Advanced searches with the CQP Query Syntax

12.1   Outline

In addition to the Simple Query Syntax introduced in Chapter 6, *BNCweb* offers
a more powerful query language for advanced users called CQP Query Syntax.
The present chapter describes this query language in detail, covering the following topics:

- Translating Simple queries to CQP Query Syntax
- Searching with regular expressions (instead of wildcards)
- Using BNC annotation that is not available in Simple Query Syntax

12.2   Introduction

The Simple Query Syntax of *BNCweb* offers rich functionality combined with
clear and intuitive notation, making it useful even for experienced users. Behind
the scenes, however, these queries are automatically translated into the more
formal and verbose syntax accepted by *BNCweb*'s query engine, the *Corpus
Query Processor* (CQP) of the *IMS Open Corpus Workbench*. The *Corpus
Workbench* is a stand-alone tool that can be used to search any corpus that is in
the right format. The information contained in this chapter therefore has potentially much wider applications, in that it can be applied to investigations of other
corpora, whether independently or in conjunction with the BNC.

While the Simple Query Syntax has been fine-tuned to support all common
query requirements, there are a number of situations where the CQP Query Syntax offers an important advantage. Various examples of linguistically interesting
queries that are not possible in Simple Query Syntax can be found later in this
chapter. In order to be able to execute a CQP query, all you have to do is to select "CQP syntax" in the "Query mode" drop-down menu before running the
query. Note that this menu may automatically switch back to "Simple query"
when you return to the page in order to enter a new query. Like Simple queries,
CQP queries can be restricted to certain texts or speakers, or to a customized
subcorpus (cf. Chapters 4 and 10).

Section 12.3 introduces the basic concepts and notation of the CQP Query
Syntax, points out the major differences from Simple Query Syntax, and explains how automatic translations of Simple queries generated internally by
BNCweb can be accessed from the QUERY HISTORY. After reading this section,
you should be able to make sense of such automatically translated queries and

use them as a starting point for your own experiments with CQP. The rest of the chapter gives a systematic description of the CQP Query Syntax, repeating and expanding on features that have only been sketched briefly before. Throughout the chapter, the focus is on those aspects of CQP queries that are most relevant to *BNCweb* users. More information on the *IMS Open Corpus Workbench* and its *Corpus Query Processor* can be found at http://cwb.sourceforge.net/.

12.3   From Simple queries to CQP syntax—a primer

To get a first impression of CQP Query Syntax, let us begin with a simple search for the fixed word sequence *birds of a feather*. On the STANDARD QUERY page, set the "Query mode" drop-down menu to "CQP syntax" and type the following query into the search box:

```
"birds"  "of"  "a"  "feather"
```

If you press [Start query] now, 7 hits should be displayed. There are a few obvious things to note here. As in the equivalent Simple query `birds of a feather` (which you may recall from Chapter 6), individual tokens (i.e. words and punctuation symbols) are separated by blanks. In addition, the CQP Query Syntax requires each token to be enclosed in quotation marks. Either single or double quotes can be used. If you pre-type your queries in a word processor and then paste them into the *BNCweb* search box, make sure that the quotation marks are straight vertical quotes (" or ') rather than curly typographic quotes ("..." or '...', which are automatically inserted by many word processors).[1]

You may also have noticed that *BNCweb* returned far fewer hits for this query than for the corresponding Simple query (25 hits). The reason is that CQP queries do not offer a global option to ignore case, which is the default for Simple queries. For case-insensitive matching, an explicit modifier `%c` has to be appended to each token, similar to the `:c` modifier in case-sensitive Simple queries. The modifier does not have to be attached directly to the token, so both of the following are possible:

```
"birds"%c  "of"%c  "a"%c  "feather"%c

"birds" %c  "of" %c  "a" %c  "feather" %c
```

Run this query now to check that you get all 25 hits. As in Simple Query Syntax, you can also specify a `%d` modifier to ignore accents and other diacritics, or combine both modifiers `%cd`. To find all spelling variants of *déjà vu*, enter

---

[1]   Your word processor should give you the option of turning off this automatic formatting of quote marks ("smart quotes").

```
"deja"%cd "vu"%cd
```

The CQP Query Syntax also uses a number of "metacharacters" that have a special function in the query language and need to be escaped (i.e. protected with a preceding backslash \) if you want to search for the literal character. Keep in mind that these are not exactly the same as in Simple queries (for instance, you can use the comma , as a literal character in CQP queries, but you have to write \^ and \$ if you want to search for the actual caret or dollar symbols).

Metacharacters in the CQP Query Syntax:
The following punctuation characters have a special meaning within quoted strings and must be preceded by a backslash (e.g. \?) if they are used literally.

. ? * + @ ( ) [ ] { } | ^ $

The same tokenization rules—defining how text is split into w-units and c-units—apply as explained in 3.5.3 ("Basic queries: searching words and phrases"). In order to search for *[he] will, won't he?*, the CQP query would have to be as follows:

```
"will" "," "wo" "n't" "he" "\?"
```

Compare this to the corresponding Simple query in 6.3 and make sure that you understand the formal differences between the two versions. If you need to match special characters such as accented letters or non-alphabetic symbols explicitly, you can enter them either directly or in the form of HTML entities, as described in 6.10 ("Matching special characters"). All letters and symbols in the Latin-1 character set are fully supported; other characters (including Greek letters) have to be used with care (cf. the caveats at the end of 6.10).

Instead of wildcards like ? and *, CQP Query Syntax makes use of REGULAR EXPRESSIONS to formulate generalizations such as "all words that begin with *super-*", "all words that end in *-ment*", or "all words that fit the pattern *imp□ss□ble*". You may remember regular expression notation from the discussion of Simple Query Syntax, where it was used to search for lexico-grammatical patterns (6.8). While regular expressions are less intuitive than wildcards and you may need some time to get used to them, they will allow you to formulate very complex patterns with only a small set of repetition operators and other metacharacters. A full description of regular expression notation is given in Section 12.4. Here, we will only introduce the equivalents of Simple query wildcards. You should study these carefully, otherwise you may be confused as you switch back and forth between Simple Query Syntax and CQP Query Syntax.

A single arbitrary character is matched by the full stop . (sometimes also referred to as the "matchall" metacharacter). Thus, the CQP query `"imp.ss.ble"` is equivalent to the Simple query `imp?ss?ble` (but recall that the latter is case-insensitive by default, while the former requires an explicit `%c` modifier if you also want to match uppercase and mixed-case spellings). An arbitrary substring is matched by the combination `.*` (including the empty string, i.e. the substring is optional in this case) or `.+` (non-empty substrings only). The Simple query `super+listic+ous` therefore translates into `"super.+listic.+ous"%c` in CQP Query Syntax. Alternatives are enclosed in parentheses and separated by vertical bars, for example `"neighb(or|our)"`. You can append a question mark ? to make the alternatives optional, as shown in the following slightly contrived example for finding inflected forms of the verbs *reflect, inflect* and *deflect*:

> `"(re|in|de)flect(s|ed|ing)?" %c`

Similarly, * and + allow repetition of the alternatives, both individually and in arbitrary combinations.

> `"(south-|north-|east-|west-)+`
> `(south|north|east|west)" %c`

finds words like *south-east, west-north-west*, and even *north-east-south-west*. It would have been very difficult to formulate a similar query in the Simple Query Syntax. Can you work out a Simple query that finds sequences of four cardinal points such as the example *north-east-south-west* above?[2]

Queries involving parts of speech and lemmas are written in a formal and somewhat verbose notation. The part-of-speech tag and headword/lemma are treated as linguistic ATTRIBUTES of a token, named `pos` (part of speech), `class` (simplified part-of-speech tag, also called lemma class), `hw` (headword) and `lemma` (combination of headword and lemma class). A query involving one or more of these attributes is formulated in CQP syntax as a so-called TOKEN EXPRESSION. The structure of a token expressions consists of an attribute name

---

2   One solution is `[south,north,east,west]-[south,north,east,west]-` `[south,north,east,west]-[south,north,east,west]`. This query only matches sequences with exactly four items such as *north-east-south-west*, of course, and you would have to add similar patterns for three, two (as in *south-east*), or more than four items. Examples of this kind show how much more powerful the regular expressions of CQP Query Syntax are than wildcards in Simple Query Syntax.

on the left, an operator (such as "="), and on the right in quotation marks a pattern (or regular expression) that the attribute value has to match. The entire expression is enclosed in square brackets [...], indicating that it refers to a single token. For instance, to search for the headword LIGHT, you have to type

```
[hw = "light"]
```

With the query [pos="AJS"] you can find adjectives used in superlative degree. Note that no %c modifiers are needed, as the headword annotation in the BNC is always in lowercase, and part-of-speech tags are always in uppercase. A special attribute named word represents the original word form of a token, so a query like "super.+"%c is merely a convenient shorthand for the explicit token expression

```
[word = "super.+"%c]
```

> Note that each token (i.e. a lexical item or a punctuation mark) requires a separate token expression to be matched. Consequently, it is not possible to match the word sequence *he is happy* with the query [word = "he is happy"%c].

Multiple constraints can be combined with & (for logical AND). The full token expression matches only if all constraints are satisfied. Typical examples of such complex expressions combine the word and pos attributes, or hw and class. To find *can* as a noun, enter

```
[word = "can"%c & pos = "NN.*"]
```

(you may notice that this word is quite often mistagged in the BNC annotation). Similarly, type [hw = "light" & class = "VERB"] to match the headword LIGHT as a verb, and not as a noun or adjective.

A token expression without any constraints will match every token in the corpus. This so-called "matchall" expression must be written in the form [ ] without blanks between the two brackets. It corresponds to the use of + to match an arbitrary token in Simple queries. The token can be made optional by appending a question mark [ ]?, corresponding to the use of * to represent an optional token in Simple Query Syntax. Thus, the query

```
[hw = "bring"] []? "forward"%c
```

finds instances of the phrasal verb *to bring forward*, optionally with an arbitrary word between verb and particle such as in *brought it forward* or *bringing this forward*.

Searching for lexico-grammatical patterns works in exactly the same way as in Simple Query Syntax, including the use of XML tags to match sentence boundaries etc. Now may be a good time to go back to 6.8 ("Matching lexico-grammatical patterns") and review the query syntax for sequences of words introduced there. Note that CQP queries make use of this regular expression notation at two levels: for matching individual words and their annotations, and for the description of lexico-grammatical patterns. Such internal consistency makes it easier to learn and remember the powerful syntax of this query language.

You should now have sufficient knowledge of the CQP Query Syntax to read and understand automatically translated versions of Simple queries, which you can look up in the QUERY HISTORY and which provide an excellent starting point for your own experiments with CQP queries. As an example, enter the Simple query

```
_AJ* as (a)? _{N}
```

and run it to find *good as gold* and approximately 7,500 other hits. Now go to the QUERY HISTORY page (cf. 4.7.1) and click on the link "Show in CQP-Syntax" in the header of the "Query" column. At the top of the query history, you should now see the automatically translated query, as shown in Figure 12.1.

No.	Date	Query (Show as simple query)	Restriction	No. of hits
1	01.07.2008, 23:37:17	[pos = "AJ.*" %c] [word = "as" %c] ([word = "a" %c])? [pos = "(N.*IZZ0)"]	-	7561
2	01.07.2008, 23:36:59	[word = "rather" %c] [word = "than" %c] ([pos = "VVI" %c] I [pos = "VVB" %c])	-	2411
3	01.07.2008, 23:36:51	[word = "head" %c & pos = "N.*" %c]	-	33042
4	01.07.2008, 23:36:39	[lemma = "(merit)_.*" %c] [word = "further" %c] [word = "investigation" %c]	-	4

Figure 12.1:   Automatic translation of Simple queries into CQP syntax in the QUERY HISTORY function

In your experiments with CQP Query Syntax, you may sometimes make a mistake and be presented with an error message like the one in Figure 12.2. Don't be intimidated by the wealth of information provided here and the highly technical description of the problem. In most cases, the error message also indicates where the error occurred (highlighted by a frame in the screenshot). If you take a close look at this part of the query, you can often spot your mistake quite easily. In the example, the user accidentally typed uppercase %C instead of the correct lowercase %c for case-insensitive matching.

Error message

**** CQP ERROR ****
CQP Error:
CQP Syntax Error: parse error, expecting `IMPLIES' or `'|" or `'&" or `']"

shcorp_1210538466 = [pos = "AJ." %c] [word = "as" %c] ([word = "a" %C <--
Synchronizing until next ';'...
PARSE ERROR

Figure 12.2:   Typical error message for syntax errors in a CQP query

A common source of problems is forgetting to change the query mode to "CQP syntax" (in particular since it automatically reverts to the default when you select "New Query" from the post-query options menu on the Query result page). Since *BNCweb* usually cannot guess whether you intended to write a Simple query or a CQP query, it will display an incomprehensible error message—or simply find no hits—after converting the putative Simple query automatically into nonsensical CQP syntax.

Tasks:

a) Write a CQP query that finds inflected forms of the verb *start*, as well as related verbs such as *restart*, *kick-start* and *jump-start*. Include a constraint in the query to ensure that every hit is indeed tagged as a verb.

b) In order to familiarize yourself further with CQP Query Syntax, go through the Simple Query Syntax examples in Chapter 6 and try to rewrite each one as a CQP query. You can easily check your solutions by running the original queries in "Simple query" mode and then looking up the corresponding CQP syntax in the QUERY HISTORY. Don't worry if you came up with a different solution than the one suggested by *BNCweb*: there are usually many equally valid ways of looking for the same information. Make sure that your query is correct by running it and comparing the results to those of the Simple query.

12.4   Regular expressions

The CQP Query Syntax is based on a systematic formal notation known as regular expressions, which is widely used by computational linguists and computer scientists for searching and analyzing text files. This formalism is not as intuitive and easy to learn as the wildcards of Simple Query Syntax, but once you have mastered the art of regular expressions, you will be able to search for much more complex patterns than with a Simple query.

Instead of special-purpose wildcards for different kinds of substrings (?, * and + in Simple queries), regular expressions offer the "matchall" metacharacter . (full stop), which matches any single character. This matchall can be combined with a range of general repetition operators—already familiar from phrase patterns in the Simple Query Syntax (Section 6.8)—to describe arbitrary substrings of various lengths. The box below lists all combinations with usage examples (middle column) and their equivalents in Simple Query Syntax (right-hand column).

Matching arbitrary substrings with regular expressions:		
Notation	Description / examples	Wildcard
`.`	arbitrary character (exactly one) e.g. `"s.ng"` ➔ *sing, sang, sung, song, syng, s8ng, s!ng ...*	`?`
`.?`	optional arbitrary character (zero or one) e.g. `"f.?ee"%c` ➔ *fee, free, FIEE, ...*	`[?,]`
`.*`	arbitrary substring (zero or more char's) e.g. `"work.*"` ➔ *work, works, worked, worker, workshop, ...*	`*`
`.+`	nonempty substring (one or more char's) e.g. `"work.+"` ➔ *works, worked, worker, workshop, ...* but not *work*	`+`
`.{n,m}`	between *n* and *m* arbitrary characters e.g. `"work.{1,2}"` ➔ *works, worked, worker, ...* but not *work, working, workshop*	n/a
`.{n,}`	at least *n* arbitrary characters (*n* or more) e.g. `"work.{4,}"` ➔ *workings, workshop, ...* but not *works, worked*	`????*` etc.
`.{0,m}`	at most *m* arbitrary characters (*m* or fewer) e.g. `"o.{0,2}n"` ➔ *on, own, open, oven, ...* but not *obtain, occupation, ...*	n/a

Remember that regular expressions in CQP are always case-sensitive, but the full stop . matches both uppercase and lowercase letters—as well as digits, punctuation symbols, accented letters, etc. You must add the "ignore case" modifier `%c` so that `"s.ng"%c` matches the *[Hang] Seng* stock market index or *[Kim Il] Sung*, but `".ing"` always finds *King* as well as *king*. In a similar way, you can add the modifier `%d` to match accented letters or combine both modifiers into `%cd`. The queries `"d.j."` and `".e.a"%d` both find the word *déjà*, and the latter also matches the capitalized form *Déjà* (but not *DÉJÀ*).

The repetition operators listed above can also be applied to a single literal character instead of the matchall. This is convenient e.g. for matching both singular and plural forms (`"works?"` ➜ *work, works*) or spelling variants (`"colou?r"` ➜ *colour, color*). If you want to see some different spellings of *aargh*, try the CQP query

```
"a{2,}rgh" %c
```

Bear in mind that repetition operators only apply to a single character immediately to their left. If you want to make a longer substring optional or allow it to be repeated, it has to be enclosed in parentheses `(...)`. As a visual reminder, the box below lists repetition operators for substrings together with typical usage examples. Note that most of these queries do not have equivalents in the Simple Query Syntax.

Repetition operators for multi-character substrings:

`(...)?`	optional substring e.g. `"(un)?easy"` ➜ *easy, uneasy*
`(...)*`	zero or more repetitions of substring e.g. `"(anti-)*pop"` ➜ *pop, anti-pop, anti-anti-pop, anti-anti-anti-pop, ...*
`(...)+`	one or more repetitions of substring e.g. `"(anti-)+pop"` ➜ *anti-pop, anti-anti-pop, ...* but not *pop*
`(...){n,m}`	between *n* and *m* repetitions of substring e.g. `"(ha){2,4}"` ➜ *haha, hahaha, hahahaha*
`(...){n,}`	at least *n* repetitions of substring e.g. `"(ha){3,}*"` ➜ *hahaha, hahahaha, ...* but not *ha, haha*
`(...|...|...)`	alternatives separated by | symbols between parentheses, with optional repetition operator e.g. `"ask(s|ed|ing)?"` ➜ *ask, asks, asked, asking*

The parenthesized substring may be a full regular expression itself, and the same holds for each |-separated alternative. In this way, very complex expressions can be put together from the simple building blocks introduced above.

Alternatives and repetition operators are often used to describe various combinations of morphological suffixes in a compact way. If you want to search for nominalizations ending in *-ness*, *-ity*, *-ment* and *-tion* as well as their plural forms *-nesses*, *-ities*, *-ments* and *-tions*, you can use the regular expression

```
".{3,}(ness(es)?|it(y|ies)|(tion|ment)s?)"
```

Take a moment to tease apart this complicated expression and understand how it matches the eight different endings. We require at least 3 characters in the "stem" part before the ending in order to weed out false matches such as *city* and *station*. This is a common trick that we will refine later in this section.

Task:
A characteristic property of regular expressions is that any given problem can usually be solved in many different ways. Try to come up with three different queries that match exactly the inflected forms of the verb *to work*, i.e. *work, works, worked* and *working*. How many alternative formulations can you find for the nominalization example above?

You will find quite often that the alternatives in a parenthesized group are just single letters. For instance, to search for inflected forms of the verb *to sing*, but not e.g. the noun *song*, you might type the query `"s(i|a|u)ng"%c`. If you have been wondering whether there are English words with more than three vowels in a row, you could use the query `".*(a|e|i|o|u){4,}.*"%c`. Regular expression syntax offers a more compact notation for this special case: you can enclose single characters in square brackets and omit the vertical bars between them, forming a so-called character class:

```
"s[iau]ng" %c  and  ".*[aeiou]{4,}.*" %c
```

Within a character class, the hyphen (–) is interpreted as a metacharacter and denotes an entire range of characters. Thus, `[a-z]` stands for any (unaccented) lowercase letter and is much more convenient than spelling out all possibilities: `[abcdefghijklmnopqrstuvwxyz]`. Likewise, `[A-Z]` stands for an uppercase letter and `[0-9]` for an arbitrary digit. Since these ranges depend on the internal ordering of characters, they should only be used for letters and digits. Otherwise, results are quite unpredictable: `[A-z]` also matches *[* and *]*, while

[a - z] reports a syntax error, and [, - ;] matches all digits in addition to various punctuation symbols. Multiple character ranges can be combined, e.g. [a - z 0 - 9 \ -] for digits, letters and hyphens (note the backslash required for the literal use of - in a character class). A character class can also be negated with an initial caret ^; for instance, [^ a - z] matches any character except for lowercase letters. This negation is interpreted in a very literal sense: the matched characters include uppercase letters, digits, all punctuation symbols and even accented lowercase letters (which do not fall into the range a - z). Unfortunately, "positive" and "negative" specifications cannot be combined in a character class. If you want to match any lowercase letter except for *e*, you have to list the "positive" ranges explicitly: [a - d f - z].

Accented letters (as well as some other special characters) are fully supported by CQP regular expressions and can easily be matched with the %d modifier. To be precise, all Latin-1 characters that can directly be entered in the Simple Query Syntax (cf. 6.10) also work in CQP queries. However, other characters that have to be entered as HTML entities (e.g. Greek letters, see Appendix 4) cannot be used in character classes and will not be recognized by the . metacharacter. These restrictions result from technical limitations of the regular expression implementation used by CQP and the internal representation of the corpus data.

You have now been introduced to the complete regular expression syntax supported by CQP queries, but it will take some time and practice before you become accustomed to the typical usage patterns and "idioms" of regular expressions. Teaching such design techniques that help you unleash the full potential of regular expressions is far beyond the scope of this book. If you are new to regular expression notation, you should work your way through a good textbook (e.g. Friedl 2006) or one of many online resources that are available. For instance, the Wikipedia entry at http://en.wikipedia.org/wiki/Regular_expression gives an extensive description of regular expression syntax and provides some links to good online tutorials. You need to be aware of two things when reading other material on regular expressions:

1. There are different "dialects" of regular expression syntax. CQP implements a version known as POSIX regular expressions. Further extensions offered by some other dialects are often described in textbooks and online tutorials, but they will not work in CQP queries.

2. Regular expressions are often used for searching substrings in long blocks of text and they are typically presented in such a way by introductory texts. In CQP queries, regular expressions are always matched against a complete word form (or linguistic annotation string). The metacharacters ^ and $, which are normally used to "anchor" regular expression matches to the start and end of a line, have no meaningful function in CQP. How-

ever, they still need to be escaped if they are used literally (e.g.
`"\$100m"` to match *$100m*).

Tasks:

a) Write a regular expression query to find words that follow the orthographic pattern *VCCVCCVCCVCC*..., i.e. at least four repetitions of a group that is formed by a vowel followed by exactly two
   consonants (each repetition may use a different vowel and consonants, of course). Use character classes to match the consonants
   and vowels. Can you take advantage of character ranges to write
   the class for consonants in a concise way?

b) Find all word forms in the BNC that contain exactly three instances of the letter *t* or exactly three instances of the letter *r*. If
   you are new to regular expressions, the solution will very likely
   not be obvious to you. A good strategy in such a situation is to
   start with a simpler query—e.g. all words that contain at least
   three *t*s—and then improve it gradually to weed out unwanted
   matches. Finally, make sure that you haven't missed anything (can
   you think of any words that should be matched but don't show up
   in the results?) and combine your regular expression with an
   analogous one for the *r*s.

12.5   Part-of-speech and headword/lemma queries

Each token in the BNC is annotated with a part-of-speech tag, headword and
various other bits of linguistic information, referred to as "attributes" of the token. In contrast to Simple queries, CQP syntax allows you to access all these attributes in a consistent way, although the notation is somewhat unwieldy. You
have to specify the desired attribute as well as a regular expression that its value
has to match, in the general form:

[attribute = "regular expression"]

Such a combination of attribute name and regular expression is called a "constraint", and the complete expression in square brackets—which specifies one or
more constraints on a single token—is referred to as a "token expression". For
instance, in order to search for (inflectional) superlatives with the part-of-speech
tag AJS, you would type `[pos = "AJS"]`; or simply `[pos = "AJ.*"]` to
find all adjectives. If you want to match all forms of the headword LIGHT (in its

noun, verb and adjective readings[3]), you have to use the `hw` (headword) attribute: `[hw = "light"]`. The familiar modifiers `%c` (ignore case) and `%d` (ignore accents) can be appended to the quoted string, but are rarely useful (since lemmas are always in lowercase and part-of-speech tags in uppercase). The following table lists all relevant attributes in the special version of the BNC used by *BNCweb* and gives their values for the past participle *Gone* (in sentence-initial capitalized spelling) as an example.

Token attributes in *BNCweb*:		
`word`	original word form ("surface form")	`Gone`
`pos`	part-of-speech tag	`VVN`
`hw`	headword	`go`
`class`	word class (simplified part-of-speech tag / lemma category)	`VERB`
`lemma`	combination of headword + word class	`go_VERB`
`type`	type of token (w: word, c: punctuation, x: missing text)	`w`

As you can see from this table, the "surface" form of a token in the original text is also treated as an attribute, with the special name `word`. A word form query like `"love.*"%c` is therefore just a convenient shorthand notation for the explicit form `[word = "love.*"%c]`. The `class` attribute specifies a simplified part-of-speech tag or "lemma class", which does not make inflectional distinctions (see Section 6.7, but note that the abbreviations N, V, A, $ and INT are not available). The `lemma` attribute combines the headword (`hw`) and its lemma class (`class`), separated by an underscore character (`_`); i.e. it treats the noun *light*, the verb *to light* and the adjective *light* as distinct entities. As an example, consider the Simple query `{+ate/V}` (a verb ending in *-ate*), which translates into CQP Query Syntax as `[lemma = ".+ate_VERB"]`.

The attribute `type` distinguishes between words (w) and punctuation symbols (c), corresponding to the w-units and c-units of the original BNC annotation. A third type of token refers to missing elements in the text (either because they were unclear in recordings and could not be transcribed, or because they had to be deleted for privacy reasons). These are indicated by the type code x. If you want a concordance of all such elements, enter the query `[type = "x"]`.

---

3 The complete list of inflected forms is *light, lights* for the noun reading, *light, lights, lighted, lit, lighting* for the verb reading, and *light, lighter, lightest* for the adjective reading.

Token expressions can specify constraints on several different attributes, which are combined with & (the symbol for logical AND) and must all be satisfied. For example, in order to match past participles of verbs beginning with *super-*, you would type

```
[hw = "super.+" & pos = "VVN"]
```

Note that this expression is equivalent to the Simple query {super+}_VVN.

Optimizing CQP queries

Multiple constraints in a token expression are evaluated from left to right, and their ordering can have a substantial impact on the time it takes to execute a query. In the example above, CQP first looks for all instances of words beginning with *super-* (about 22,000 tokens), and then checks their part-of-speech tags. If the two constraints had been swapped, resulting in the formally equivalent query [pos = "VVN" & hw = "super.+"], CQP would first locate all 2 million past participles in the BNC and then match each one against the regular expression. Unsurprisingly, the second query is more than 50 times slower than the first. The most efficient solution makes use of the lemma attribute to restrict the search space even further: [lemma = "super.+_VERB" & pos = "VVN"]. This query only has to check about 2,300 instances of verbs beginning with *super-* and is more than twice as fast as the original query. Note that there are no differences in performance when the queries are executed a second time, since query results are temporarily cached by the *BNCweb* server (cf. Chapter 13).

Individual constraints in a token expression can be negated by using != ("does not match") instead of = to connect the attribute name to the regular expression. Such "negative" constraints, which are not possible in Simple Query Syntax, are particularly useful in combination with other, "positive" constraints. For instance, you can easily find words ending in *-ing* that are not present participles, without having to specify all the possible part-of-speech tags of such words:

```
[word = ".+ing" & pos != "VVG.*"]
```

The regular expression VVG.* is used here instead of a literal string VVG to ensure that the ambiguity tags VVG-AJ0 and VVG-NN1 are excluded from the result set, too. If constraints are combined with | (the symbol for logical OR) instead of &, only one of the conditions has to be satisfied. For example, if you want to find a token that is either a verb ending in *-ize* or a nominalization of such a verb (aptly ending in *-ization*), you might write this query:

```
[hw = ".+ize" & class = "VERB"
 | hw = ".+ization" & class = "SUBST"]
```

Note that the constraints combined by | are themselves complex expressions. Since & binds more tightly than | (programmers say that & has "higher precedence"), no parentheses are required to ensure correct order of evaluation in this case. It is also possible to negate a parenthesized subexpression by preceding it with ! (for logical NOT), but this operator is rarely needed: the query `[word=".+ing" & !(pos="VVG.*")]` is completely equivalent to `[word=".+ing" & pos!="VVG.*"]`.

Such combinations of constraints with AND (&), OR (|) and negation (! or !=) are called "Boolean expressions". A token expression in CQP Query Syntax may contain a Boolean expression of arbitrary complexity, as the following contrived example illustrates. Assume that you need to find words starting with *super-* that are either adjectives ending in *-ous*, *-able* or *-ive*, or nominalizations ending in *-ity* or *-ness*. To achieve this goal, you want to combine a prefix constraint for *super-* with a subexpression that matches either an appropriate adjective or an appropriate noun:

```
[hw="super.+" &
 (class = "ADJ" & hw=".*(ous|able|ive)"
  | class = "SUBST" & hw = ".*(ity|ness)") ]
```

The complex constraint in the middle line matches adjectives ending in *-ous*, *-able* or *-ive*, and the one in the bottom line matches nouns ending in *-ity* or *-ness*. The two constraints are combined with logical OR (|), so that only one of them has to be satisfied for each matching token. Parentheses are essential in this case: if they were omitted, the query would match every noun ending in *-ity* or *-ness*, in addition to adjectives starting with *super-* and ending in *-ous*, *-able* or *-ive*.

Tasks:

a) It is easy to search for (lexical) verb forms that begin with *be-* and end in *-en*. Write a CQP query for this purpose, as well as an equivalent Simple query. Then go to the query history and compare the automatic translation made by *BNCweb* with your CQP query.

> b) Now, work out a CQP query for the more difficult problem of
>   finding verbs that begin with *be-* and do not end in *-en*. Can you
>   solve this problem in Simple Query Syntax as well?
>
> c) In how many different ways can you rephrase the query for verbs
>   ending in *-ize* and nouns ending in *-ization* above? Try using other
>   attributes such as `pos` and `lemma` in your reformulations. Can
>   you rewrite the query in the form of a single constraint, i.e. with-
>   out the use of logical operators? Is there an equivalent Simple
>   query? If you wish, include variants with *-ise* and *-isation* as well.

12.6   Lexico-grammatical patterns and text structure

Queries for lexico-grammatical patterns and other sequences of words are constructed from token expressions (either the full form enclosed in square brackets
or the shorthand notation for word forms), using the same repetition operators
and groups of alternatives as in the Simple Query Syntax and in regular expressions for string matching. A table of these operators can be found in Chapter 6
(Section 6.8) for Simple queries and Section 12.4 for regular expressions. It is
repeated below for the special case of skipping arbitrary tokens. If the repeated
pattern consists of a single token expression, parentheses may be omitted, e.g.
`"that"%c?` instead of `("that"%c)?` for an optional *that*. The Simple query
for basic prepositional phrases given in Section 6.8 and repeated here for convenience:

    _{PREP} (_{ART})? (_{A}|_{ADV})* _{N}

translates into CQP Query Syntax in a straightforward way (we have used the
table of part-of-speech abbreviations from Section 6.7 and simplified a little):

    [class="PREP"] [class="ART"]?
      ([class="ADJ"] | [class="ADV"])*
        [class="SUBST"]

In order to match an arbitrary token, specify a token expression in square brackets without any constraints. This special "matchall" expression `[]` has to be
written without blanks between the opening and closing bracket. It plays the
same role as the matchall character `.` in regular expressions for strings. You can
combine the matchall expression with any of the repetition operators to skip a
certain number of tokens.

Skipping tokens with repetition operators:

[ ]	skip exactly one arbitrary token
[ ] ?	optional token (may be skipped)
[ ] *	skip any number of tokens (optional)
[ ] +	skip one or more tokens
[ ] {n,m}	skip at least n and at most m tokens
[ ] {$n,$}	skip at least n tokens
[ ] {$0,m$}	skip up to m tokens

If you want to find *cat* and *dog* within a distance of 3 to 5 tokens of each other (i.e. *dog* must be the 3rd, 4th or 5th token following *cat*, or vice versa), use [ ] {2,4} to skip two, three or four tokens in between:

```
( [hw="cat"] [ ]{2,4} [hw="dog"]
| [hw="dog"] [ ]{2,4} [hw="cat"] )
```

The first alternative in this query finds instances where *cat* precedes *dog*, and the second alternative finds instances where *dog* precedes *cat*.[4] Note that this type of proximity query is much more flexible than the Simple query notation described in 6.9. If you take a closer look at the query results, you will notice that some of the hits cross sentence boundaries (i.e. *cat* occurs in a different sentence than *dog*), which is probably not what you were looking for. Append the filter within s to the end of the query to ensure that every query hit is contained in a single s-unit:

```
( [hw="cat"] [ ]{2,4} [hw="dog"]
| [hw="dog"] [ ]{2,4} [hw="cat"] ) within s
```

Similar restrictions using within can be appended to the end of any CQP query, and can refer to any text region or typographical mark-up such as s (s-unit), p (paragraph), u (speaker turn), head (heading or caption), quote (quotation), item (list item) and hi (highlighted text). If you replace within s by within u in the query above, every hit will be contained in a single turn, but you will find that one of them crosses an s-unit boundary within the turn. The within restriction is a particularly useful function since it is well known that language varies significantly across different portions of a text.

---

4   We have used the hw attribute for convenience here. The constraint [hw="dog"] also matches the verb *to dog*, of course, and it would be more appropriate to write [lemma="dog_SUBST"]. This does not affect the outcome of the query, though, as no instances of the verb co-occur with *cat* in the BNC.

Of course, the modified query will only match in the spoken part of the BNC because it requires matches to be inside speaker turns (`<u>` ... `</u>` regions in the BNC mark-up). This "side effect" of `within` can be exploited to search for typographical mark-up by ensuring that hits are contained in `<hi>` ... `</hi>` regions. Type `"very"%c within hi` to find highlighted instances of *very* (recall that you have to display the extended context of a query hit to see the typographical highlighting on screen). Another example is the query

```
[pos="NN.*"] [hw="be"] "like"
   []{0,2} [pos="NN.*"] within quote
```

which identifies simple comparisons (such as *my heart is like a singing bird*) within quotations. Only one `within` clause can be specified for each query, so it is not possible e.g. to search both for list items (`within item`) and headings (`within head`) at the same time.

If you only need to know whether a single token is highlighted or part of a heading, quotation, etc., you can also use the name of the respective region as a constraint in the token expression. For example, `[word="very"%c & hi]` is equivalent to the query `"very"%c within hi` above. With this notation, you can combine multiple types of regions into a complex Boolean expression. The following query finds the name *Thatcher* both in headings and in list items:

```
[word = "Thatcher" & (head | item)]
```

Keep in mind that such constraints only apply to an individual token: the query `[hw="cat"] []{2,4} [hw="dog"] within hi` ensures that the entire phrase from *cat* to *dog* is highlighted (e.g. *cat chased by the dog*), while the version `[hw="cat" & hi] []{2,4} [hw="dog"]` only requires *cat* to be highlighted; *dog* may not be highlighted at all (e.g. *cat chased by the dog*) or may be highlighted separately from *cat* (e.g. *cat chased by the dog*).

It is also possible to test whether a token is at the start or end of a particular region, using special built-in functions `lbound(...)` and `rbound(...)`. The query

```
[hw="very" & lbound(hi)]
```

finds a region of highlighted text that begins with the word *very*, while

```
[hw="very" & rbound(hi)]
```

finds a region that ends in the word *very*. Of course, the query results always include cases where only the word *very* is highlighted, because it is then both at the start and at the end of the region. These built-in functions are particularly useful in combination with other constraints. The query

```
[hw="very" & hi & !lbound(hi) & !rbound(hi)]
```

finds highlighted instances of *very* that are neither at the start nor at the end of the highlighted region. A typical usage pattern of `lbound(...)` is to search for capitalized words that are not in sentence-initial position. The following query identifies instances of the word form *To* in headings, but neither at the start of the heading nor at the start of any other s-unit within the heading:

```
[word = "To" & head & !(lbound(head) | lbound(s))]
```

If you find it difficult to make sense of such complex Boolean expressions, try reading them aloud, pronouncing & as "and", | as "or" and ! as "not". The example above might thus be paraphrased as "word form *To* and within heading and not at the start of a heading or s-unit".

> **Task:**
> Especially in newspapers, headings often make very elliptical use of language, e.g. by leaving out short "filler" words such as *were, has* and *been*. You could begin exploring this kind of language by formulating a query for occurrences of a present or past participle at the beginning of a heading. (You will need to look up the POS-tags for participles in the *BNC Reference Guide*.) What kind of grammatical constructions do the examples illustrate? How often do these patterns appear at the start of sentences that are not within headings?

You can use the same XML tags as in Simple Query Syntax to match the start and end points of regions. For instance, `<hi> [hw="very"]` finds *very* at the start of a highlighted region, and `[hw="very"] </hi>` at its end, exactly like the queries with `lbound(hi)` and `rbound(hi)` above. Use tags in pairs to match a single, complete region:

```
<hi> [hw="very"] </hi>
```

requires that only *very* is highlighted, but not the surrounding words. A similar example looks for superlatives such as *biggest* and *most important* that are highlighted individually:

```
<hi> ([pos="AJS"] | "most" [pos="AJ0"]) </hi>
```

If you want to compile a list of all headings and captions in the BNC, allow an arbitrary number of tokens to be skipped between the start and end tag:

```
<head> []* </head>
```

All structural mark-up described in Section 3 of the *BNC Reference Guide* is supported. If you look at the examples given there, you will notice that XML tags marking the start of a region often contain attributes that provide additional information about the region. For instance, `<hi rend="it">` ... `</hi>` denotes text in italics; other common values of the `rend` attribute are `bo` (bold), `ul` (underlined), `lo` (for subscripts) and `hi` (for superscripts). Such "tag attributes" can be tested in CQP queries with a syntax that is similar to their appearance in the original XML files. To find all subscripts in the BNC, type

```
<hi_rend="lo"> []* </hi_rend>
```

Two quirks of the CQP query syntax have to be noted here. First, there must be an underscore (_) between tag name (`hi`) and attribute name (`rend`), which are separated by a blank in the original XML file. Second, if you want to match a complete region, the corresponding end tag has to include the attribute name as well: `</hi>` does not give correct results in the example above.[5]

A complete listing of tag attributes and the meanings of their values can be found in Section 3 of the *BNC Reference Guide*—click on the XML elements listed there to display full information. Here, we give a few examples that are likely to be useful. If you want to see all material from a particular speaker, use the `who` attribute of `<u>` tags, which gives the speaker ID for each turn:

```
<u_who="PS2SM"> []* </u_who>
```

Captions are sometimes represented as paragraphs of type `caption` (or `caption:byline`, etc.). Execute the following query to obtain a list of all such captions.

```
<p_type="caption.*"%c> []* </p_type>
```

As you can see, constraints on tag attributes allow full regular expression notation including the `%c` and `%d` modifiers. This is particularly convenient for attributes that can take arbitrary values and do not use a fixed set of categories. One example are spelling corrections made by the BNC editors, which are marked by `<corr>` tags with an attribute named `sic` for the original spelling.

---

5   If you try both versions of the query, you will see that `<hi_rend="lo"> []* </hi>` misses some 700 hits found by the correct form.

To get an impression of the problems that native speakers have with the placement of apostrophes, type

```
<corr_sic=".*'.*"> []* </corr_sic>6
```

Multiword units, e.g. complex prepositions like *in front of*, are split into separate
tokens in the BNC, but enclosed in <mw> ... </mw> tags with attributes pos
(part-of-speech tag, e.g. PRP), hw (headword, e.g. in front of), class
(lemma class, e.g. UNC) and lemma (e.g. in front of_UNC) that apply to
the entire multiword unit. The query for prepositional phrases formulated at the
beginning of this section can be improved by allowing complex prepositions in
addition to the single-word prepositions matched by [class="PREP"] (we
are using the full part-of-speech tagset here to achieve better balance of precision and recall):

```
([pos="PR.*|TO0"] | <mw_pos="PRP"> []* </mw_pos>)
    [pos="AT.*|DT.*"]?
        ([pos = "AJ.*"]|[pos="AV.*"])* [pos="NN.*"]
```

Finally, you should be aware of another idiosyncrasy of the internal representation used by CQP. If regions are nested within regions of the same name, an index specifying the level of nesting is appended to the tag names. For instance,
some captions have been encoded as nested paragraphs of type caption and
can be found with the queries <p_type1="caption"> []* </p_type1>
and <p_type2="caption"> []* </p_type2>. In most cases, it will be
sufficient to search for maximal regions without nesting indices, though.

Tasks:

a) Is *data* singular or plural? Write a CQP query that matches the
   word *data* followed by a singular verb, and a query that matches
   data followed by a plural verb (allowing for optional adverbials
   between the noun and the verb). When you take a closer look at
   the query hits, you will often find that *data* is part of a prepositional phrase modifying the true subject of the clause. Try to re-
   phrase your query in order to avoid such false positives (of course,
   you will have to sacrifice recall in order to improve the precision
   of the query). Hint: make sure that *data* is the first noun in the sentence; you may need to start your query with <s> to achieve this.

---

6   Note that *BNCweb* does not display the content of <corr> tags with the sic attribute in
    the Query result page. However, if you view the larger context of an individual query hit
    (cf. 4.4.4), the original form will be displayed in light grey within square brackets.

b) It seems plausible to assume that contracted forms of *not* and auxiliary verbs are used particularly often in headings in order to save
   space. Verify this hypothesis by writing separate CQP queries that
   match the full and contracted forms within and outside headings
   (marked `<head>` ... `</head>`). Calculate the ratio between the
   frequency of the full and the contracted form in each case. You
   should also use the online *Corpus Frequency Wizard* (see 5.6) to
   test whether the observed differences are significant. Note that you
   have to enter the frequency of the contracted form as "frequency
   count", and the sum of the frequencies of full and contracted form
   as "sample size".

c) How do songs and poems end? In the BNC, a poem or song consists of one or more lines of verse marked by `<l>` ... `</l>` tags;
   the entire piece is enclosed in `<lg>` ... `</lg>` (see Section 3.2.4
   of the *BNC Reference Guide* for an example). Write a CQP query
   that makes use of this annotation in order to find the last line of
   each song and poem in the BNC. Can you also work out a query
   that matches the third line of each song and poem? (You will find
   that it is impossible to match only the third line, but you can write
   a query that matches the first three lines.)

12.7   Advanced features of CQP queries

This section introduces some highly advanced features of the CQP Query Syntax that constitute a substantial extension over the functionality of Simple Query
Syntax (in addition to regular expressions and extended matching of XML tags
covered in previous sections). You may prefer to tackle this part of the chapter
only when you feel comfortable with basic CQP queries and have worked
through all the tasks above.

   Both Simple queries and CQP queries rely on regular expression notation for
matching sequences of words. Despite the great flexibility of regular expressions, which you will have come to appreciate by now, there are inherent limits
on the kinds of patterns that can be searched. It is impossible, for example, to
find expressions such as *from time to time* or *from cover to cover*, i.e. the general pattern *Prep N_1 Prep N_2* where N_1 and N_2 refer to the same noun (lemma):
$N_1 = N_2$. Such additional constraints linking multiple tokens cannot be formulated in regular expression notation. You can easily search for any particular
noun, e.g. the noun *time* with the Simple query `_{Prep}  {time/N}`
`_{Prep}  {time/N}`, but this approach is both tedious (because you have to
perform dozens of queries) and incomplete (because you will only find nouns

that you expect to appear in this construction). The required query might infor-mally be paraphrased as

"find sequences *Prep N₁ Prep N₂* such that $N_1 = N_2$".

CQP query syntax allows you to mark individual tokens with named labels, much like the subscripts in the intuitive description above. Since labels have to start with a letter, we call them `n1` and `n2` instead of 1 and 2. The connector "such that" is represented by the symbol `::` in CQP query syntax and introduces a **GLOBAL CONSTRAINT** that specifies relations between multiple tokens (while the constraints in token expressions only refer to a single token). This global constraint allows us to represent the condition $N_1 = N_2$, but we need to make ex-plicit in what sense N_1 and N_2 are equal—here it is with respect to the `lemma` attribute. The informal description above therefore translates into the following CQP query:

```
[pos = "(PR.*|TO0)"] n1:[pos = "NN.*"]
  [pos = "(PR.*|TO0)"] n2:[pos = "NN.*"]
    :: n1.lemma = n2.lemma
```

If you want to rule out accidental matches across a sentence boundary,[7] append `within s` after the global constraint. Once you have become familiar with the notation for labels and global constraints, it should be easy to write similar que-ries, starting from an informal paraphrase and translating them piece by piece into CQP query syntax. The global constraint is a full Boolean expression, so multiple conditions can be specified and, if desired, negated.

Several built-in functions can be applied to labels as well. The `f()` function determines the frequency of a lemma, word form or part-of-speech tag in the en-tire BNC. If you are not interested in *time* and other high frequency nouns in the query above, you can weed them out by setting a cut-off frequency of (say) 1,000 occurrences, as follows:

```
[pos = "(PR.*|TO0)"] n1:[pos = "NN.*"]
  [pos = "(PR.*|TO0)"] n2:[pos = "NN.*"]
    :: n1.lemma = n2.lemma & f(n1.lemma) < 1000
```

Some basic arithmetic for such frequency counts can be performed with the ad-dition and multiplication functions `add()` and `mul()`. If you want to find com-binations of an infrequent adjective with a much more frequent noun— i.e. can-didates for what some researchers call "upward collocations"—try

---

7   E.g. *Signs **of Spring**. **In Spring**, the weather becomes warmer and ...*

```
adj:[pos="AJ.*"] noun:[pos="NN.*"]
   :: mul(f(adj.lemma), 1000) < f(noun.lemma)
```

and generate a frequency breakdown to find examples like *prep school, halcyon days* and *elapsed time*. In this example, the part `mul(f(adj.lemma), 1000) < f(noun.lemma)` states that the noun has to be at least 1000 times more frequent than the adjective, but this factor can easily be changed and combined with other constraints on the individual frequencies of the two words.

Two labels are defined implicitly and can always be used in the global constraint: `match` points to the first token of the current query hit, and `matchend` to its last token. We could thus have written the previous query more concisely:

```
[pos="AJ.*"] [pos="NN.*"]
   :: mul(f(match.lemma), 1000)
      < f(matchend.lemma)
```

The explicit form with `adj` and `noun` labels is recommended, though, as it is easier to read for most users. Implicit labels are particularly useful in combination with the built-in function `distabs()`, which calculates the (absolute) distance between two tokens. If you are interested in very long prepositional phrases, combine a suitable PP query (you may copy one of the examples from the previous section, or write your own improved query) with the global constraint `:: distabs(match, matchend) >= 7`. The query result will now only include PPs spanning 8 or more tokens (so that the distance between the first and last token is at least 7).

With the help of labels, it is also possible to access the values of XML tag attributes for any regions enclosing a labeled token. This allows you to look up words in a specific BNC document, uttered by a particular speaker, or even find a sentence by its document name and running number (this is impracticable with ordinary XML tag notation, as the relevant start tag may be far away from the current token and cannot be included in the query pattern). If you are interested in the use of noun phrases by speaker `PS2SM`, try this or a similar query:

```
[pos="AJ.*"] [pos="NN.*"] :: match.u_who = "PS2SM"
```

If you want to locate sentence number 800 (`<s n="800">`) in document EES (`<text id="EES">`) without switching to the BROWSE A TEXT feature, type

```
<s_n="800"> []* </s_n> :: match.text_id = "EES"
```

As a more interesting example, if you are looking for uses of the word *conclusion* within the first 50 sentences of a BNC text, execute the following query:

```
[hw="conclusion"] :: int(match.s_n) <= 50
```

Note how the built-in function `int()` has to be applied to use the value of an attribute in a numeric comparison.

The BNC also includes information about paralinguistic "events" such as page breaks, background noises, coughs, laughter and other non-verbal sounds, pauses, and changes in voice quality (see Section 4.3 of the *BNC Reference Guide* for a detailed listing of events to be found in the spoken material). In *BNCweb*, an additional attribute named `flags_before` collects all events that happen immediately before the current token. Different events are identified by the codes `pb` (for page break), `shift` (for a shift in voice quality), `vocal.*` (for non-verbal sounds such as coughs and laughter), `pause` (for significant pauses) and `event.*` (for various noises and all other events). Since multiple events may be present for a single token, this attribute is matched with the special `contains` operator instead of `=`. In order to find *to*-infinitives interrupted by a pause, you can use the following query:

```
"to" [pos = "V.*I" & flags_before contains "pause"]
```

Note that the codes for non-verbal sounds and other events have to be matched by regular expressions, since these codes are always extended with a free-form description of the sound or event. Use alternatives in the regular expression to match multiple codes:

```
"to" [pos = "V.*I" & flags_before contains
      "(pause|vocal.*)"]
```

If you want to exclude a certain type of event, use `not contains` (in analogy to `!=`). The `flags_before` attribute also provides some information about missing words, which have either been deleted for anonymization purposes (code `gap`) or were unclear in speech recordings and could not be transcribed (code `unclear`). *BNCweb* treats such gaps in the text as separate tokens with the property `[type="x"]`, though, so they can be matched in the normal, more intuitive way. For a concordance of deleted telephone numbers, use the following query:

```
[type = "x" & word = ".*gap:telephone.*"]
```

Since most *BNCweb* users are more interested in linguistic patterns than in typography, both query languages ignore the presence or absence of whitespace between tokens. Thus, `"can"%c "not"%c` (as well as the corresponding Simple query `can not`) matches both *cannot* and the uncommon spelling *can not*.

Information about whitespace has not entirely been lost, though, and is taken into account when results are displayed. It is also represented in the flags_before attribute by the code space. To find the spelling *can not*, use the query

```
"can"%c [word="not"%c & flags_before
     contains "space"]
```

If you only want the single-word spelling, the required query is

```
"can"%c [word="not"%c & flags_before
     not contains "space"]
```

Finally, a special feature of the CQP Query Syntax allows you to exert some control over the matching strategy used by *BNCweb*. By default, the query processor uses a form of shortest match policy called "early matching" in order to keep query hits short. As a consequence, optional elements at the start of a query are included if possible, while those at the end of the query are never included. For example, the query

```
[pos = "AJ.*"]* [lemma = "time_SUBST"]
```

will include all adjectives that immediately precede an instance of *time*, but will match only the noun when there are no adjectives. The query

```
[pos = "AJ.*"]{2,}
```

is intended to find sequences of two or more adjectives. However, it will always match exactly two adjectives—the minimum number required to satisfy the specified constraints—even if they are part of a longer sequence (in this case, several overlapping hits are returned). There is a simple trick to ensure that each query hit comprises all consecutive adjectives: specify an additional token that is not an adjective.

```
[pos = "AJ.*"]{2,} [pos != "AJ.*"]
```

If you prefer not to include the additional token in the query hits, you can mark it as a "look-ahead expression" by enclosing it in [:...:] instead of simple square brackets:

```
[pos = "AJ.*"]{2,} [: pos != "AJ.*" :]
```

Unfortunately, this trick is limited to repetitions of single token expressions and cannot be used e.g. for enumerations of adjectives:

```
[pos = "AJ.*"] ("," [pos="AJ.*"])+
```

Future versions of *BNCweb* may provide more control over the matching strategy and more sophisticated look-ahead functionality.

Tasks:

a) Search for superlatives (both inflectional as in *greatest* and periphrastic as in *most important*) within captions (marked by `<p type="caption.*">`) and within sub-headings (marked by `<head type="SUB">`). Use a global constraint involving the implicit `match` label to formulate this query.

b) Sometimes people use multiple exclamation marks to make a very emphatic point. In the BNC, each exclamation mark in such a sequence is treated as a separate token. What are the longest groups of exclamation marks in the corpus? Write a query that matches all exclamation marks in a sequence, not just the first two or three.

12.8   Exercises

1. *The quest for the very longest and most unbelievably complicated prepositional phrase imaginable.* English noun phrases and prepositional phrases are relatively simple constructions compared e.g. to the monstrosities allowed by the German language.[8] Nonetheless, prepositional phrases can sometimes become quite long (an example from the BNC is *with pseudo-Victorian and other bogus 'historical' styles*). Use *BNCweb* to find further examples of very long prepositional phrases. First, you need to expand and refine the query given earlier in this chapter so that it matches more complex patterns. Then, use the built-in `distabs()` function to remove the shorter prepositional phrases from the query hits. What is the longest example you can find? How many "false positives" are there among the query hits?

2. *Coordination of English verbs.* The English language makes extensive use of coordination, both at the level of phrases (*the old man and the calm sea*)

---

8   For instance, in German newspapers you will often find prepositional phrases such as *mit ihren für die an der Peripherie und Semi-Peripherie des Systems lebenden Völker untragbaren Folgen.*

and at the level of individual words (*the religious beliefs and practices of their parents*). When two verbs are coordinated, they will usually also agree in their morpho-syntactic properties, i.e. they carry the same part-of-speech tag. For instance, one would normally not coordinate a past-tense and present-tense verb, as in *Peter arrived and lives in Paris*. It is easy to search for such coordination patterns in Simple Query Syntax, e.g. for simple past tense with the query _VVD _CJC _VVD. However, this requires a separate query for every possible part-of-speech tag, and you would have to tally up the corresponding frequency counts from the DISTRIBUTION feature if you wanted e.g. to compare the frequency of this construction in spoken and written English. Fortunately, such complications can be avoided with the help of CQP Query Syntax.

a) Write a CQP query that matches a lexical verb followed by a coordinating conjunction and another lexical verb, using a global constraint to make sure that the first and second verb carry the same part-of-speech tag. What are the most frequent combinations of verbs that occur in this coordination pattern? Would you expect the pattern to be more common in written than in spoken English?

b) As a linguist, you may be more interested in (apparent) violations of the rule stated above, i.e. in cases where the part-of-speech tags of the two verbs are different. You should be able to find such examples with a small modification of your CQP query from part a). Why is it important to rule out ambiguity tags here?

c) When looking at the hits of the previous query, you will have noticed that many of them result from tagging errors in the BNC (e.g. expressions like *all that has been written or said* with the second past participle (VVN) mistagged as past tense (VVD)). Can you find examples that are not due to tagging problems? Add constraints to your query in order to remove the most common tagging errors from the query hits. What other kinds of false positives did you encounter?

3. *Cognate objects in English.* Explore the use of cognate objects in English, i.e. constructions where the object of a verb is the verb's noun form, e.g. *to dream a dream*. More complex examples are *fight a good fight* and *smelt an interesting smell*. Also, note that the two forms don't have to be identical, as is the case in *he slept a troubled sleep*.

a) Begin with a query for simple verb + object constructions in active voice. Your query should match a lexical verb followed by a noun phrase, making sure that the verb and the head of the noun phrase belong to the same headword. You can reuse the NP query developed in the first exercise here.

b) Write a second query for the corresponding constructions in passive voice. This query should match a noun followed by a passive verb pattern, ensuring that the noun and the lexical verb belong to the same headword. You can reuse the query for passives from the second exercise in Chapter 6 here, converting it into CQP syntax first.

c) Both queries will return relatively few hits, so you need to maximize their recall. Which optional elements might appear between the verb and the noun? Extend your queries accordingly.

d) Evaluate the precision of your final queries by manual inspection of a random sample. Recall that you can use the *Corpus Frequency Wizard* (Section 5.6) to extrapolate the result to the full set of query hits. How many of the false positives are due to tagging errors in the BNC?

13 Understanding the internals of *BNCweb*: user types, the cache system and some notes about installation

13.1 Outline

This chapter concerns practical issues in the running of *BNCweb*. It is geared towards different types of readers, ranging from a standard *BNCweb* user to the system administrator who is responsible for the installation and maintenance of a *BNCweb* server. The following points will be covered:

- *BNCweb* users: standard users and users with administrator status
- Features of the *BNCweb* interface which normally remain hidden to standard users
- User settings
- Description of the functionality of the cache system
- Some general issues that relate to the installation of *BNCweb*
- Configuration options available in the Perl library *bncConfigXML.pm*

While the more technical final section of this chapter will be particularly relevant for system administrators, all users may benefit from reading Sections 13.2 to 13.5 as this will increase their awareness of the possibilities and limitations of the system. Note that a detailed and up-to-date description of the installation process can be found on the *BNCweb* homepage at http://www.bncweb.info/.

13.2 *BNCweb* users: standard users and administrators

BNCweb is a multi-user interface to the British National Corpus. Since full access to the BNC—i.e. including access to the larger context of query results—is restricted to license holders, a standard installation of *BNCweb* will require users to provide authentication via a valid username/password combination. Although in principle, several users could share the same access account, it is strongly recommended that all users of *BNCweb* have their own username. This ensures that each standard user has access to only their own individual query history and personalized display settings (see Section 13.4.1 below). More importantly, user-defined subcorpora and saved queries—which are potentially the result of labor-intensive manual categorizations—then cannot be accidentally deleted by another user.

A newly registered user of *BNCweb* will by default have the status of a standard user. However, it is also possible to define one or several users as administrators. This type of user has access to information about all the other users who access *BNCweb* on the same server, and they also see an additional section of links—entitled "Admin features"—in the main navigation panel of *BNCweb*, which allows them to perform a number of useful maintenance tasks.

There are two ways of changing a user's status to "administrator": via a variable in the Perl library file *bncConfigXML.pm*—see Section 13.6.3 below—or with the help of the administrator tool MANAGE ADMIN ACCESS. A screenshot of the MANAGE ADMIN ACCESS feature is shown in Figure 13.1.

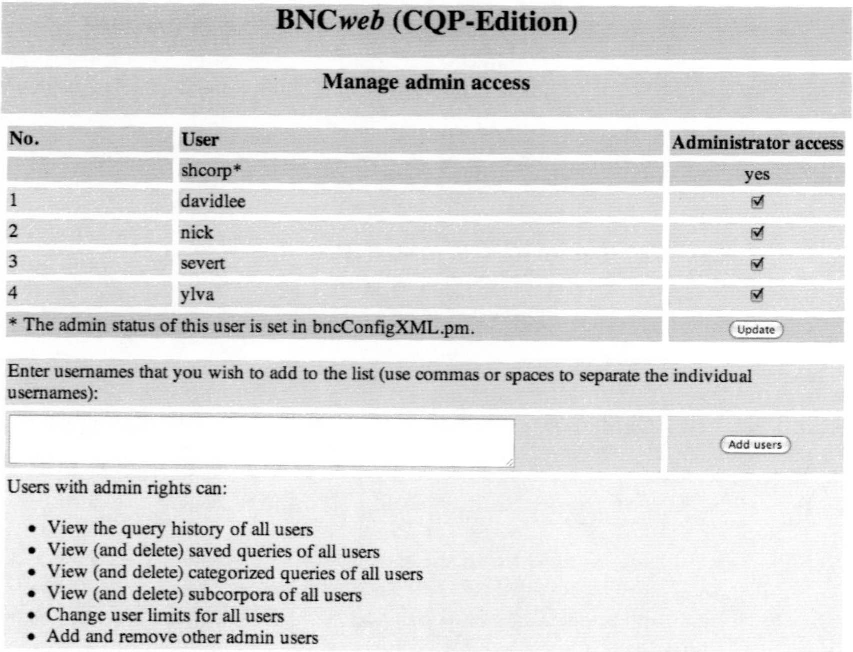

BNC*web* (CQP-Edition)

Manage admin access

No.	User	Administrator access
	shcorp*	yes
1	davidlee	☑
2	nick	☑
3	severt	☑
4	ylva	☑
* The admin status of this user is set in bncConfigXML.pm.		(Update)

Enter usernames that you wish to add to the list (use commas or spaces to separate the individual usernames):

	(Add users)

Users with admin rights can:

- View the query history of all users
- View (and delete) saved queries of all users
- View (and delete) categorized queries of all users
- View (and delete) subcorpora of all users
- Change user limits for all users
- Add and remove other admin users

Figure 13.1:   The MANAGE ADMIN ACCESS feature

In the set-up as shown in Figure 13.1, five users have been given administrator status. The first of these—the username *shcorp*—was set in the Perl library *bncConfigXML.pm*. This is indicated by the slightly darker shade of grey of the table row. The remaining four users were added by entering their usernames in the text box below the table. It is possible to add several users at the same time by typing their usernames with commas or spaces in between. The administrator status of one or several users can be revoked by un-selecting the check-box in the relevant row(s) and then clicking [Update]. It is not possible to use this feature to change the setting for any users whose administrator status is defined in the Perl library file. Please note that no check is made to see whether the usernames that are added in the box actually exist. It is thus in principle possible to assign administrator status to users before their usernames have been created.

13.3   Additional information available to administrator users

13.3.1   Overview

A *BNCweb* user with administrator status has access to user-specific information of all users. In particular, an administrator can perform the following tasks:

- View the query history of all users
- View (and delete) saved queries of all users
- View (and delete) categorized queries of all users
- View (and delete) subcorpora of all users

13.3.2   Administrator access to the Query history feature

If an administrator accesses the QUERY HISTORY feature, *BNCweb* will by default display a history of that user's own queries. In addition, however, a drop-down menu makes it possible to select the query history of any other user on the same server. A further option is available to display the queries of all users in temporal sequence. Finally, the administrator may select to view only those queries of all users which resulted in a syntax error. A screenshot of an administrator's view of the QUERY HISTORY feature is shown in Figure 13.2.

The principal reason for giving administrators access to the query history of other users is that this will help them offer support to standard users. For example, an administrator may notice that a user repeatedly enters queries that lead to syntax errors and may therefore want to contact this user and let them know about the correct syntax for this particular query. Also, users often find it difficult to recall their exact queries, e.g. when they talk to their supervisors during an office hour. In this case, it is very easy to use this administrator access to go through the query history of the user together with him or her and to suggest improvements to searches—without first having to log in as a different user.

> **Note:**
> Some users may feel uneasy about the fact that all of their queries, including their failed ones, can be viewed by (some) other users—in fact, some users may perceive this feature to be excessively intrusive, representing a "Big Brother"-type of invasion into their privacy. For this reason, we recommend that new users are immediately alerted to this functionality of *BNCweb*—and that the reasons are explained why *BNCweb* offers this type of access to administrators. It may also help to point out that the log-files of the server contain far more detailed information about the use of *BNCweb*: every single click a user makes creates an entry in the log. This is not a feature of *BNCweb* specifically but the default behavior of web-servers such as Apache.

BNC*web* (CQP-Edition)

Query history

User: [all users ⬦]   (Show queries)

The following searches were conducted with BNCweb:

No.	User	Date	Query (Show in CQP-Syntax)	Restriction	No. of hits
1	shcorp	11.05.2008, 18:15:47	however	-	59674
2	shcorp	11.05.2008, 18:15:35	nevertheless	-	7037
3	shcorp	11.05.2008, 18:15:20	at the same time	-	6921
4	davidlee	11.05.2008, 18:13:05	so_AV0 AJ*	Written texts	28404
5	davidlee	11.05.2008, 18:12:55	so_AV0 AV0	Written texts	31419
6	shcorp	11.05.2008, 18:12:15	(will_VM0|shall|sha n'tlwo n't l'll)	Spoken texts	59760
7	davidlee	11.05.2008, 18:08:40	{tumble/V}	-	836
8	lancs23	11.05.2008, 18:06:00	according	-	15660
9	lancs1	11.05.2008, 18:05:41	awfully	-	375
10	lancs23	11.05.2008, 18:04:10	according to	-	15548
11	shcorp	11.05.2008, 17:50:12	trail	-	1329
12	shcorp	11.05.2008, 16:27:14	funny	Metatextual categories: Spoken or Written: *Written* Publication date: *1975-1984*	126

Figure 13.2:   Query history of all users

In addition, administrators also have access to some basic usage statistics via the corresponding link in the "Admin features" section. The feature displays the number of queries performed by each user—ordered alphabetically or by total number of queries—during three different periods: overall, during the past year and during the past month. Please note that this feature only displays the number of queries that were performed and does not keep track of any of the post-processing features available to users of *BNCweb*. It therefore only provides rough information about the actual work-load performed by the server. For more detailed information, we recommend the use of a log-analysis tool.

13.3.3 Administrator access to user-specific data stored by other features

Three further features of *BNCweb* offer administrators access to data which belongs to users on the same server: the SAVED QUERIES feature, the CATEGORIZED QUERIES feature and the MAKE/EDIT SUBCORPORA feature. In contrast to the QUERY HISTORY feature, administrators can actively make changes to the data stored by other users. Thus, not only will administrators be able to see queries that were saved by other users, they will also be able to delete them. In the case of categorized queries, users with administrator status can view the concordances with their manually added values and make changes to them. If the administrator chooses to separate the categorized query into different saved queries (cf. Chapter 9), the resulting set will belong to the user who originally categorized the query rather than to the administrator. Finally, subcorpora of other users can be viewed, modified and deleted. Again, this functionality is provided to enable more advanced users to offer support to other users.

13.4   Customizable settings in *BNCweb*

13.4.1   Configuration settings available to standard users

All features of *BNCweb* will work "out of the box" with standard settings and new users do not have to perform any configuration routines before they can start using the system. However, users can choose to influence the behavior of some aspects of *BNCweb* through the USER SETTINGS feature, which is accessible via the main navigation panel. These user-configurable options apply to three different areas: a) the display of query results and the larger context display of a query hit, b) the default values used in the COLLOCATIONS feature, and c) the way downloaded data is formatted for the user's computer. The top half of the USER SETTINGS page is displayed in Figure 13.3.

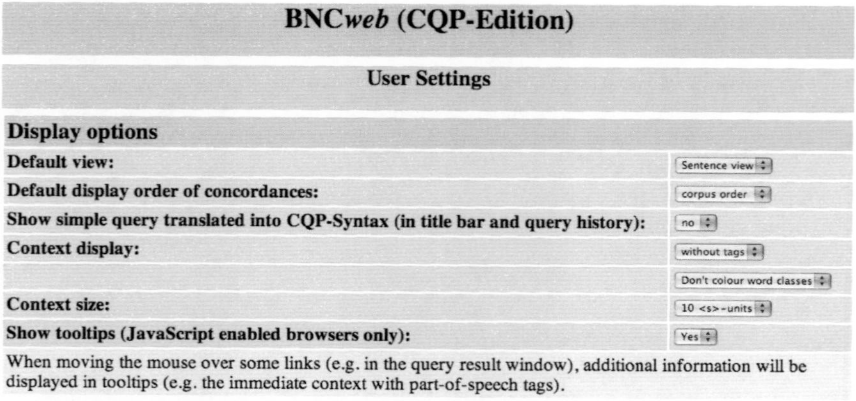

BNC*web* (CQP-Edition)
User Settings

Display options

Default view:	Sentence view ⬥
Default display order of concordances:	corpus order ⬥
Show simple query translated into CQP-Syntax (in title bar and query history):	no ⬥
Context display:	without tags ⬥
	Don't colour word classes ⬥
Context size:	10 <s>-units ⬥
Show tooltips (JavaScript enabled browsers only):	Yes ⬥

When moving the mouse over some links (e.g. in the query result window), additional information will be displayed in tooltips (e.g. the immediate context with part-of-speech tags).

Figure 13.3:   The USER SETTINGS window (top half only)

The following options are available:

- Display of concordances in "Sentence view" (default) or "KWIC-view".

- Display of concordances in "Corpus order" (default) or "Random order".

- Display of the search string in the title bar of a query result in "Simple Query Syntax" (default) or translated to "CQP-Syntax". The same setting will also determine the display of search strings in the QUERY HISTORY feature.

- Display of the larger context of a query hit with part-of-speech tags or without (default) and with colored word classes or without (default).

- Size of the context display in s-units (default: 10 s-units; maximum: 60 s-units).

- Display of "tooltips" in the Query result window (default: "yes"). These JavaScript-based boxes appear when the user hovers the cursor over certain links in concordances—see 4.4.5.

- For the COLLOCATIONS feature, users can set the calculation method (default: "log-likelihood"), minimum frequencies for collocates (default: "5") and node–collocate combinations (default: "5"), and the window size (default: "3 Left" to "3 Right")—see 8.4.

- File format for downloading data to the user's hard-drive: Operating systems (e.g. Windows or Mac OS X) differ in the way they represent newlines (i.e. the invisible "end-of-line" character or character sequence).

Although many modern text editors automatically detect newlines correctly, exchanging files that were created by downloading data from *BNCweb* with users of other operating systems may occasionally lead to unexpected results. *BNCweb* therefore gives users the option of saving downloaded data in a format that is specific to an operating system which is different from the one currently employed by the user. The default setting is "Automatic", which means that the download format will match the operating system of the user's computer.

13.4.2   Configuration settings available to administrator users

Some of the features of *BNCweb* place high demands on the server, both in terms of CPU time and disk space. Furthermore, each query that is performed and each post-processing analysis that is carried out produces additional data—and even the largest hard-disk will eventually fill up. This could for example quite quickly happen if 10 different users tried to do a collocation analysis of all nouns in the corpus (more than 25 million hits). A number of measures have been taken to make sure that *BNCweb* does not reach the limits of the hardware, even if large groups access the system at the same time.

The default behavior of these restrictions is set in a configuration file—see Section 13.6.3 below. With the help of the USER LIMITS feature, administrators of *BNCweb* can override these global settings and assign different maximum values to individual users who require access to high-frequency data that would otherwise not be available to them. A screenshot of this feature is shown in Figure 13.4.

User limits				
No.	User	Collocation feature	Sort feature	Distribution feature	Action
	DEFAULT*	250,000	250,000	1,000,000	
1	davidlee	500,000	250,000	1,000,000	Delete Change
2	jianmingwu	1,000,000	1,000,000	1,000,000	Delete Change
3	nick	500,000	250,000	1,000,000	Delete Change
4	shcorp	1,000,000	1,000,000	1,000,000	Delete Change

* The default values can be changed in the library file bncConfigXML.pm.

Enter usernames that you wish to add to the list (use commas or spaces to separate the individual usernames):

[   ]   (Add users)

Figure 13.4:   The USER LIMITS feature

As in the case of the MANAGE ADMIN ACCESS feature, the default values are displayed against a slightly darker background. Adding a user-specific limit involves two steps: first, the user needs to be added to the list by entering their username in the textbox below the table. Several users can be added at the same time by typing their usernames with commas or spaces in between. Once the button [Add users] is clicked, the page will refresh and the table will contain the newly added user(s). At this point, the values of their user limits will still be identical to the default limits. In a second step, individual values can now be changed by clicking on the relevant link in the rightmost column of the table. This is shown in Figure 13.5.

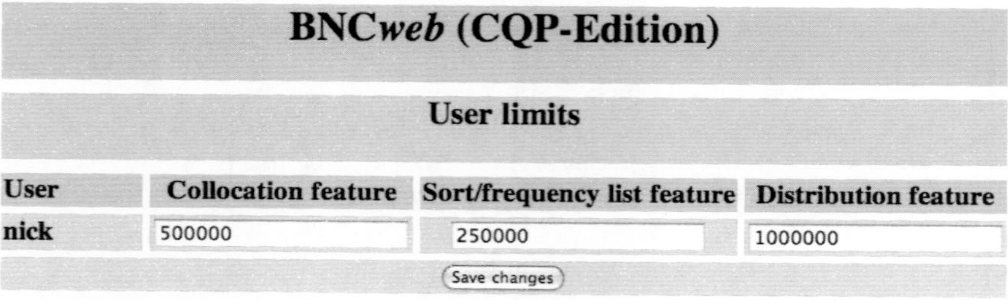

BNC*web* (CQP-Edition)

User limits

User	Collocation feature	Sort/frequency list feature	Distribution feature
nick	500000	250000	1000000

Save changes

Figure 13.5:   Changing the user limits for an individual username

If desired, these values can be set to be more restrictive than the defaults. Finally, deleting a user from the list will mean that their limits revert back to the default values.

13.5   The cache system

13.5.1   General description

With each query and each use of a post-processing feature like the COLLOCATION or DISTRIBUTION features, new data is written to the hard-disk of the server and saved as a temporary file. In order to reduce disk-space usage, *BNCweb* has an internal cache system that keeps track of previously performed queries and re-uses them if possible, even if the original query was carried out by a different user. This functionality is particularly useful for example in a classroom setting, where several users are likely to carry out the same actions on *BNCweb*. As a positive side-effect, data which is retrieved from cache is also available almost instantly. Especially in the case of more complex queries or post-processing analyses of larger query results, users may therefore experience a noticeable speed improvement for some of their actions.

The following points describe the cache system in some more detail and may help readers make the best use of its functionality:

- All standard queries—including those involving spoken or written metatextual restrictions—are cached. However, queries that are restricted to user-defined subcorpora are not cached. The reason for this is that the composition of a user-defined subcorpus can change (cf. Chapter 10) even though its name will remain the same.

- All data is cached and made available to other users as soon as the query or post-processing feature has finished executing. When several users start a collocation analysis of a large query result—or a similarly disk-intensive feature—at more or less the same time, they will therefore not have access to previously cached information and each create large amounts of data on the server. In a classroom situation, where whole groups of users may execute certain tasks at the same time, it is therefore advisable that the instructor performs these tasks in advance.

- For high-frequency features, access to cached data is granted even if the total number of hits of the query is higher than the limits that apply to the user. For example, a user who would like to perform a collocation analysis of the preposition *at* (521,623 hits), but whose user limit is set to 250,000, could still get access to the information if a different user with a higher limit has previously performed this particular collocation analysis and if the cached file for this action is still available.

- In fact, *BNCweb* uses three separate caches: one for data produced by the corpus query processor (in effect, this refers to all data required to display concordance lines), one for *MySQL* tables that are created as a result of the SORT, COLLOCATION and DISTRIBUTION features, and a third for frequency lists of subcorpora (cf. Chapters 7, 8, 10 and 11). Once the maximum size of the cached data is reached for any of the three components, the oldest items in the cache are deleted until its total size is again within the limit set in the configuration file *bncConfigXML.pm*. System administrators may wish to change the individual limits for the three different caches according to the needs of the *BNCweb* users on their server.

13.5.2 Maintenance of the cache system

Users with administrator status can view and modify the contents of the three different cache systems introduced in Section 13.5.1 by clicking on one of the three links provided in the "Admin features" section of the main navigation panel. Figure 13.6 displays a screenshot of the CQP query cache. At the time this screenshot was taken, a total of 3,781 query files had been cached on the server. While most of these files were small, queries that returned a large number of hits produced much more data. In Figure 13.6, the cached queries are ordered by size, with the largest files shown first: the first query alone (which retrieved all nouns and verbs—more than 43 million hits) resulted in about 330 megabytes of data (346,825,300 bytes). This fact nicely demonstrates the importance of having access to cached queries: if 20 users of *BNCweb* were to search for "any noun or verb" without this type of cache system, about 6.5 gigabytes of data would be produced. Contents of the cache can also be displayed in temporal order by clicking on the heading of the "Date" column.

BNC*web* (CQP-Edition)

Cached queries: 3781 files; 1,508,053,508 bytes on disk (46.82%) - Delete complete cache

No.	Query ID	Query string (without restrictions)	No. of hits	Date	Size on Disk	Action
1	shcorp_1210526224	[lemma = "(.*)_VERB" %c] | [lemma = "(.*)_SUBST" %c]	43,353,155	11-05-2008 19:18:34	346,825,300	Delete
2	shcorp_1210526143	[lemma = "(.*)_VERB" %c]	17,861,343	11-05-2008 19:16:16	142,890,804	Delete
3	uclan5_1208769967	[pos = "aj.*" %c]	7,293,751	21-04-2008 11:26:19	58,350,068	Delete
4	lancs1_1201059675	[word = "the" %c]	6,041,234	11-05-2008 19:12:49	48,329,932	Delete
5	lancs1_1209348787	[lemma = "_STOP"]	5,014,383	28-04-2008 04:13:15	40,115,124	Delete
6	lancs13_1208724793	[pos = "PNP.*" %c]	4,969,579	20-04-2008 22:53:20	39,756,692	Delete
7	lancs9_1207908808	[word = "\." %c]	4,713,133	13-04-2008 23:39:32	37,705,124	Delete
8	lancs1_1209347723	[lemma = "(\.)_.*" %c]	4,713,133	28-04-2008 03:55:30	37,705,124	Delete
9	lancs1_1209350810	[hw = "\." & class = "STOP"]	4,713,130	28-04-2008 04:47:06	37,705,100	Delete
10	lancs1_1209348713	[lemma = "_STOP"]	4,713,130	28-04-2008 04:12:00	37,705,100	Delete

Figure 13.6:   Display of the query cache

Since older contents of the cache will be automatically erased when the assigned limit is reached, manual deletion of cached files should not normally be necessary. If a system administrator wishes to free additional space on the hard-disk, manual deletion of the largest files is of course an option. However, a more convenient way would be to simply lower the limits for one or all three cache systems. When the next entry to the relevant cache is made by *BNCweb*, any old files going beyond the new limit will be automatically deleted. If a particular file has become corrupted or has for any other reason become unusable, it may nevertheless be necessary to delete it manually. This kind of action is easily performed by clicking on the relevant link in the cache table. An administrator may also choose to delete the whole cache by clicking on the corresponding link above the cache table.

In contrast to deleting saved or categorized queries, deleting cached files is not a dangerous action since these files will be automatically recreated when the same query is executed again. However, if a cached file is deleted while a feature of *BNCweb* requires access to it, an error message will be displayed. In this case, the initial query (or the chosen post-query option) may have to be re-executed to recreate the cached file.

13.6   Installation of *BNCweb*

13.6.1   Prerequisites

BNCweb has a client-server architecture: it is designed to give a (potentially large) number of concurrent users access to a server-side *BNCweb* installation via their standard Web browsers. As a result, *BNCweb* requires no special installation procedure or client program on the part of the end user—any standard Web-browser (under any kind of operating system) can be used to access the BNC via the Internet or a local area network.

On the server side, *BNCweb* consists of a set of Perl scripts that require installation on a UNIX system such as Linux, Mac OS X, Sun Solaris, etc. It might also be possible to install *BNCweb* under *Cygwin*, a Unix-like environment for the Windows operating system (http://www.cygwin.com/). However, at the time of writing, we have not heard from anybody who has successfully done this.

A detailed and updated installation manual for *BNCweb* is available at http://www.bncweb.info/, and only some basic knowledge of UNIX system administration is required for a successful installation. Please note that the installation requires access to a local copy of the original XML-version of the BNC and that it is not possible to use *BNCweb* in conjunction with the BNC Online service hosted by the British Library (http://sara.natcorp.ox.ac.uk/).

The following tools and libraries need to be installed on the server—some of which may already be pre-installed on the system:

- The *IMS Open Corpus Workbench* (http://cwb.sourceforge.net/)—a specialized indexing and query software for large text corpora with linguistic annotations

- *MySQL* 4.1 or higher—future updates of *BNCweb* may require at least *MySQL* 5.0 (http://www.mysql.com/)

- *Xsltproc*—an XSLT stylesheet processor for transforming XML documents (from the *Gnome LibXSLT* package)

- *Perl* 5.8 (version 5.6 may work, too, but might require installation of additional modules)
- Perl modules:
  - o *DBI*
  - o *DBD::mysql*
  - o *HTML::Entities*
  - o *Parse::RecDescent*

13.6.2   Time and disk-space required

During the installation process, an index of the original BNC-XML texts and a number of large MySQL tables will be compiled. Even on very fast servers, this may take several hours. A full installation of *BNCweb* takes up about 3 gigabytes of disk space. However, disk-space requirements are higher (approx. 8-10 gigabytes) during the compilation of the index of the BNC files. When *BNCweb* is used, it creates temporary files of a considerable size on the server. A cache system has been implemented to ensure that the available disk-space is used efficiently (cf. Section 13.5 above). We recommend that at least 3–5 gigabytes of free disk-space are available for these temporary files—a larger amount will be beneficial when whole groups of users access *BNCweb* at the same time.

Note:
Although *BNCweb* has a client-server architecture, it can of course also be installed—using the same installation procedure—on a single-user computer running a UNIX operating system. The web browser will then access *BNCweb* locally with the address "localhost" or "127.0.0.1". Even an entry-level notebook will provide more than sufficient computing-power for such a set-up.

13.6.3   Configuration of the Perl library *bncConfigXML.pm*

All necessary configuration settings for *BNCweb* are made via a number of variables in the Perl library *bncConfigXML.pm*. This file is located in the folder called *lib_files/* in the *BNCweb* directory. It contains two sections. Variables in the first section will need to be configured during the installation of *BNCweb*—please refer to the online installation manual for further information (http://www.bncweb.info). The second section of the file *bncConfigXML.pm* contains a number of variables which can be set to change the behavior of *BNCweb* depending on the requirements of the individual set-up. For all of these variables, default values are provided which should be adequate for a standard system. However, if the available disk-space is limited or if large numbers of users will be accessing *BNCweb* at the same time, some changes may be required to ensure that *BNCweb* runs smoothly.

As mentioned in Section 13.2, users of *BNCweb* can have one of two usage levels: standard and administrator. At least one user with administrator status has to be defined in the configuration file—this is done via the variable *$bwSuperuser*. The default value of this variable is "admin". If no *BNCweb* user with this name exists, it is necessary to modify the variable accordingly.

The value of *$bwSuperUser* can also be a regular expression, which allows you to assign admin status to a group of users. Thus, in order to give the users *admin1*, *admin2* and *admin3* administrator rights, the variable will have to look as follows:

```
$bwSuperuser = 'admin1|admin2|admin3';
```

Please note that administrator access to *BNCweb* will only be granted if the string contained in *$bwSuperuser* is a full match. In other words, it is not possible to set the variable *$bwSuperuser* to "admin" and thereby assign administrator status to all usernames that contain the sequence of letters *admin*.[1]

The remaining variables in the file *bncConfigXML.pm* are used to set global values for limiting the use of CPU und disk-intensive features of *BNCweb* (e.g. the COLLOCATIONS or SORT features). As shown in Section 13.4.2, it is possible to override these global values for individual users via the USER LIMITS feature.

The first three variables (*$bwDefaultSort*, *$bwDefaultCollocation* and *$bwDefaultDist*) refer to the maximum number of hits a query result can have for users to be able to sort the concordance, calculate collocations, and to display the distribution of hits over the different metatextual categories. The defaults are set to 250,000 for both the COLLOCATION and the SORT feature. Since the DISTRIBUTION feature produces far less data on the server and is also less CPU-intensive, the default limit for this feature is one million hits. If a user attempts to use any of these features with a query result that is larger than the values of these variables, an error message will be displayed, as shown in Figure 13.7.

Since the SORT and COLLOCATION features are particularly demanding in terms of both CPU-time and disk-space, an additional limit is put on how many users can perform a sort or collocation operation at the same time. This is set in the variable *$bwConcurrentProcesses*—the default value is "5". If the limit is

---

1 To be precise, this could be achieved with the value ".*admin.*", but it is strongly discouraged because of security concerns.

reached and a user tries to start another process, an error message will be displayed, as shown in Figure 13.8. Since it typically takes only a few seconds to calculate collocations or to sort the concordances of relatively large query results, the desired analysis can usually be conducted on trying again a few seconds later.

Disk Space Alert

The action you have requested would use up too much disk-space!

You were trying to work with 17,861,343 hits but your limit is currently set to a maximum of 1,000,000 instances.

You can perform the desired action on a random subset of your data: In the query result display, select the option "Thin..." and then enter a number up to the maximum of 1,000,000. Alternatively, if you really need access to the full set of data, please contact your system administrator who will be able to increase the limit for you.

Figure 13.7   Disk-space alert message

Too many processes...

There are already 5 collocation databases being compiled. Please use the "back"-button of your browser and try again in a few moments.

Figure 13.8:   "Too many processes" alert message

The final three variables ($bwFileSize$, $bwMaxMySQLSize$ and $bwMax-FreqlistMySQL$) determine the maximum disk space (in bytes) that is available for the internal cache system. The default value for all three variables is 3 gigabytes (3,221,225,472 bytes). The free disk space on the server needs to be larger than the sum of these three variables.

References

Baayen, R.H. (2008): *Analyzing Linguistic Data: A Practical Introduction to Statistics Using R*. Cambridge: Cambridge University Press.

Ball, C. (1994): "Automated text analysis: cautionary tales", *Literary and Linguistic Computing*, 9(4), 295-302.

Baroni, M. & S. Evert (in press): "Statistical methods for corpus exploitation", *Corpus Linguistics. An International Handbook*, ed A. Lüdeling & M. Kytö. Berlin: Mouton de Gruyter, Chapter 36. Available at <http://purl.org/stefan.evert/PUB/BaroniEvertHSK38_manuscript.pdf> (accessed 2.7.2008).

Beaman, K. (1984): "Coordination and subordination revisited: syntactic complexity in spoken and written narrative discourse", *Coherence in Spoken and Written Discourse*, ed. D. Tannen. Norwood, N.J.: Ablex. 45-80.

Berber-Sardinha, T. (2000): "Comparing corpora with WordSmith Tools: How large must the reference corpus be?", (Workshop on Comparing Corpora). Available at <http://acl.ldc.upenn.edu/W/W00/W00-0902.pdf> (accessed 2.7.2008).

Biber, D., S. Johansson, G. Leech, S. Conrad & E. Finegan (1999): *Longman Grammar of Spoken and Written English*. London: Longman Addison Wesley.

Biber, D., S. Conrad & R. Reppen (1988): *Corpus Linguistics. Investigating Language Structure and Use*. Cambridge: Cambridge University Press.

Burnard, L. (2007): *Reference Guide for the British National Corpus (XML Edition)*. Available at <http://www.natcorp.ox.ac.uk/XMLedition/URG/> (accessed 2.7.2008).

Chomsky, N. (1962): "A transformational approach to syntax", Paper given and transcript of discussion, *Third Texas Conference on Problems of Linguistic Analysis in English, May 9–12, 1958*, ed. A. A. Hill. Austin, Texas: The University of Texas, 124-169.

Clark, H.H. & E.V. Clark (1977): *Psychology and Language: An Introduction to Psycholinguistics*. New York: Harcourt Brace Jovanovich.

Collins COBUILD Advanced Learner's English Dictionary. 5th edition. 2006. Glasgow: Harper Collins.

DeGroot, M.H. & M.J. Schervish (2002): *Probability and Statistics*. Boston: Addison Wesley. 3rd edition.

Ellegård, A. (1953): *The Auxiliary "Do": The Establishment and Regulation of its Use in English*. Gothenburg Studies in English, 2. Stockholm: Almqvist & Wiksell.

Evert, S. (2006): "How random is a corpus? The library metaphor", *Zeitschrift für Anglistik und Amerikanistik*, 54(2), 177-190.

Evert, S. (in press): "Corpora and collocations", *Corpus Linguistics. An International Handbook*, ed. A. Lüdeling & M. Kytö. Berlin: Mouton de Gruyter, Chapter 58. Available at <http://purl.org/stefan.evert/PUB/Evert2007HSK_ extended_manuscript.pdf > (accessed 2.7.2008).

Friedl, J.E.F. (2006): *Mastering Regular Expressions*. 3rd edition. Sebastopol, CA and Farnham, UK: O'Reilly.

Garside, R. (1996): "The robust tagging of unrestricted text: the BNC experience", *Using Corpora for Language Research*, ed. J. Short & M. Short. London: Longman. 167-80.

Garside, R. & N. Smith (1997): "A hybrid grammatical tagger: CLAWS4", *Corpus Annotation: Linguistic Information from Computer Text Corpora*, ed. R. Garside, G. Leech & A. McEnery. London: Longman. 102-21.

Gries, S.Th. (in press): *Quantitative Corpus Linguistics With R: A Practical Introduction*. New York: Routledge, Taylor & Francis Group.

Hoffmann, S. (2005): *Grammaticalization and English Complex Prepositions. A Corpus-Based Study*. London: Routledge.

Hommerberg, C. & G. Tottie (2007): "*Try to* or *try and*? Verb complementation in British and American English. *ICAME Journal* 31, 45-64.

Kennedy, G. (1998): *An Introduction to Corpus Linguistics*. London and New York: Longman.

Lapata, M., S. McDonald & F. Keller (1999): "Determinants of adjective-noun plausibility", *Proceedings of the 9th Conference of the European Chapter of the Association for Computational Linguistics (EACL 1999), Bergen, Norway*. 30–36.

Lee, D.Y.W. (2001): "Genres, registers, text types, domains, and styles: Clarifying the concepts and navigating a path through the BNC jungle", *Language Learning & Technology* 5(3), 37-72.

Leech, G. & N. Smith (2000): *Manual to Accompany the British National Corpus (Version 2) with Improved Word-class Tagging*. UCREL: Lancaster University. Available at <http://www.natcorp.ox.ac.uk/docs/bnc2postag_ manual.htm> (accessed 2.7.2008).

Lehmann H.-M., P. Schneider & S. Hoffmann (2000): "BNCweb", *Corpora Galore: Analysis and Techniques in Describing English*, ed. J. Kirk. Amsterdam: Rodopi. 259-266.

McEnery, T., R. Xiao & Y. Tono (2005): *Corpus-based Language Studies: an Advanced Resource Book*. London: Routledge.

McEnery, T. & A. Wilson (2001): *Corpus Linguistics*. 2nd edition. Edinburgh: Edinburgh University Press.

Meyer, Ch.F. (2002): *English Corpus Linguistics. An Introduction*. Cambridge: Cambridge University Press.

Oakes, M.P. (1998): *Statistics for Corpus Linguistics*. Edinburgh: Edinburgh University Press.

Quirk, R., S. Greenbaum, G. Leech & J. Svartvik (1985): *A Comprehensive Grammar of the English Language*. London: Longman.

R Development Core Team (2008): *R: A Language and Environment for Statistical Computing*. Vienna, Austria: R Foundation for Statistical Computing. See also <http://www.r-project.org/> (accessed 2.7.2008).

Rayson P., D. Berridge & B. Francis (2004): "Extending the Cochran rule for the comparison of word frequencies between corpora", *Le poids des mots: Proceedings of the 7th International Conference on Statistical analysis of textual data (JADT 2004), Louvain-la-Neuve, Belgium, March 10-12, 2004*, ed G. Purnelle, C. Fairon & A. Dister. Louvain, Belgium: Presses universitaires de Louvain. 926-936.

Scott, M. (1997): "PC analysis of key words—and key key words", *System* 25(1), 1-13.

Schiffrin, D. (1987): *Discourse Markers*. Cambridge: Cambridge University Press.

Sinclair, J.McH. (1996): EAGLES. *Preliminary Recommendations on Corpus Typology*. Available at <http://www.ilc.cnr.it/EAGLES96/corpustyp/corpustyp.html> (accessed 2.7.2008).

Smith, N., P. Rayson & S. Hoffmann (2008): "Corpus tools and methods, today and tomorrow: Incorporating linguists' manual annotations", *Literary and Linguistic Computing*. 23(2), 163-180.

Stenström, A. (1994): *An Introduction to Spoken Interaction*. London and New York: Longman.

Stubbs, M. (1995): "Collocations and semantic profiles: On the cause of the trouble with quantitative studies", *Functions of Language* 1, 23–55.

Stubbs, M. (1996): *Text and Corpus Analysis: Computer-assisted Studies of Language and Culture*. Oxford & Cambridge, MA: Blackwell.

Tottie, G. (1986): "The importance of being adverbial; Adverbials of focusing and contingency in spoken and written English", *English in Speech and Writing: A Symposium*, ed. G. Tottie & I. Bäcklund. Uppsala: Almqvist and Wilksell International, 93-118.

Glossary

AMBIGUITY TAG
An ambiguity tag is a part-of-speech tag in the BNC that has been used wherever the automatic tagging software was unable to definitively decide which tag to assign to a word. An ambiguity tag consists of a hyphenated pair of tags: for example "AJ0-AV0", where the choice between adjective ("AJ0") and adverb ("AV0") is left open. The first element of an ambiguity tag may, however, be taken to be slightly more likely. There are 30 different ambiguity tags used in the BNC—a full list can be found via the link "The CLAWS-5 tagset" on the **MAIN NAVIGATION PANEL** of *BNCweb*.
See also: **TAG, ANNOTATION**

ANNOTATION
Linguistic information attached to individual words or other selected parts of a corpus. In the BNC, the part-of-speech tag "NN1", for example, indicates that the word is a singular common noun. Another kind of annotation identifies headwords and simplified parts of speech (see **LEMMA**). Annotation is one type of **MARK-UP** in the corpus.
Most forms of annotation are inserted automatically with specialist software. However, annotations can be added manually as well—see Chapter 9.
Note: in computational linguistics, "annotation" is typically used to describe the *process* of inserting annotations, rather than the product itself.
See also: **METATEXTUAL MARK-UP**

ATTRIBUTE
In the CQP Query Syntax, pieces of linguistic annotation attached to individual tokens (words and punctuation symbols) are called "attributes". Each attribute provides one kind of information, e.g. part-of-speech tags (`pos` attribute) or headwords (`hw` attribute). The original word form or punctuation symbol can also be understood as an attribute, which is named `word` in CQP queries. XML tags representing text structure, typographical mark-up, etc. are sometimes referred to as "structural attributes". See Section 12.5 for a complete list of (token-level) attributes offered by *BNCweb*.
See also: **ANNOTATION, MARK-UP, METATEXTUAL MARK-UP**

C-UNIT
A unit of punctuation, such as comma, semicolon, long dash and full stop (or period).
See also: **W-UNIT, S-UNIT**

CASE-INSENSITIVE
In a case-insensitive query, no distinction is made between upper and lower case letters. Thus, queries for *Reading, reading* and *READING* all return exactly the same Query result. Case-insensitive searches are the default in Simple Query Syntax.
See also: **CASE-SENSITIVE**

CASE-SENSITIVE
In a case-sensitive query, upper and lower case forms of a letter are treated differently. Thus, a case-sensitive query for `Reading` will find only instances of *Reading*, but not *reading* or *READING*.
See also: **CASE-INSENSITIVE**

COLLOCATION
The habitual co-occurrence of words/linguistic items in close proximity to one another. For example, if you look up the word *jubilee*, you will tend to find the following words (the collocates) nearby: *silver, diamond, golden, Queen's, line.* The term "collocation" is very broad, and allows varying degrees of collocability (or collocational strength), which is measured by any of a number of statistical formulae (e.g. log-likelihood, mutual information). See Chapter 8 for a detailed discussion.

CONCORDANCE
A listing of all the occurrences in the corpus of the **QUERY ITEM**, together with some surrounding context in the form of words to the left and right. In *BNCweb*, a concordance forms part of a **QUERY RESULT**.
   BNCweb offers two modes of displaying concordance lines: "sentence view" and "KWIC view". In sentence view, each example that matches the search item is displayed with one **S-UNIT** of context. In KWIC view (i.e. Key Word In Context view), each matching example is displayed on a single line, and the search item appears as node in a fixed, central position. As well as being browsed, concordance lines can be manipulated by a range of *BNCweb* functions that are available via the post-query options menu (e.g. **SORT**, **DISTRIBUTION**, **COLLOCATIONS**, etc.)
See also: **NODE**

CONTEXT-GOVERNED COMPONENT (CG)
Spoken material in the BNC (comprising 6,175,896 words) that was collected in particular settings or contexts. Examples include: sports commentaries, sales demonstrations, lectures, political speeches and legal proceedings. Speech in the CG component tends to be more formal than that in the other major category of

spoken data in the BNC, namely the **DEMOGRAPHICALLY SAMPLED COMPONENT**.

CORPUS POSITION
A unique number identifying each token in the corpus, used internally within *BNCweb* for processing queries. Only visible when a Query result is saved to the user's local computer with the DOWNLOAD feature. The purpose of downloading corpus position is to enable transfer of concordance lines from *BNCweb* to other applications (e.g. Microsoft *Excel*) and back again. See 9.6.

CQP QUERY SYNTAX
One of the two formats used to enter queries in *BNCweb*. In general, the notation used in CQP syntax is more verbose than that of the **SIMPLE QUERY SYNTAX**. Although in many respects the same queries can be expressed in either CQP syntax or Simple Query Syntax, the former allows some advanced queries that cannot be expressed in the latter. See Chapter 12 for a full reference of the query syntax. Queries in this format can also be run in other tools (and on other corpora) that make use of the CQP query engine. For more general information on CQP, refer to http://cwb.sourceforge.net/.
See also: **TOKEN EXPRESSION**

DERIVED TEXT TYPE
A text type that subsumes a number of the more specific **GENRE** categories contained in the BNC. For example, the derived text type "Other published written material" subsumes the genre categories "W:advert", "W:hansard", "W:institut_doc", "W:instructional", "W:letters:personal", "W:letters:prof", "W:misc" and "W:pop_lore". The other derived text types in the written component are "Academic prose", "Non-academic prose and biography", "Fiction and verse", "Newspapers" and "Unpublished written material". In the spoken component, the category "Spoken conversation" matches the single genre "S:conv" (i.e. the **DEMOGRAPHICALLY SAMPLED COMPONENT**), while the category "Other spoken material" comprises the 23 other spoken genres that make up the **CONTEXT-GOVERNED COMPONENT**.

DEMOGRAPHICALLY SAMPLED COMPONENT
Spontaneous spoken conversation material in the BNC (comprising 4,233,962 words) that was collected by 153 **RESPONDENTS**, who were recruited according to sociodemographic sampling criteria such as age, sex, and social class. Respondents were asked to record their interactions with other people over a two to seven day period. Recordings were made non-surreptitiously, i.e. all participants knew that they were being recorded. Speech in the demographically sampled

component tends to be more informal than that in the other major category of spoken data in the BNC, namely the **CONTEXT-GOVERNED COMPONENT**.

DESCRIPTIVE FEATURE

A classificatory feature of the corpus that was not part of the **SELECTION CRITERIA**, but added *post hoc*—on the basis of observed evidence—because it was determined to be useful for researchers. Examples of such features include "sex of target audience", "accent/dialect of speaker" and the 70 genre categories.

DESCRIPTIVE STATISTICS

Miscellaneous frequency data obtained on the use of a linguistic item/feature in a corpus. Examples include the frequency of *lovely* uttered by different age groups of speaker, the frequency breakdown of a query result and the nouns that occur most often with the adjective *dangerous*. While descriptive statistics can provide interesting insights into patterns of language, the findings usually need to be combined with a qualitative analysis of individual concordance lines (and their contexts) to gain a clearer understanding of the usage of the feature being examined.

DISPERSION

An indication of how well dispersed or "spread" the occurrences of a search item are across the texts of the BNC, or across selected parts of it. For example, the nouns *antibiotic* and *freon* each occur ten times in the spoken component of the BNC. However, while *antibiotic* is found in ten different texts (i.e. a ratio of 10:10), *freon* appears in only a single one (i.e. a ratio of 1:10). This points to the fact that *freon* is a more specialist term than *antibiotic*. Note that dispersion is not an absolute measure but depends on the number of hits of a Query term— see 7.2.3.

See also: **DESCRIPTIVE STATISTICS**, **RAW FREQUENCY**, **NORMALIZED FREQUENCY**

DOMAIN

The subject field, or broad topic area, of a BNC text (applies to both written and spoken texts). For example, within spoken texts there is a domain called "business", which includes company talks and interviews, trade union talks, sales demonstrations, business meetings, and consultations. The domain categories form part of the **SELECTION CRITERIA** in the compilation of the corpus.

ESCAPE SEQUENCE

An escape sequence is a backslash followed by a letter which acts as a **WILDCARD** in Simple Query Syntax. For instance, the escape sequence \u stands for a single uppercase letter, and the escape sequence \D for an arbitrary number of digits. A full list of escape sequences available in Simple Query Syntax is given in 6.6. Note that backslashes are also used to match certain punctuation symbols (e.g. \? to search for a question mark or \, to search for a comma). This is because these symbols, called **METACHARACTERS**, have special functions in *BNCweb* queries; for example, the wildcard ? matches any single character. We refer to the use of the backslash with punctuation symbols as "escaping", while "escape sequence" stands for the combination of the backslash with an ordinary letter.

GENRE
The genre categories recognized in the corpus were identified in independent research by David Lee. "Genre" here refers to a culturally recognized grouping of texts according to some conventionally recognized language-external criteria such as purpose, setting, and participants. The BNC genres can be high-level/broad (e.g. "business/commerce texts", which lumps together many different types of text) or low-level/specific (e.g. "Hansard", which refers to the official transcripts of parliamentary speeches). Other examples of genres contained in the BNC are: prose fiction, print advertisements, school essays, face-to-face conversations, and university tutorials.
See also: **DERIVED TEXT TYPE, DOMAIN**

GLOBAL CONSTRAINT
A Boolean expression (cf. 12.5) added to the end of a CQP query, separated from the main query by a double colon (: :). In this way, conditions involving multiple tokens can be expressed. For example, it is possible to put limits on the length of a query match (e.g. finding noun phrases that consist of 6 or more tokens) or to make sure that two words are identical (e.g. in expressions like *day after day* or *piece by piece*)—see 12.7.

HEADWORD
A headword is a set of wordforms consisting of a basic uninflected form and its inflectional variants. The headword WRITE, for example, represents the wordforms *write, writes, wrote, writing* and *written*. Headwords do not distinguish between different wordclasses. Thus, the headword PLAY covers both the wordforms of the verb (i.e. *play, plays, played* and *playing*) and of the noun (i.e. *play* and *plays*).
See also: **LEMMA**

LEMMA
In *BNCweb*, a lemma is the combination of the **HEADWORD** and the **SIMPLIFIED TAG** for a given word. Thus, the lemma *play_VERB* represents all the wordforms

of the verb *to play*. In Simple Query Syntax, you can search for the verb lemma PLAY by way of the query {play/VERB} (or the shorthand {play/V}).

MAIN NAVIGATION PANEL
Term used to refer to the links on the left hand side of *BNCweb* pages that are available to the user without first performing a query.

MARK-UP
A cover term for data included in a corpus that describes (i) the source (authors, speakers) of a text (METATEXTUAL MARK-UP), (ii) structural features of a text, such as the location of headings, paragraphs and speaker turns, as well as typographical aspects, e.g. highlighting or use of superscript numbers, and (iii) linguistic characteristics of the text (linguistic ANNOTATION).
See also: TAG

METACHARACTER
Certain punctuation symbols that have a special meaning in *BNCweb* queries. For instance, the question mark ? stands for an arbitrary single character (letter, digit or punctuation mark) in Simple Query Syntax. In order to match the actual punctuation symbol, it has to be preceded by a backslash (also known as "escaping" the metacharacter). For instance, you need to type \? to match an actual question mark. Metacharacters and their precise meanings are different in Simple Query Syntax (see 6.3) and CQP Query Syntax (see 12.3).
See also: ESCAPE SEQUENCE

METATEXTUAL MARK-UP
Factual data about the source or provenance of a corpus text—e.g. for a written text, the author, publication date and target audience; for a spoken text, the age and education level of any speakers. The main use of metatextual mark-up in *BNCweb* is as the basis for restricting queries to subsets of the BNC.
See also: ANNOTATION, MARK-UP, TAG

NODE
1. The position occupied by the QUERY ITEM in a CONCORDANCE. In a KWIC-format concordance, the node will be in the center of each concordance line. Concordances can also be sorted relative to the node.
2. In a collocation analysis, the term "node" refers to the word or expression for which collocates are determined. In *BNCweb*, this use of "node" coincides with the first use, since collocation analyses center on query items shown in the node position of a concordance.

NORMALIZED FREQUENCY
A frequency value that has been adjusted to take account of the size of the corpus, or the size of the portion of the corpus, over which a query has been run. In this book, we express normalized frequencies as frequencies per million words (pmw). Normalized frequencies are essential when making comparisons between unevenly sized sections of the BNC—or across different corpora.
See also: RAW FREQUENCY

PART-OF-SPEECH, see TAG

POST-QUERY OPTIONS MENU
The drop-down menu on the "Query result" page of *BNCweb* that lists the options available for manipulating or analyzing a CONCORDANCE. Examples include SORT, COLLOCATIONS and CATEGORIZE HITS.

PRECISION
The proportion of instances in a Query result that are actually valid, that is they successfully match what was targeted in the search. Precision is usually expressed as a percentage figure. For example, if a search for *will* as a noun returns 100 hits and 2 of those turn out not to be nouns, precision is 98% (98 valid hits out of 100).
See also: RECALL

QUERY ITEM
The word or sequence of words (including punctuation marks) matched by a QUERY TERM and displayed in the NODE position of a CONCORDANCE.

QUERY RESULT
The output produced by *BNCweb* in response to a query by the user. The query result is in two parts: (i) basic frequency information about the number of occurrences of the search item in the corpus—displayed in the title bar—and (ii) a CONCORDANCE of all the examples of the query item in the corpus.
See also: QUERY ITEM, QUERY TERM

QUERY TERM
The string you use to start a query. In its simplest form, a query term is a single word token (e.g. `absolutely`). More complex query terms can contain wildcards, regular expressions and repetition operators, and may also make use of the POS-tagging and headword/lemma information annotated in the BNC—see Chapters 6 and 12.

RAW FREQUENCY
The actual number of occurrences or hits of a linguistic item in the whole BNC or in selected parts of it.
See also: **NORMALIZED FREQUENCY**

RECALL
The proportion of all relevant instances (i.e. those cases you intended to find) that are retrieved by a corpus search. Recall is usually expressed as a percentage figure. If there are 200 instances of *will* as a noun in a corpus and your search only finds 150, recall is 75% (150 ÷ 200 × 100).
See also: **PRECISION**

REGULAR EXPRESSION
Regular expressions are a compact notation for describing repetition, optionality and alternatives in sequences of characters (word forms and annotations) or sequences of tokens (e.g. lexico-grammatical patterns). In CQP Query Syntax, regular expressions are used both at the level of characters and at the level of tokens. For example, `"super.+"` matches a word beginning with *super-* followed by one or more arbitrary characters, while `[pos="AT0"]?` `[pos="AJ."]+` `[pos="NN."]` matches a sequence of an optional article, one or more adjectives, and a common noun. Note that the + symbol has the same meaning (i.e. 'one or more') in both uses.
   Simple Query Syntax allows regular expression notation only at the level of tokens, while simpler wildcards are used at the level of characters (e.g. `super+` for words beginning with *super-*). The full syntax of regular expressions is explained in Sections 12.4; their application at the level of tokens is described in Sections 6.8 and 12.6.
See also: **WILDCARDS, METACHARACTERS, REPETITION OPERATOR**

REPETITION OPERATOR
In **REGULAR EXPRESSION** notation, repetition operators are **METACHARACTERS** that indicate that a certain part of the expression may be repeated and/or is optional. The most frequently used repetition operators are ? (optionality), * (0 or more repetitions) and + (1 or more repetitions). A specific number of repetitions or a range can be specified in curly brackets, e.g. `{3}` (exactly 3 repetitions) or `{5,10}` (between 5 and 10 repetitions).

RELATIVE FREQUENCY, see NORMALIZED FREQUENCY

RESPONDENT
In the BNC, respondents are the individuals who recorded the spoken dialogue material (unplanned conversations) in the **DEMOGRAPHICALLY SAMPLED**

COMPONENT of the corpus. Respondents were selected on the basis of their demographic profile—for example, as being of a certain age or socioeconomic class (see 3.5). The data recorded by the respondents was sampled from a two to seven day period. It is important to be aware that respondents are just a few among the many speakers represented in the corpus. *BNCweb* allows you to restrict your queries to texts recorded by specific kinds of respondents (e.g. "respondent age between 25 and 34"). However, since the results of such queries will include utterances by other speakers, usually it is preferable to apply speaker-specific restrictions instead.

S-UNIT

A sentence or sentence-like unit within a BNC text. S-units are numbered sequentially in the corpus. Together with the text ID, this number forms the information needed to refer to any hit that you retrieve from the corpus using *BNCweb* (e.g. G42: 22). The texts in the spoken component of the BNC have also been divided into s-units, even though it is at times difficult to segment spoken language into sentences,
See also: W-UNIT, C-UNIT.

SAMPLING VARIATION

If you take two samples from the same language (e.g. two corpora compiled in exactly the same way, or two random samples from a query result), the frequency of a word or expression will usually differ—to a greater or lesser degree—between the samples. The difference results from the random selection of texts for the corpora (or hits from a query result) and is therefore referred to as "sampling variation". In order to make reliable generalizations about language, it is necessary to apply statistical techniques that correct for sampling variation. See 5.6 for a detailed account of sampling variation and appropriate statistical procedures.
See also: STATISTICAL SIGNIFICANCE

SELECTION CRITERIA

Specifications defining the kind and proportion of material to be included for the compilation of the corpus. For example, the selection criteria for the written component of the BNC are time (i.e. date of publication), text domain, and medium (e.g. books vs. periodicals).
See also: DESCRIPTIVE FEATURE

SIMPLE QUERY SYNTAX

One of the two formats used to enter queries in *BNCweb*. As the name suggests, the Simple Query Syntax is designed to be easy to learn and apply: only a limited number of codes and conventions are used. See Chapter 6 for a full refer-

ence of the query syntax. Although their format is simple, Simple query expressions can be combined so as to retrieve quite complex linguistic patterns from the corpus.
See also: **CQP QUERY SYNTAX**.

SIMPLIFIED TAG

Also called "lemma class". One of the 11 high-level part-of-speech tags that are derived from the more fine-grained tags in the CLAWS-5 tagset. For example, the simplified tag "ADV" subsumes the more specific tags "AV0", "AVP", "AVQ" and "XX0". In *BNCweb*, a simplified tag in combination with a **HEADWORD** forms a **LEMMA**.

STATISTICAL SIGNIFICANCE

In order to draw conclusions about language from a finite corpus—or to extrapolate from a small sample to a full set of query hits—it is necessary to apply statistical techniques that determine whether differences between two samples can be explained by **SAMPLING VARIATION** or whether they point to actual differences e.g. between two language varieties. If sampling variation can be ruled out as an explanation, the observation is said to be statistically significant. A quantitative measure of statistical significance is the so-called "p-value", which specifies the risk that the observed difference is merely due to random variation. Any p-value below 5% (or preferably 1%) is generally accepted as a significant result. See 5.6 for details.

SUBCORPUS (plural form: *subcorpora*)

In theory, a subcorpus is any subsection of a corpus. In practice, the contents of a subcorpus tend, as with the corpus itself, to be more principled, determined by factors such as subject matter and medium of production. *BNCweb* makes it possible to define a subcorpus flexibly by several methods (see Chapter 10). Typical examples of subcorpora are: medical texts, emails, academic written texts, academic written texts on law, texts to do with news and current affairs, spoken conversations among young people, or utterances by female speakers.

TAG

"Tag" is a general term that is sometimes used interchangeably with "mark-up", but many corpus linguists use "tags" mainly to refer to "linguistic tags"—i.e. annotations, particularly part-of-speech (POS) annotations. A full list of POS-tags can be found in Appendix 2 and via the link "The CLAWS-5 tagset" in the **MAIN NAVIGATION PANEL** of *BNCweb*. In the BNC, words are also annotated with a simplified tagset, containing 11 high-level tags. These tags were assigned by collapsing the detailed tags into larger categories (e.g. CJC, CJS, CJT → CONJ). See also: **MARK-UP, ANNOTATION, SIMPLIFIED TAG, LEMMA**

TOKEN

1. A cover term for **W-UNITS** and **C-UNITS** (i.e. words and punctuation), the basic items annotated with linguistic information such as part-of-speech tags in the BNC.

2. More generally in corpus linguistics, "token" refers to single occurrences of running words in a text (typically this equates to w-units in the BNC), as opposed to word "types", i.e. unique word forms. The type/token-ratio can be a useful measure for describing general differences between text types (e.g. in terms of lexical richness).

TOKEN EXPRESSION

In CQP Query Syntax, a token expression matches a single token and is usually enclosed in square brackets [...]. Two or more matching conditions may be combined by using a Boolean operator. For example,

```
[(word = "can"%c) & (pos != "VM0")]
```

finds the word *can* tagged as anything but a modal verb (i.e. as a noun or lexical verb). The token expression [word = "funny"] can be abbreviated to "funny".

See also: **ATTRIBUTE, GLOBAL CONSTRAINT, REGULAR EXPRESSION**

W-UNIT

The smallest linguistic unit recognized by the automatic part-of-speech tagger CLAWS. In most cases, w-units correspond to orthographic words. Exceptions are contracted forms (e.g. *she's*) and fused forms (e.g. *gonna*), which CLAWS treats as separate tokens. The word count returned in a *BNCweb* Query result refers to the number of w-units only.

See also: **S-UNIT, C-UNIT**.

WILDCARDS

Wildcards are punctuation symbols with a special function in Simple Query Syntax. They allow the range of individual word forms matched by a query to be generalized. Examples include:

? for a single, arbitrary character
      s?ng will find *sing, sang, song, sung,* etc.
* for zero or more arbitrary characters
      sing* will find *sing, sings, singer, singingly, single* etc.
+ for one or more arbitrary characters
      sing+ will find *sings, singer, singingly, single,* etc. but not *sing*

See also: **REGULAR EXPRESSION**

Appendix 1: Genre classification scheme

Genre classification scheme (devised by David Lee): short genre labels and detailed descriptions of the genres

Written texts: 46 genres

Code	Description
W:ac:humanities_arts	academic prose: humanities
W:ac:medicine	academic prose: medicine
W:ac:nat_science	academic prose: natural sciences
W:ac:polit_law_edu	academic prose: politics law education
W:ac:soc_science	academic prose: social & behavioural sciences
W:ac:tech_engin	academic prose: technology computing engineering
W:admin	adminstrative and regulatory texts, in-house use
W:advert	print advertisements
W:biography	biographies/autobiographies
W:commerce	commerce & finance, economics
W:email	e-mail sports discussion list
W:essay:school	school essays
W:essay:univ	university essays
W:fict:drama	excerpts from two modern drama scripts
W:fict:poetry	single- and multiple-author collections of poems
W:fict:prose	novels & short stories
W:hansard	Hansard/parliamentary proceedings
W:institut_doc	official/govermental documents/leaflets company annual reports etc.; excludes Hansard
W:instructional	instructional texts/DIY
W:letters:personal	personal letters
W:letters:prof	professional/business letters
W:misc	miscellaneous texts
W:news_script	TV autocue data
W:newsp:brdsht_nat:arts	broadsheet national newspapers: arts/cultural material
W:newsp:brdsht_nat:commerce	broadsheet national newspapers: commerce & finance
W:newsp:brdsht_nat:editorial	broadsheet national newspapers: personal & institutional editorials & letters-to-the-editor
W:newsp:brdsht_nat:misc	broadsheet national newspapers: miscellaneous material
W:newsp:brdsht_nat:report	broadsheet national newspapers: home & foreign news reportage
W:newsp:brdsht_nat:science	broadsheet national newspapers: science material
W:newsp:brdsht_nat:social	broadsheet national newspapers: material on lifestyle leisure belief & thought
W:newsp:brdsht_nat:sports	broadsheet national newspapers: sports material

W:newsp:other:arts	regional and local newspapers: arts
W:newsp:other:commerce	regional and local newspapers: commerce & finance
W:newsp:other:report	regional and local newspapers: home & foreign news reportage
W:newsp:other:science	regional and local newspapers: science material
W:newsp:other:social	regional and local newspapers: material on lifestyle, leisure, belief & thought
W:newsp:other:sports	regional and local newspapers: sports material
W:newsp:tabloid	tabloid newspapers
W:non_ac:humanities_arts	non-academic/non-fiction: humanities
W:non_ac:medicine	non-academic: medical/health matters
W:non_ac:nat_science	non-academic: natural sciences
W:non_ac:polit_law_edu	non-academic: politics law education
W:non_ac:soc_science	non-academic: social & behavioural sciences
W:non_ac:tech_engin	non-academic: technology, computing, engineering
W:pop_lore	popular magazines
W:religion	religious texts, excluding philosophy

Spoken texts: 24 genres

Code	Description
S:brdcast:discussn	TV or radio discussions
S:brdcast:documentary	TV documentaries
S:brdcast:news	TV or radio news broadcasts
S:classroom	non-tertiary classroom discourse
S:consult	*mainly* medical & legal consultations
S:conv	face-to-face spontaneous conversations
S:courtroom	legal presentations or debates
S:demonstratn	'live' demonstrations
S:interview	job interviews & other types
S:interview:oral_history	oral history interviews/narratives, some broadcast
S:lect:commerce	lectures on economics commerce & finance
S:lect:humanities_arts	lectures on humanities and arts subjects
S:lect:nat_science	lectures on the natural sciences
S:lect:polit_law_edu	lectures on politics, law or education
S:lect:soc_science	lectures on the social & behavioural sciences
S:meeting	business or committee meetings
S:parliament	BNC-transcribed parliamentary speeches
S:pub_debate	public debates, discussions, meetings
S:sermon	religious sermons
S:speech:scripted	planned speech, whether dialogue or monologue
S:speech:unscripted	more or less unprepared speech, whether dialogue or monologue
S:sportslive	'live' sports commentaries and discussions
S:tutorial	university-level tutorials
S:unclassified	miscellaneous spoken genres

Appendix 2: Part-of-speech tags

List of part-of-speech (POS) tags with descriptions

Tag	Description
AJ0	Adjective (general or positive) (e.g. *good, old, beautiful*)
AJC	Comparative adjective (e.g. *better, older*)
AJS	Superlative adjective (e.g. *best, oldest*)
AT0	Article (e.g. *the, a, an, no*)
AV0	General adverb: an adverb not subclassified as AVP or AVQ (see below) (e.g. *often, well, longer* (adv.), *furthest*)
AVP	Adverb particle (e.g. *up, off, out*)
AVQ	Wh-adverb (e.g. *when, where, how, why, wherever*)
CJC	Coordinating conjunction (e.g. *and, or, but*)
CJS	Subordinating conjunction (e.g. *although, when*)
CJT	The subordinating conjunction *that*
CRD	Cardinal number (e.g. *one, 3, fifty-five, 3609*)
DPS	Possessive determiner-pronoun (e.g. *your, their, his*)
DT0	General determiner-pronoun: i.e. a determiner-pronoun which is not a DTQ or an AT0.
DTQ	Wh-determiner-pronoun (e.g. *which, what, whose, whichever*)
EX0	Existential *there*, i.e. *there* occurring in the *there is...* or *there are...* construction
ITJ	Interjection or other isolate (e.g. *oh, yes, mhm, wow*)
NN0	Common noun, neutral for number (e.g. *aircraft, data, committee*)
NN1	Singular common noun (e.g. *pencil, goose, time, revelation*)
NN2	Plural common noun (e.g. *pencils, geese, times, revelations*)
NP0	Proper noun (e.g. *London, Michael, Mars, IBM*)
ORD	Ordinal numeral (e.g. *first, sixth, 77th, last*) .
PNI	Indefinite pronoun (e.g. *none, everything, one* (as pronoun), *nobody*)
PNP	Personal pronoun (e.g. *I, you, them, ours*)
PNQ	Wh-pronoun (e.g. *who, whoever, whom*)
PNX	Reflexive pronoun (e.g. *myself, yourself, itself, ourselves*)
POS	The possessive or genitive marker *'s* or *'*
PRF	The preposition *of*
PRP	Preposition (except *of*) (e.g. *about, at, in, on, with*)

PUL	Punctuation: left bracket, i.e. *(* or *[*
PUN	Punctuation: general separating mark (*.* , *!* *:* *;* *−* and *?*)
PUQ	Punctuation: quotation mark (*'* and *"*)
PUR	Punctuation: right bracket, i.e. *)* or *]*
TO0	Infinitive marker *to*
UNC	Unclassified items which are not appropriately considered as items of the English lexicon.
VBB	The present tense forms of the verb BE (except for *is* and *'s*), i.e. *am, are, 'm, 're* and *be* (subjunctive or imperative)
VBD	The past tense forms of the verb BE: *was* and *were*
VBG	The *-ing* form of the verb BE: *being*
VBI	The infinitive form of the verb BE: *be*
VBN	The past participle form of the verb BE: *been*
VBZ	The *-s* form of the verb BE: *is, 's*
VDB	The finite base form of the verb DO: *do*
VDD	The past tense form of the verb DO: *did*
VDG	The *-ing* form of the verb DO: *doing*
VDI	The infinitive form of the verb DO: *do*
VDN	The past participle form of the verb DO: *done*
VDZ	The *-s* form of the verb DO: *does, 's*
VHB	The finite base form of the verb HAVE: *have, 've*
VHD	The past tense form of the verb HAVE: *had, 'd*
VHG	The *-ing* form of the verb HAVE: *having*
VHI	The infinitive form of the verb HAVE: *have*
VHN	The past participle form of the verb HAVE: *had*
VHZ	The *-s* form of the verb HAVE: *has, 's*
VM0	Modal auxiliary verb (e.g. *will, would, can, could, 'll, 'd*)
VVB	The finite base form of lexical verbs, comprising the indicative, imperative and present subjunctive (e.g. *forget, send, live, return*)
VVD	The past tense form of lexical verbs (e.g. *forgot, sent, lived, returned*)
VVG	The *-ing* form of lexical verbs (e.g. *forgetting, sending, living, returning*)
VVI	The infinitive form of lexical verbs (e.g. *forget, send, live, return*)
VVN	The past participle form of lexical verbs (e.g. *forgotten, sent, lived, returned*)
VVZ	The *-s* form of lexical verbs (e.g. *forgets, sends, lives, returns*)
XX0	The negative particle *not* or *n't*
ZZ0	Alphabetical symbols (e.g. *A, a, B, b, c, d*)

Appendix 3: Quick reference to the Simple Query Syntax

Basic word form searches

- To search for word forms, simply type them into the query field and click [Start query]: `glitterati` → *glitterati*
- Use wildcards for unspecified letters, and prefix or suffix searches:

> ? for a single arbitrary character
> `s?ng` → *sing, sang, song, ...*
> * for zero or more characters
> `*able` → *able, table, capable, suitable, available, ...*
> + for one or more characters
> `+able` → *table, capable, suitable, ...* but not *able*
> ??+ for three or more characters, etc.
> `??+able` → *capable, ...* but not *able, table, unable, stable*

- Combine multiple wildcards: `*oo+oo*` → *Voodoo, schoolroom, ...*
- Protect wildcards and other metacharacters with backslash \ to match the literal character (called "escaping" the metacharacter):

> `\?` → *?*
> `?` → *a, b, c, ..., A, B, C, ..., 1, 2, 3, ..., ., !, ?, ...*

Simple Query Syntax uses the following metacharacters:

> `? * + , : @ / ( ) [ ] { } _ - < >`

- List comma-separated alternatives (optionally including wildcards) in square brackets:

> `??+[able,ability]` → *capable, capability, availability, ...*
> `neighbo[u,]r` → *neighbour, neighbor*

- Searches are case-insensitive by default: the queries `bath`, `Bath` and `BATH` find the same matches (viz. the three word forms *bath, Bath* and *BATH*). Set the "Query mode" drop-down menu to "Simple query (case-sensitive)" to distinguish between *AIDS* and *aids*, for example.
- Use `:d` modifier to ignore accents: `fiancee:d` → *fiancée, fiancee* (see Section 6.10 and Appendix 4 for details on matching special characters).

Matching parts-of-speech (POS)

- Search for a word form with a specific POS tag by linking them with an underscore _. Wildcards can be used both for word form and POS tag:

```
lights_NN2 →  plural noun lights, but not the verb form lights
*ly_AJ0     →  adjectives ending in -ly (e.g. daily)
super+_V*   →  verb forms starting with super-
```

- You can also search by POS tag only: _PNX → any reflexive pronoun
- See Appendix 2 for a complete listing of POS tags used in the BNC.
- Use simplified POS tags enclosed in curly braces: super+_{VERB} for verb forms starting with super- (no wildcards allowed in simplified tags).
- List of simplified POS tags (Table 3.8 shows comparison with full tagset):

A, ADJ	adjective	INT, INTERJ	interjection
N, SUBST	noun	PREP	preposition
V, VERB	verb	PRON	pronoun
ADV	adverb	$, STOP	punctuation
ART	article	UNC	other / uncertain
CONJ	conjunction		

- Keep in mind that part-of-speech tags have been assigned by an automatic software tool and are not always correct (try e.g. beer_{N} can_{N}).

Headword and lemma queries

- Search by headword, enclosed in curly braces: {light} finds the forms *light, lights, lit, lighted, lighting, lighter* and *lightest* (but not the nouns *lighting* and *lighter*).
- In *BNCweb*, the lemma is a combination of headword and simplified POS tag, separated by a slash /. A lemma query distinguishes e.g. between the noun, verb and adjective reading of LIGHT:

```
{light/V} →  light, lights, lit, lighted, lighting (tagged as verb)
{light/N} →  light, lights (tagged as noun)
{light/A} →  light, lighter, lightest (tagged as adjective)
```

Word sequences

- Queries can consist of multiple words, e.g. `talk of the town`
- All words and punctuation symbols ("tokens") are separated by blanks; possessives (*Peter's*) and contracted forms (*they've, gonna*) must be split:

    `he will , wo n't he \?` ➔ *he will, won't he?*

- Each query item in a sequence can make full use of wildcards, part-of-speech constraints, and headword or lemma searches:

    `{number/N} of _{A} _NN2` ➔ *numbers of younger men, ...*

- Use + to skip an arbitrary token, or * for an optional token. Combine + and * for larger gaps, e.g. `+++**` to skip between 3 and 5 tokens.

    `{eat} * up`   ➔ *eat up, ate up, eat it up, eaten all up, ...*
    `{eat} + up`   ➔ *eat it up, eaten all up, ...* but not *eat up, ate up*
    `{eat} ++* up` ➔ *up* at a distance of 3 or 4 tokens after *eat*

Advanced lexico-grammatical patterns

- Use regular expression notation (Sections 6.8 and 12.4) for alternatives, optional elements and repetition within a sequence:

`(_{A})?`	optional adjective
`(_{A})*`	zero or more adjectives (optional)
`(_{A})+`	one or more adjectives (non-optional)
`(_{A}){2,4}`	between two and four adjectives
`(...|...|...)`	matches one of the alternatives indicated by ...
`(...|...|...)*`	alternatives with repetition (optional)
`(...|...|...)+`	alternatives with repetition (non-optional)
`(...|...|...){2,4}`	between two and four repetitions of the given alternatives (may be mixed in any order)

- Regular expression notation can be nested to match complex patterns:

    `the (most _AJ0 | _AJS) {man}`
        ➔ *the biggest men, the most attractive man, ...*
    `the (most (_AV0)? _AJ0 | (_AV0)? _AJS) {man}`
        ➔ plus: *the very richest men, the most supremely stupid men, ...*
    `_{PREP} (_{ART})? ((_{ADV})? _{A})* _{N}`
        ➔ "a preposition; followed by an optional article; followed by any number of adjectives (zero or more), each of which may optionally be preceded by an adverb; followed by a noun"

XML tags

- XML start and end tags can be inserted in query expression to match the
  boundaries of a region, e.g. the start (`<s>`) or end (`</s>`) of an s-unit:

  `<s> but`   → s-unit beginning with *but* (or *But*)
  `_{ART} </s>`   → article at end of s-unit (mostly errors)

- To match a complete region, skip all tokens between the start and end tag:

  `<quote> (+)+ </quote>` → list of all quotations in the BNC
  `<mw> (+)+ </mw>`   → list of all multiword units

- Some useful XML tags in the BNC:

`<s> … </s>`	s-unit
`<p> … </p>`	paragraph
`<u> … </u>`	speaker turn
`<head> … </head>`	heading or caption
`<quote> … </quote>`	quotation
`<item> … </item>`	list item
`<hi> … </hi>`	highlighted text
`<mw> … </mw>`	multiword unit

Proximity queries

- Special syntax for searching one item within a specified range of another:

  `kick <<s>> bucket` → *kick* and *bucket* in the same sentence
  `{kick/V} <<s>> bucket_NN1` (can use POS/lemma constraints)
  `day <<3>> night`   → *day* and *night* within range of 3 tokens
  `day <<5<< night`   → *night … day* (within 5 tokens)
  `day >>5>> night`   → *day … night* (within 5 tokens)

- Only the left element ("target") will be highlighted on the result page. The
  right element is considered as a "constraint" that must be satisfied.

- Multiple constraints can be chained:

  `{day} <<5>> {month} <<5>> {year}`

  In this case, *day* must co-occur with *month* as well as *year* in a 5-token
  window; only *day* will be highlighted on the Query result page.

- Proximity queries can be nested with parentheses:

  `{waste/V} <<s>> (time <<3>> money)`

Here, the verb *waste* must co-occur with *time* as well as *money* in the same sentence; but *time* and *money* must be closer together (within a 3-token window).
Again, only instances of *waste* will be highlighted.

Appendix 4: HTML-entities for less common characters

HTML entities used in *BNCweb* for less common characters (i.e. excluding Latin-1 characters):

&alpha;	□	&OElig;	Œ	&#x100;	□	&#x165;	□
&amp;	&	&oelig;	œ	&#x101;	□	&#x16B;	ū
&beta;	β	&Omega;	Ω	&#x103;	ă	&#x16F;	ů
&Beta;	B	&omega;	ω	&#x105;	ą	&#x175;	ŵ
&bull;	•	&Omicron;	O	&#x107;	ć	&#x176;	Ŷ
&chi;	χ	&omicron;	o	&#x109;	ĉ	&#x177;	ŷ
&darr;	↓	&Phi;	Φ	&#x10C;	Č	&#x17A;	ź
&Delta;	Δ	&phi;	φ	&#x10D;	č	&#x17C;	ż
&delta;	δ	&pi;	π	&#x10F;	ď	&#x17D;	Ž
&epsilon;	ε	&Pi;	Π	&#x111;	đ	&#x17E;	ž
&Epsilon;	E	&prime;	′	&#x113;	ē	&#x2010;	-
&eta;	η	&Prime;	″	&#x119;	ę	&#x2015;	—
&gamma;	γ	&Psi;	Ψ	&#x11A;	Ě	&#x2126;	Ω
&Gamma;	Γ	&psi;	ψ	&#x11B;	č	&#x2153;	⅓
&ge;	≥	&radic;	√	&#x127;	ħ	&#x2154;	⅔
&gt;	>	&rarr;	→	&#x12B;	ī	&#x2155;	⅕
&hearts;	♥	&rho;	ρ	&#x139;	Ĺ	&#x2156;	⅖
&hellip;	...	&rsquo;	'	&#x13A;	ĺ	&#x2157;	⅗
&infin;	∞	&Scaron;	Š	&#x141;	Ł	&#x2158;	⅘
&iota;	ι	&scaron;	š	&#x142;	ł	&#x2159;	⅙
&kappa;	κ	&Sigma;	Σ	&#x144;	ń	&#x215A;	⅚
&lambda;	λ	&sigma;	σ	&#x146;	ņ	&#x215B;	⅛
&larr;	←	&sim;	~	&#x148;	ň	&#x215C;	⅜
&le;	≤	&tau;	τ	&#x14D;	ō	&#x215D;	⅝
&lowast;	*	&theta;	θ	&#x155;	ŕ	&#x215E;	⅞
&lsquo;	'	&Theta;	Θ	&#x158;	Ř	&#x2218;	°
&lt;	<	&trade;	™	&#x159;	ř	&#x2243;	≃
&mdash;	—	&Upsilon;	Y	&#x15A;	Ś	&#x25BE;	▼
&Mu;	M	&upsilon;	υ	&#x15B;	ś	&#x25CB;	○
&mu;	μ	&xi;	ξ	&#x15D;	ŝ	&#x266D;	♭
&ndash;	–	&Yuml;	Ÿ	&#x15E;	Ş	&#x266E;	♮
&nu;	ν	&zeta;	ζ	&#x15F;	ş	&#x266F;	♯
		&Zeta;	Z	&#x163;	ţ	&#x2713;	✓

Index

—A—

accented letters 97, 104, 116-17, 217, 223, 225

admin features 246, 249, 254

administrator 245-49, 251, 253, 254, 257

ambiguity tag 38-39, 106, 107, 118, 212, 228, 242

annotation 25, 38, 41, 42, 44, 46, 95, 101, 103, 124, 219, 220, 225, 227, 236, 255
(manual) 161-84

association measure 141, 142, 145, 147, 149-58, 159

association score 143, 152, 157-58

authentic language 16, 18, 20

—B—

BNC see British National Corpus

BNC index 198, 199

Boolean expression 229, 232, 233, 237

British National Corpus 4, 10, 11, 14, 17, 19, 20, 26, 27-46, 53, 54, 56, 60, 74, 163, 185, 193, 195, 212, 239, 245

browse a text 66-67, 179, 238

—C—

cache system 158, 252-55, 256, 258

case-insensitive 97, 117, 188, 216, 218, 221

categorize hits 162-70, 179, 181, 183

categorized query 167, 168, 169, 249, 255

categorization mode 165-67, 169

CG. See context-governed component

chi-squared (test) 84, 85, 90, 91, 152, 208

Chomsky 20

CLAWS 38, 42, 162n

collocation 139-60, 161, 167, 202, 249, 250, 253, 257-58
(settings) 142-43, 145, 158, 160
(upward) 237

competence 20, 20-21, 22, 23

complex prepositions 21-23

concordance 4, 11, 48, 50-54, 65, 112, 124, 132, 148, 161, 162, 165, 175-76, 250

confidence interval 80-83, 85, 86, 88, 89, 90

configuration settings 249-52, 256

context-governed component 33-35, 37

contracted form 42, 77-78, 96

COPAC 195-97

corpus 13, 15-20, 24

Corpus Frequency Wizard 81-86

corpus linguistics 14, 18-20, 23, 83

corpus order 53-54, 79, 87, 250

corpus position 176, 181, 182

corpus types 24-26

Corpus Workbench. See *IMS Open Corpus Workbench*

CQP Query Syntax 215-43

critical value(s) 85-89, 208

c-unit 41-42

—D—

default category 164

demographically sampled component 32-34, 36-37

derived text type 30-31

descriptive feature 28, 29, 30-31

descriptive statistics 8-9, 18, 75,
124, 134

diacritics 97, 216

dialogue 35

Dice coefficient 145, 156-57

dispersion 50, 62, 121, 122, 128-31

distribution 8-9, 30, 119-131, 173

domain 28-29, 32, 33-34, 75-76,
119, 120, 129, 195

download 134, 146, 162, 174, 175-
77, 181, 212, 250-51

DS. See demographically sampled
component

duplicate passages 44

—E—

effect size 86, 89, 150, 151, 154,
155, 156, 157

errors in the BNC 43-45

escape 95-96, 104, 217, 226

escape sequence 104-106

exact binomial test 87-88

Excel. See Microsoft *Excel*

expected frequency 141, 143, 150,
151, 152, 153, 155, 156

explore genre labels 200

extrapolate/extrapolation 54, 80-82,
83, 86, 88, 174

—F—

file-frequency extremes 130

filename (see also text ID) 28n, 53,
66

Fisher's exact test 84, 89

fpmw. See normalized frequency

frequency breakdown 133-36, 137

frequency comparison 83-84, 89

frequency list 158, 210-14

frequency per million words (see
also normalized frequency) 60,
63, 71, 76, 121, 183

—G—

genre 30-1, 32, 124-28, 186, 188,
193-95, 200, 204, 212-13

global constraint 237-38

Greek letter(s) 116, 117, 217

—H—

headword 40-41, 44, 103, 106-109,
145, 210, 211, 218-19, 226-30,
235

HTML entity 116-17, 217, 225, 283

hypothesis 19, 87, 88

hypothesis test 80, 83-84, 87, 90,
151

—I—

IMS Open Corpus Workbench 215,
216

infix query 104

installation 255-58

introspection 19, 20, 21

—K—

key keyword 209

key word in context. See KWIC

keyword/title scan 195-98, 204

keyword (library) 195-98, 204

keyword (statistical concept) 204-10

KWIC 52, 54, 132, 250